Secret Origin of the Golden State Killer :
Visalia Ransacker

Jackie,
Thanks for reading.
It's a much more satisfying
story now that the case has
been solved!
— Kat Winters

Jackie,
Thank you for
reviewing the book.
Hope you enjoy it.
Keith Komos

written by

KAT WINTERS and KEITH KOMOS

For more information:

Trial website: http://www.goldenstatekillertrial.com

Visalia Ransacker website: http://www.visaliaransacker.com

Golden State Killer website: http://www.goldenstatekiller.com

E-mail: coldcase.earons@gmail.com

Twitter: https://www.twitter.com/coldcasewriter

DEDICATION

The journey itself can affect us just as much as the destination. This book is dedicated to that journey. We remember now the lives that were so unjustly taken away, the difficult road walked by survivors, the pain felt by families, and the terror felt by communities affected by the Visalia Ransacker / East Area Rapist / Golden State Killer. We also remember the tenacious spirits that were able to find love, light, and hope in spite of it all.

To the Law Enforcement personnel who never gave up, to the public who continued to press for justice, to the families and survivors who overcame the odds, and to everyone affected by this case – this book is dedicated to you.

Table of Contents

Supplemental Material

COPYRIGHT NOTICE REGARDING MAPS

A NOTE ABOUT THE ARREST

In April 2018, a man named Joseph James DeAngelo was arrested for the Visalia Ransacker / East Area Rapist / Golden State Killer crimes. While DeAngelo has already been charged with various murders in the Golden State Killer series, he has yet to be charged with anything related to the Visalia Ransacker series and he has yet to be tried in a court of law for any of the crimes.

In the interest of preserving DeAngelo's right to a fair trial, which is his constitutional guarantee, this edition of the book does not delve deeply into the circumstances of his life. The events surrounding his identification and arrest are discussed, but Joseph DeAngelo is considered innocent of anything described in this book until proven otherwise in a court of law. If and when any significant changes occur regarding the status of this or any major development in the Visalia Ransacker case, we'll update the book with the relevant information.

To follow the court proceedings related to this case, visit the trial blog: www.goldenstatekillertrial.com

To follow major developments in the case, please visit our websites: www.visaliaransacker.com and www.goldenstatekiller.com

Thank you for understanding and for giving the criminal justice system the room it needs to operate effectively.

Introduction

The Visalia Ransacker.

They didn't have his DNA. They didn't *think* they had his fingerprints. And there wasn't a witness alive who could identify him in a lineup.

So who *was* he?

Was he the plump, jittery "baby" caught squealing under an officer's flashlight? Or was he the lean, vicious killer with "deliberate" and "angry" movements and a vice-like grip who murdered a college professor in cold blood?

Did he really spend two years ransacking house after house in the same small area, committing well over 100 sexually motivated crimes before vanishing without a trace?

And did he really move on to become one of the most notorious serial killers of all time – the East Area Rapist / Golden State Killer?

After forty-five years of investigation, it seems enough evidence has mounted to finally give us the answer.

Yes. On all counts.

But make no mistake – to deal with the Visalia Ransacker case is to deal with uncertainty, even now. Some of the mysteries are finally in the process of being solved – but there are still many more questions to answer.

Why would a man lay siege to a community, killing one of its most beloved residents? How could he commit so many crimes in a small area in such a short period of time? How can we use evidence and behavior to fill in the gaps?

Mysteries are solvable – so everything available on the Visalia Ransacker is in this book, and much of the information we present is offered to the public for the first time. We lay out the raw facts of the case, taking our time to travel through the crime series in chronological order, pointing out important developments along the way.

But this book provides more than a litany of facts related to a cold case. To read this book is to actually witness the birth and evolution of a deranged killer. The pale, round face peeking over fences and into windows as he silently observed the pretty girls, their nervous boyfriends, and the warm family moments. The moment he took that first step, crossing the threshold and entering their world as an invader. The theft of keepsakes, collections, personal items, and sentiment. The undergarments belonging to the mothers and daughters removed from drawers and arranged deliberately on beds in an embarrassing display. Masturbation at some of the crime scenes – sexual pleasure derived from the spoil of their sanctity. The crimes *feeding* the obsession rather than relieving it. Hues of anger added – furniture pushed over, wine dumped onto the floor, medication poured down the sink, family photos destroyed, and a Sunday School pin smashed on the fireplace. Guns and ammunition stolen. Stalking. Harassing phone calls. Noisy prowlers. A masked man bounding down the stairs. An attempted kidnapping. A man shot to death. Two attempted entries while the occupants were home. An officer shot at.

2

Size nine Converse shoe prints everywhere.

This was the Visalia Ransacker. A serial killer honing his "craft" on the innocent people of a small agricultural town in Central California. He hovered over the area like a thick fog for over two years and then he vanished, never to be heard from again.

Or so they thought. Six months later, a masked man invaded a bedroom in an area east of Sacramento called Rancho Cordova – two hundred miles away from where the Visalia Ransacker had haunted the night. This man, dubbed the "East Area Rapist," began a string of serial assaults that lasted for three years. And then, it seemed the East Area Rapist himself had vanished as well.

But he hadn't – he'd simply evolved. Three hundred miles away from the serial rape attacks, a string of murders began. Santa Barbara County. Ventura. Dana Point. Irvine. They were eerily similar in M.O. to the East Area Rapist but unconnected for years.

There wasn't always agreement if the Visalia Ransacker was the same man as the East Area Rapist / Golden State Killer, but there *was* agreement that an offender as tenacious as the Visalia Ransacker typically wouldn't stop at that particular phase of his apparent evolution. And he hadn't.

To be fair, the sloppy, reactionary murder committed by the Visalia Ransacker looked nothing like the methodical, tactical executions performed by the man later dubbed the "Golden State Killer." Under all of these different monikers and in all of these different areas, he committed crimes for at least twelve years. More than two hundred burglaries. Fifty rapes. At least thirteen murders.

After 1986, it seems the killings stopped. Other than heavy, whispered phone calls to former victims, nothing more from this unique brand of offender materialized.

The cases, most of them still unconnected, went cold. The unidentified perpetrator remained free.

Traditional police work could do little to move the needle against such an organized and meticulous criminal. It was in the lab where the first advances were made.

In 1996, ten years after his last known homicide, DNA linked murders committed in Ventura County, Dana Point, and Irvine to one common unidentified subject. In 2001, three of the "East Area Rapist" assaults were tied by DNA to that group of murders, and the portrait of a serial rapist who'd moved over three hundred miles to become a serial *killer* began to emerge.

For the next seventeen years, that's basically all that was known – that this offender known as the East Area Rapist / Golden State Killer had raped victims in their homes from 1976 to 1979 and that he'd gone on to systematically rape and murder his victims from 1979 to 1986. Police who once worked on the cases separately now worked together to solve something bigger than themselves.

The criminal remained unidentified for forty years. He'd been careful... *very* careful. There were no fingerprint matches. No one knew what he looked like. No one knew where he had come from. Had he truly started in the east area of Sacramento, or had this tactical and polished offender cut his teeth somewhere else? The first East Area Rapist attack clearly wasn't his first crime. So what was?

Some investigators felt that the answer could be found in Visalia, somewhere underneath all of those strange and nearly forgotten "Visalia Ransacker" crimes. A lot of work was done to test this hypothesis. Some of the evidence was convincing. Some of it pointed *away* from a connection. Nothing could be found to either prove or *disprove* the idea that the Visalia Ransacker went on to become the Golden State Killer. But whether an individual investigator felt that there was a connection or not, he or she maintained hope that a break in one case would invariably mean a break in the other.

And it did. Investigators have recently closed the gap. Police now state unequivocally that the notorious Golden State Killer committed his first known murder while operating as the prolific "Visalia Ransacker."

This is a game-changer, and it means that we can finally trace the offender back to an earlier starting point. Due to the immense size and scale of the Golden State Killer case and how little is known about his origins, it seems imperative to examine the Ransacker case closely to see what can be gleaned from it. Every crime committed by the EAR/GSK has been studied and analyzed for years, but the Ransacker crimes have not had that luxury. This crime spree, during which the offender was just as prolific as his more well-known stints as the East Area Rapist and Golden State Killer, holds many secrets. Study of it not only illuminates his evolution, but it gives insight into the techniques and motivations that were integral parts of his later crimes.

The seeds of what he later became are already starkly visible in the Visalia Ransacker series. Examining the Golden State Killer before he had the plan, the polish, and the execution reveals a man with an unbridled urge to satisfy his twisted desires but no idea how to do it. He learns as he goes, and indeed *we* learn about *him* as he goes.

This book is a full examination of the Visalia Ransacker crime series, a resurrection and an overhaul done with a fresh start and a critical eye. Through the countless details that are presented in this book, new connections are made, new frameworks can be developed, and loose ends are tied between his early crimes and his later ones. Through the organization, discovery, and presentation of this material, it's our hope that this book will finally help the public put this offender under a microscope and assist them in figuring out that elusive "why." In the pinning down of his comings and goings, the thought process behind different clusters of attacks, the deciphering of some of his victimology, and the study of his methods, we'll step through this series together and weave new threads.

We observe him as he commits every single known crime in the VR series. Our approach isn't a narrative – it's a case-by-case examination of his movements, his behaviors, and his methods. Some may find it a little dry. Others may appreciate the facts-only approach that spends little time theorizing and a lot of time working through the treasure trove of data. The narrative shapes itself.

While this work can be considered an encyclopedia of the Ransacker case, to peg it as merely a reference tool might be selling it short. Our hope is that it can be used as an asset to other cases and as a springboard to high-level discussion. The chances are high that the Visalia Ransacker / Golden State Killer is responsible for even *more* crimes, and this book may even provide guidance and clues that can help solve countless *other* offenses as well.

So join us as we discover the *Secret Origin of the Golden State Killer* in the *Visalia Ransacker* series.

The crimes that took over forty years to untangle still have much more to reveal.

The Visalia Ransacker

No lights. No movement.

They were gone.

He circled the perimeter, trying windows as he went. No luck. They'd locked them all before leaving.

He pried at one of them. It wouldn't give. He tried another. The frame gave way slightly, and through sheer force, he was able to open it the rest of the way. He crawled inside.

Rain drummed softly on the roof above. The noise was bothersome – a couple of times he'd even unplugged heating units so that he could hear better.

Should he close the drapes? Which lights should he turn on? Which windows or doors should he open to allow himself a quick escape should the residents come home and interrupt him?

This house seemed more vacant than others. Indeed, the couple would be gone for another two days. Rather than open multiple windows or wedge chairs under doorknobs, he merely opened a single window and pulled the screen inside with him.

Then he made his way to the master bedroom, fairly confident that he could spend as long as he wanted to without being disturbed.

* * *

The shattered glass from the window told them all they needed to know.

The burglary wasn't discovered until the couple returned home. Their back door, which they'd left locked, had been unlocked from the inside. A window next to it was wide open, as it had been for two nights now.

The police were just as furious as the homeowners – the ransacking had occurred on a night when the department was out in force. The officers were specifically *looking for the Ransacker*. If it was luck, it was uncanny – they'd patrolled two weekends in a row and both times, he'd offended right under their noses. It was a cat and mouse game – and they were the mice.

The victims were given paperwork to fill out. Despite the drawers being dumped out, jewelry box contents on the floor, and clothing all over the bedrooms, a few hours of cleaning and taking inventory revealed that the burglary had not been as extensive as they'd feared. Their feeling of safety was shaken, but in a way, they were relieved. The stolen property list that they filled out had only one item on it.

"Piggybank."

This was the Visalia Ransacker. An unholy mix of man and child. A risk-averse tactician with an animalistic impulsiveness. A violent, sexually motivated monster with an affinity for shiny objects and pocket change. A man who could curb his appetite for crime just long enough to select and plan the safest entry into the most vulnerable homes, but who couldn't modulate his own urges well enough to stop offending even on the very street where he was wanted for murder.

It seemed he'd appeared fully-formed on an April night in 1974 with barely a hint of where he'd come from. When he was again swallowed up by the night in December 1975, the mystery of where he'd disappeared to had become just as potent as the mystery of his origin.

But mysteries are made to be solved.

Modus Operandi

First, we need to cover the basics. The Ransacker had a unique way of operating, and the signature behaviors he performed at crime scenes usually left little doubt that the same man was committing all of the crimes attributed to him.

The typical VR crime went through the following steps:

1) While the residents were out of town or out of the home for the evening, the Ransacker would enter an open window, an unlocked window, or he would pry open an entrance. He sometimes entered by slipping the lock on a door or by forcing open a sliding glass door, but he typically entered through large windows.

2) Once inside the residence, he would open one or more additional exit points (again, usually windows), often pulling the screens into the home from the inside. He would usually leave the screens on or near a bed. He then had multiple options for a quick escape should the homeowners return unexpectedly, and the open windows had the added benefit of allowing him to hear what was going on outside – a family approaching the door, a car pulling into a driveway, approaching sirens, etc. He sometimes wedged a chair under the doorknob on the front door or engaged the chain lock in an effort to

slow down the residents should they come home while he was still there. Sometimes he put cans, cups, or trinkets against the inside of the doors so that he'd have a better chance of hearing the residents return.

3) With all of this in place, he would then begin ransacking the home. He'd open every drawer in the house and usually rummage through the contents. Bedrooms were his particular focus.

4) He collected up all of the women's undergarments that he could find, and he would toss them onto the floor, onto the bed, or onto some other surface in the house. He'd usually arrange them in particular ways and in a deliberate fashion. For instance, he'd stack all of the panties on pillows, line up all of the bras, make a pattern with the lingerie and nightgowns, or create some other intentional display.

5) The VR would sometimes find hand lotion or bring his own, usually Jergens brand. Investigators theorized that he was masturbating at some of the scenes. They based this theory on the way he rearranged some of the photos of women and girls who lived at the residence, panties that had been balled up nearby, the presence of a pornographic magazine that he'd found and left out, and/or smears of lotion located in the home.

6) He would often cause a bit of damage or destruction beyond what was necessary to break into the home. He pushed over bookshelves, poured wine onto carpet, sprayed shaving cream onto furniture, dumped medication down the sink, and sometimes destroyed or cut up bras or panties.

7) The Ransacker would steal keepsakes and collectibles from the home. Personal items, piggybanks, class rings, wedding rings, engraved bracelets, a personalized locket, coin collections, stamp collections, and Blue Chip stamps. One of his "calling cards" was that

he would sometimes take a single earring from a pair - a fact that would sometimes be discovered by the victim long after the burglary. Occasionally, the items he took would be found discarded in a nearby yard. He also showed his propensity for violence by stealing firearms, ammunition, a knife, a hammer, and a billy club. He sometimes stole practical items that seemed to be for his own personal use, such as packaged t-shirts, glue, canned food, dishes, binoculars, and a stereo.

Escalation

As the series wore on, it became clear that the motivation for all of this was sexual in nature. While the ransacking crimes were more well-known to police, it was learned that the VR was a prolific peeper and prowler as well. Shoe prints found at multiple scenes all matched each other, and those same shoe prints could be found under windows and in yards all over town. The Ransacker clearly had several "peeping routes" that he'd settled into.

His crimes escalated, and he began stalking specific families and women. In the early morning hours of September 11th, 1975, he even attempted to kidnap a teenage girl – a young lady that he'd been peeping at since at least February. He entered her home while the family was asleep and in the process of dragging her away, the girl's father, Claude Snelling, woke up and confronted him. Without hesitation, the Ransacker shot him to death.

Rather than leave the small area where he was wanted for murder, the Ransacker brazenly continued to offend and even continued his escalation pattern. Calls to police increased – especially reports of peeping and prowling. The VR began stalking potential targets more aggressively, and he began to harass potential victims by phone. His peeping and ransacking continued at a frantic pace, and he even attempted to enter two occupied homes in the middle of the night.

Confrontation

In December 1975, a vigilant homeowner noticed fresh shoe prints under her daughter's window. The Ransacker had already been peeping at her daughter and he'd burglarized the apartment over her garage, so she wasted no time in calling the police.

The next night, two officers decided to stake out the residence. Predictably, the Ransacker showed up to peep at the girl. An officer named William McGowen confronted him, finally seeing the offender's face clearly in the process. Chaos ensued – the Ransacker feigned surrender and shot at McGowen. Luckily, the bullet only hit the officer's flashlight. He walked away relatively unharmed.

The Ransacker escaped that night, somehow evading a bloodhound and dodging a dragnet set up by seventy police officers. It was the last time that the Ransacker was confirmed to be in Visalia, though careful research and good police work ended up filling in a few blanks and identifying possible events occurring both before and after the bulk of the series.

Because of the Claude Snelling homicide, the Visalia Ransacker can still be prosecuted for murder in Visalia. It's unknown if that will ever occur, but there are plenty of mysteries, clues, and facts that await in the pages that follow – all of which add new and revealing brushstrokes to the portrait of this notorious serial offender.

Summer 1973

Visalia, California is an agricultural community situated off of Route 99 between Fresno and Bakersfield. In the mid 1970s, it was the kind of place where people were still friendly, neighbors still knew each other, and a sense of community was still pervasive.

It was also the time and place where a budding serial killer began cutting his teeth. While the burglaries committed by the VR began in earnest around April 1974, some investigators believe that the criminal actually began his activities as early as 1973.

Toward the middle of the year, a particular house on South Demaree Street was targeted by prowling activity. A few weeks later, it was the scene of a ransacking / burglary. Unfortunately, the reports for these incidents are unavailable or lost, as are the details, but the incidents have appeared on the official lists of Ransacker events for decades. These crimes were some of the first inklings that a unique type of offender had begun operating in the area.

VR #001 – *Prowler*
May 1973 | S Demaree Street

-NOT CONFIRMED TO BE RELATED-

A corner house on South Demaree Street experienced prowling activity. Because the report is missing, we can only present this event as being *possibly* related – there isn't enough documentation available to know if it was truly a Visalia Ransacker crime or not.

While the vast majority of the book will deal with events that we can conclusively tie to the Ransacker due to M.O. or physical evidence, there are a few incidents (particularly in 1973) that don't have enough data to fully bring them into the fold as being the work of the actual individual known as the Visalia Ransacker. In order to keep our presentation of the subject "pure," anytime that an incident can't be tied to the VR through M.O. or physical evidence, we label it with "NOT CONFIRMED TO BE RELATED" at the beginning of the entry. It would be irresponsible to leave these incidents out of the discussion completely since almost everything mentioned in this book is (or was at one time) believed to be the work of one man, but we're sticklers for evidence and clean research.

This prowling incident occurred in May 1973. Interestingly enough, May 1973 was also the month that Joseph James DeAngelo, the man who allegedly committed the Visalia Ransacker crimes, began working as a police officer in Exeter – a town about a dozen miles east of Visalia. While working there, it appears that he actually lived in Visalia.

Around this general timeframe, DeAngelo took about four hundred hours worth of classes at Kings County Public Safety Academy (a police academy affiliated with the College of the Sequoias in Visalia).

VR #002 – *Ransacking*
June 1973 | S Demaree Street

-NOT CONFIRMED TO BE RELATED-

The same house that had experienced prowling activity in May was broken into and ransacked extensively. Again, most of the documentation is unavailable.

The location of this crime was in the far southwestern corner of the burglary grid, near the intersection of West Whitendale Avenue and South Demaree Street. This is a notable point on the map because the Visalia Ransacker never ventured further south than West Whitendale Avenue, and he never ventured further west than South Demaree Street. Because this was such an interesting location, investigators have weighed it heavily when trying to determine an origin point for the offender.

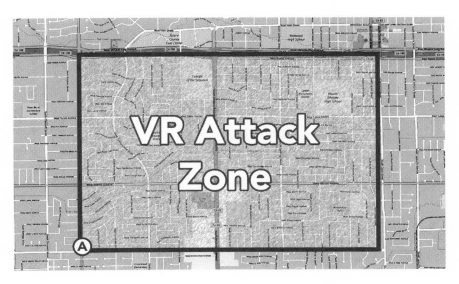

The marker shows the location of the S Demaree St ransacking in relation to the "VR Attack Zone." All of the ransackings took place within this box.

Even though there isn't a lot of information available on these two incidents, officers investigating the Visalia Ransacker crime series did determine that this was most likely the first known ransacking.

After this event, several months passed before there was any more possible activity. Some have suggested that the quiet months makes this pair of incidents less likely to be related, but it wasn't uncommon for the Visalia Ransacker / East Area Rapist to slow down considerably during the summer. If the South Demaree Street events (or *any* of the 1973 events) *were* him, then he seemed to be starting out slowly in the area. His later phases would show a man who offended much more prolifically.

September 1973

Months passed between the ransacking on South Demaree Street and the next flurry of activity possibly attributable to the Ransacker.

The events in this chapter didn't appear on the police's radar until after the Ransacker had seemingly left the area in 1976. At that time, investigators were combing through old files and fielding new tips. As they did this, a few prowling incidents from September 1973 grabbed their attention.

This chapter will be one of the oddest ones in the book – none of these events are confirmed to be the work of the Visalia Ransacker. Nevertheless, they seem to be some of the most talked-about and most frequently-cited prowling events in the entire case.

Their popularity is no mystery – not only are these run-ins incredibly interesting, but these reports and confrontations occur in areas that the VR was known to prowl later on.

We'll explain why some of these sightings might or might not be related as we tackle them one-by-one.

VR #003 – *Prowler*
September 3rd, 1973 | W Kaweah Ave

-NOT CONFIRMED TO BE RELATED-

At 8:15 PM on Monday, September 3rd, a residence on West Kaweah Avenue experienced prowling activity.

A fifteen-year-old girl was in her bedroom when she heard a noise at her window. She opened her blinds to see a man standing in her flowerbed. He was peeping in at her through her window. He took off as soon as he realized he'd been spotted, but not before the girl got a good look at him.

She described the prowler as a white male, mid-twenties, with short, light blonde hair. He had a round face that was "very smooth."

West Kaweah Avenue, where this took place, is a street that factors prominently into the VR crime series. It runs east/west from South Mooney Blvd to South Encina Street, and it lies just south of West Noble Avenue and State Route 198. State Route 198 is the northern border of the VR's attack zone, and South Mooney Blvd runs vertically and cuts it in half. The incident occurred on a portion of West Kaweah Avenue located just north of the Mt. Whitney High School – and the school is a location that plays a significant role later on.

At the time of this writing, the home where this incident occurred is heavy with tall, thick foliage. Photos of what it looked like in the 1970s are hard to come by, but if the heavy foliage existed back then, it's easy to see why a prowler might have been attracted to this residence.

We mentioned the close proximity to Mt. Whitney High School, but another significant location was within walking distance – a pair of homes on West Feemster Avenue that also experienced prowling activity in September. But first, more activity at *this* residence.

VR #004 – *Prowler*
September 10th, 1973 | W Kaweah Ave

A week later at 9:00 PM on Monday, September 10th, 1973, the same home on West Kaweah Avenue experienced prowling activity once again. This time, it was the girl's mother who spotted something.

Late in the evening, the woman walked from her residence to the curb where her car was parked. As she did, she heard a noise near her fence. She turned to find a man leaving her backyard.

He ran at a slow pace away from the houses and toward the curb, and as he started making his way westbound, he noticed the woman standing there observing him. He stopped, looked startled for a moment, and then turned to face the general direction of her backyard and shouted, "Catch you later, Sandy!" The woman's name was not Sandy, and she felt that he was speaking to an imaginary person.

The woman described the exact same man that her daughter had seen: a white male, twenty to thirty years old, 5'10" or 5'11", medium build, with a round face and short, blonde hair.

While researching these incidents, we found that this family's troubles didn't end on September 10th. The mother and daughter heard noises at their windows for several weeks after this event took place, and the noises and prowling activity appeared to continue into mid-October. On October 10th, 1973 at 10:00 PM, the mother and two of her friends spotted the same man at her sliding glass door. He was peering into her home.

The description she gave remained the same, though she added that he seemed to have a heavier lower half and that he moved with a strange gait. These two characteristics came up several times in descriptions of the Visalia Ransacker, and these were even some of the same adjectives used in the description given by a police officer who came face-to-face with the VR in December 1975.

When it comes to these incidents on September 3rd and 10th, it should be pointed out that both of them were reported as occurring on a Monday between 8:00 PM and 9:00 PM. Having a prowler on the same premises, on the same day of the week, and at roughly the same time is evidence of a significant pattern. If this prowling is related to the VR, then it seems the Visalia Ransacker was free on Monday nights in early September 1973. This is a slightly different pattern than the one he shows later, because for the bulk of his crime spree in Visalia, he offended on weekends.

It definitely seems that this household was targeted, and the observation of the prowler speaking to an imaginary accomplice matches up with some of the other activity that we'll discuss (even past the VR series into the East Area Rapist crimes).

It should be noted that there's no physical evidence or glaring M.O. components that tie these events to the Visalia Ransacker series, and it's possible that this was the work of another peeper or prowler.

VR #005 – *Prowler*
September 1973 | W Feemster Ave

-NOT CONFIRMED TO BE RELATED-

Sometime in September, a residence on West Feemster Avenue suffered prowling activity. The exact date of the activity is unknown, but many of the circumstances and details were captured.

It was late in the evening, and it had been dark outside for about an hour. A sixteen-year-old girl living with her family on West Feemster Avenue was in her bedroom. When she happened to look out her window, she noticed a pale, round-faced man staring in at her from a few feet away. When he was noticed, he darted away.

It's unknown if this activity was related to the Visalia Ransacker, but it wouldn't be the last time that this address experienced suspicious activity.

VR #006 – *Prowler*
September, 1973 | W Feemster Ave

-NOT CONFIRMED TO BE RELATED-

A week or two after the first prowling incident on West Feemster, another incident occurred after dark.

The same young lady was in her house. As her boyfriend approached the residence, he noticed a man emerging from Evan's Ditch, a drainage canal located across the street. The boyfriend paused and watched the man as he sank to his belly and wormed his way military-style toward the house. When the prowler arrived at the window, the boyfriend approached him.

"Hey! What are you doing?"

The man took off running, but the boyfriend caught up to him and cornered him in the yard.

"Looks like this guy's got us here, Ben!" the prowler said in a high-pitched, nervous voice. His body language indicated that he was frightened, though it may have been an act.

The boyfriend asked him various questions. "Who are you? What were you doing at my girlfriend's window?"

The man mumbled his replies and seemed to be making sidesteps to get away. He continually looked around. As the boyfriend started to close in on him, the man's voice became lower and a bit more menacing, though his nervous posture didn't go away. The man's eyes locked onto the boyfriend and his hand crept toward his jacket pocket. The boyfriend took a few steps back – he was under the impression that the prowler was reaching for a gun.

His escape now clear, the man told the boyfriend to leave him alone, and he began walking toward the front yard. The boyfriend followed at a safe distance. The man glanced back every five or six steps to make sure that he wasn't being followed too closely. He headed east on West Feemster Avenue, then turned left and went north on South Sowell Street.

The boyfriend, who had spent two or three minutes with the subject, described him in detail. He was a white male, 5'10", in his mid-twenties, about 185 lbs, with a large/heavy frame. His hair was a light, sandy blonde color and it was described as greasy or stringy.

His skin was very pale, and his face was unusually round and very smooth, like a baby's face. Despite the age estimate, the boyfriend felt that the subject couldn't grow facial hair. His eyes were "squinty," and his lower lip protruded a bit. He had a "pug nose." His ears were described as small and fat.

His lower half was pronounced, with large legs and thighs. His shoulders were described as rounded and sloping. Arms and legs seemed stocky and a little short for his frame. He ran at a medium pace, and was described as having an awkward gait.

The subject's voice had a strong hint of an "Okie" accent, which somewhat common for the area. His speech was described as "flat," "slow," or "monotone."

He wore a brown jacket with tight cuffs.

The location of these incidents on West Feemster Avenue was quite far away from the May/June events on S Demaree St – nearly three miles – but this actually took place right in the heart of future Visalia Ransacker activity. The West Feemster Avenue and West Kaweah Avenue incidents were less than a mile from each other, basically separated on the map by the high school.

As we noted at the beginning of this entry, this sighting may not be related to the Visalia Ransacker. Over three years after these encounters occurred, the Visalia Police Department (with cooperation from these two witnesses and the woman next-door who *also* experienced prowling activity) felt that they'd identified the man responsible. This man, who had confessed to one peeping incident, was investigated and cleared of any other Visalia Ransacker activity. Generally, this is the consensus.

However, some investigators felt that the peeper angle was never properly vetted and that the person may have been misidentified. Others felt that he'd been properly identified but mistakenly cleared as the Ransacker. Yet another group of investigators pointed to a statement by the officer who came face to face with the VR in December 1975, and the statement said that the peeper who was identified looks very similar to the Ransacker, but that they looked like two different men.

As if that weren't confusing enough, the house next-door to this residence was *definitely* burglarized by the Visalia Ransacker on

August 23rd, 1975 – a fact that some investigators point to as making this incident and some of the related ones a bit more suspicious.

The silver lining in this situation is that the description, behavior, and location of these prowling incidents gels with some of the other data that's available on the Ransacker, (including the West Kaweah Avenue events described at the beginning of the chapter and even the McGowen shooting), so neither acceptance nor rejection of the West Feemster Avenue entries as canon does much to take away from or add to any avenue of research.

January 1974

In January 1974, it was Déjà vu for the folks on West Feemster Avenue. Four months after the much-discussed prowler had been confronted at their home, they again experienced strange activity. Their next-door neighbors did as well.

VR #007 – *Prowler*
January 1974 | W Feemster Ave

-NOT CONFIRMED TO BE RELATED-

At 10:30 PM on some date in January (exact date is unknown), the same residence on West Feemster Avenue once again had a prowler on the premises. It appeared to be the same man who had approached the residence before.

If it *was* the same man, returning to the location where he had been discovered and seen so clearly showed a particular kind of brazenness and obsession with certain victims. Regardless of whether the prowler was the Visalia Ransacker or not, this was a trait that the VR would become known for.

VR #008 – *Prowler*
January 1974 | W Feemster Ave

-NOT CONFIRMED TO BE RELATED-

At 11:00 PM on some date in January (the exact date is unknown), the residence next-door experienced prowling activity. In this instance, the woman looked outside to see a man staring into her window. Upon being noticed, he ran back and nimbly jumped over the fence.

The woman described the prowler as having a round, pale face and small eyes. She noted that he held a screwdriver in his left hand.

Nearly three years later, she was contacted by the Visalia Police Department. At that time, she told the officers that the prowling incident previously described was actually the second time that she had seen the prowler, but she couldn't remember when the first incident happened.

Despite a thorough investigation by police, it's unknown for sure whether these prowling incidents had anything to do with the incidents in September, or if they had anything to do with the Visalia Ransacker at all.

The geography in these cases always deserves a bit of analysis – time and location are always among the most concrete facts that we have to work with in cold cases. These two homes on West Feemster were in a bit more of a secluded area than the home on West Kaweah Avenue that had been prowled in September. They were directly across from Evan's Ditch – a canal that runs through various parts of the city. It's been theorized that the VR (and perhaps other prowlers as well) used this ditch to get around town easily without having to use the street. When the VR began operating as the East Area Rapist in Sacramento, this was again one of the methods he used to traverse the neighborhoods incognito.

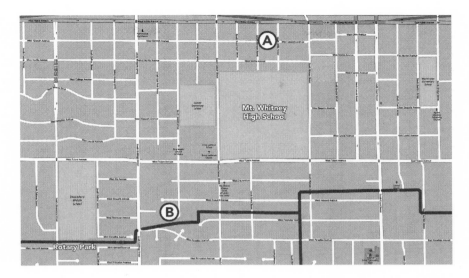

The locations of the prowling incidents in September 1973 and January 1974. Evan's Ditch is represented by thick lines, and it may have been used by the prowler to traverse the area without having to use the street.

A) September incidents on West Kaweah Ave

B) Prowling incidents in September and January on W Feemster Ave. Incidents took place at two residences situated next-door to each other.

The fact that the same prowler appeared to be peeping into *two* houses on West Feemster instead of just one may indicate that he wasn't targeting either of the women specifically, but rather, he was prowling the street itself. This road was short, it dead-ended, and there were houses located on only one side of the street. It was a fairly secluded spot, thick with cover, and with multiple options for escape if the prowler were to be discovered. A criminal just warming up and beginning to commit these types of crimes (or one targeting a new area for the first time) might've found this location an ideal place to get his feet wet.

An image of this portion of Evan's Ditch as it looks today. Photo by Bill Harticon.

The First Ransackings

The police now feel strongly that the VR was spending quite a bit of time peeping and prowling the city in order to learn the lay of the land, identifying potential victims as he went. If the Ransacker truly landed in town in May 1973 like they've always theorized due to the South Demaree Street activity, then it took a while for him to start burglarizing homes on a regular basis.

What's perhaps a bit telling about this case is that the VR seemed to have a very specific modus operandi from the get-go. Once the ransackings began in the springtime, they were peculiar enough and unique enough to be tied to the same offender even without any physical evidence. It's clear that from the start, the offender had a solid idea of what types of activities excited him. He also had a solid idea of how to avoid detection – none of the homeowners or neighbors noticed anything out of the ordinary during the timeframe of the actual burglaries, and nothing was found at any of the scenes that could be tied back to any particular individual.

VR #009 – *Ransacking*
March 19th, 1974 | W Walnut Ave

-NOT CONFIRMED TO BE RELATED-

Sometime on Tuesday, March 19th, a home on West Walnut Avenue was broken into.

We don't have any reports or documentation for this event, so it's unknown for sure if the VR's distinctive behaviors were present. It's sometimes listed as a possible Visalia Ransacker burglary, so we're including it here with the usual caveat that we can't vouch for its position in the VR canon.

More information could be forthcoming in the near future – now that the VR series is finally being studied more closely by additional jurisdictions due to its tie to the Golden State Killer case, it's possible that lost or forgotten reports will turn up.

VR #010 – *Ransacking*
April 6th or 7th, 1974 | S Linda Vista St

Sometime between Saturday, April 6th at 7:30 PM and Sunday, April 7th at 11:00 AM, a ransacking occurred at a single-story house on South Linda Vista Street. The victims were out of town when the burglary occurred.

The offender attempted to pry open a door, but he was unsuccessful. He found an unlocked window and used it to enter the residence.

Once inside, he ransacked every room. Clothing was dumped onto the floor, and the burglar stole a piggybank full of coins before exiting through a sliding glass door.

The resident was a fifty-year-old woman, and her daughter was a student at Mt. Whitney High School.

This home on South Linda Vista Street had a bigger backyard than most of the properties in the area, which could've been a significant geographical attraction for the offender. Perhaps he'd hidden in the yard to make sure that his targets weren't home, or he'd needed a staging area, or he'd needed a wide berth to jump fences in his travels between Linda Vista and Whitney (the other street that he targeted around the same time).

This incident is usually considered the first confirmed ransacking of the Visalia Ransacker series. Surprisingly, even though it's an early crime, there are a lot of behaviors here that remain consistent throughout 1974 and 1975: the dumping of the clothing onto the floor (particularly women's clothing and underwear), entry while the residents aren't home, and a fascination with piggybanks and coins.

The obvious pry marks at the door and the initial failure to enter the residence can be looked at through two different lenses – one explanation is that perhaps this was a sign of a fledgling burglar who didn't quite know what he was doing. The other is that maybe he just didn't care and or he was lazy, looking for the easiest way in with minimal amount of effort and not worrying about leaving sloppy "work" behind.

When the entire VR series is looked at as a whole, it's clear that breaking into a home gracefully was never the Ransacker's forte. There were *several* doors and windows that bested him over the years. Unsuccessfully prying at this door and failing to gain entry through it was par for the course.

VR #011 – *Ransacking*
April 6th or 7th, 1974 | S Whitney St

Sometime between Saturday, April 6th at 6:00 PM and the afternoon hours of Sunday, April 7th, the Visalia Ransacker hit a home on South Whitney Street. The victims were out of town for the weekend.

The VR entered the single-story house by prying open a sliding glass door. Once inside, he ransacked every room. Just like the ransacking on South Linda Vista Street, he stole a piggybank with coins inside.

This was the first known ransacking where the perpetrator used an improvised alarm system. The Ransacker was known to occasionally take cups or trinkets and put them against doors or on doorknobs in such a way that they'd fall to the ground or make a loud noise if the doors were opened from the outside. It ensured that if the residents came home in the middle of a ransacking, he'd be alerted by the sound of the items crashing down and he'd have a chance to escape. To facilitate a quick getaway, he'd usually leave one or more windows open.

At this scene, he left items inside both the front *and* back doors.

While the South Demaree Street ransacking in June 1973 is often suspected to be the work of the Visalia Ransacker, most of the other possible events tied to him before March and April 1974 were mere prowlings. The use of the "alarm system" this early on in the crime spree is very telling – perhaps he'd thought about his crimes quite a bit before going into them full-swing, or maybe he'd studied the art of burglarizing homes, or it's even possible that he'd been a small-time burglar somewhere else before coming to Visalia. These theories and more will be explored later.

The victim in this case was an adult male, and there were other residents living in the home as well.

The police dusted for evidence and found a few latent prints that didn't match the family. They didn't match any known burglar in the area either, so they were saved on specialized fingerprint cards for possible matching or identification should the offender hit again.

This was the first known time that the Visalia Ransacker hit South Whitney Street (called Whitney Lane and Whitney Drive at the time of the crimes). It certainly wouldn't be the last. The Ransacker would visit again and again, and a year and a half after starting his burglaries on Whitney, he would actually commit a murder on the street – just a few houses away from where *this* crime took place, in fact.

Again, the geography is worth a look. The clues that can be found here help give us an idea of where he was coming from and where he might've been going to during each night where he was active. Through the study of the crime locations and the surrounding topography, various deductions about origins and pathways through the neighborhoods can be made.

In this particular instance, assuming that the ransackings were done back-to-back like other burglaries later in the series, one has to wonder which method he chose when crossing from South Linda Vista Street over to South Whitney Street. Since the house that he ransacked on Linda Vista was up toward Noble Avenue, did he cross through a backyard to get to Noble and then hop over to Whitney, or did he go all the way back down to West Campus Avenue and take the street? The following map shows the two ransackings we just discussed, as well the two that we'll discuss next:

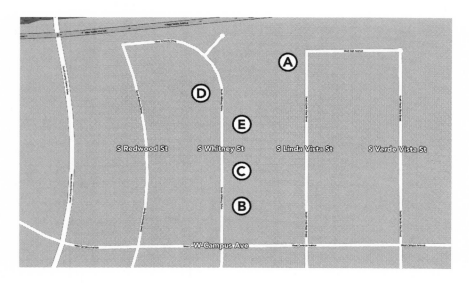

The area where the April 1974 ransackings occurred. This is often considered "ground zero" for the offender – not only is it the location where he started, but it's the area where significant events like the murder of Professor Claude Snelling took place on September 11th, 1975.

A) April 6th: Ransacking on Linda Vista

B) April 6th: Ransacking on Whitney

C) April – exact date unknown: Ransacking on Whitney

D) April – exact date unknown: Ransacking on Whitney

E) September 11th, 1975 Murder of Claude Snelling

Other April 1974 Ransackings

There were two more incidents attributed to the Ransacker during the month of April. No reports exist on these. Unfortunately, much of the information from *several* early Ransacker incidents is no longer available or was never captured adequately. It's a common issue with very old cases, and the police in April 1974 had no idea that they were dealing with a serial offender. At the time, there was no way of knowing what was important to note and what wasn't. On the surface, these seemed like nuisance burglaries. Low-loss and low-damage.

VR #012 – *Ransacking*
April 1974 | S Whitney St

A ransacking occurred at a house on South Whitney Street. Several items were stolen.

The approximate date and the exact address of this burglary is known, and little else. It occurred only two houses to the north of VR #011, so it's possible that this ransacking took place late on April 6th or early on April 7th like the two we've already discussed.

Some of these missing or incomplete reports were a little frustrating as we were compiling our research together, but as we said in the intro, it's understandable. Oftentimes the burglaries weren't reported right away. The dollar amount of the items stolen was usually small, and at some of them, nothing was stolen at all. There typically wasn't a lot of damage at the scene. Many homeowners simply shrugged them off or reported them when it was convenient for them.

VR #013 – *Ransacking*
April 1974 | S Whitney St

Another ransacking occurred at a house on South Whitney Street. Several items were stolen. Like VR #012, the address is known but no report exists. It's possible that this ransacking occurred on the same night as the other Whitney and Linda Vista ransackings.

While it's unfortunate that no detailed information exists for these two incidents, we do know that they were brought into the fold due to matching M.O. and other factors that were observed at the scene. They were clearly perpetrated by the same offender that burglarized the other homes in April.

This cluster we're dealing with is obviously significant – the first four official ransackings. Traditionally, profilers and police like to look closely at the earliest known crimes. Mistakes are often made and the thought-process of an offender in his or her fledgling state is more apparent. Investigators throughout the years have paid particular attention to *this* ransacking within the cluster, because the Visalia Ransacker actually returned to this home and ransacked it *again* on February 2nd, 1975. The VR was known to do this a few times, and each time he did it, it seemed to mark a significant turning point the series. Early February 1975 was when he seemed to be doing a *lot* of prowling and peeping in this same area, and it's the month when Claude Snelling, the Golden State Killer's first known murder victim, first found the Visalia Ransacker on his property.

First May 1974 Series

While it's possible to make the case that all of the April ransackings occurred on one night, that certainly wasn't the story in May. Perhaps emboldened by the fact that he burglarized four different homes and yet no one had figured out who he was, the Ransacker began upping the ante.

Throughout the East Area Rapist / Golden State Killer series, we often see that the month of May corresponds to a significant uptick in the offender's activity. This month, May 1974, was no exception. It was here that he really began to sink his teeth into his routine as the Visalia Ransacker.

Side note: Another notable "May" occurred in 1977 when he was the East Area Rapist. He committed five home-invasion rapes and several burglaries – a significant number of crimes. May 1986 was also notable, because it was the month where he committed his last known murder. At that point, he'd taken nearly a five-year break from offending between July 1981 and May 1986, so his return was a significant deviation from pattern.

VR #014 – *Ransacking*
May 4th, 1974 | S Dollner St

At approximately 8:30 PM on Saturday, May 4th, the Ransacker pried open a window at a single-story house on South Dollner Street. He entered the residence while the victims were away for the evening.

While inside, he opened a couple more windows – most likely to leave himself a means of escape if the residents returned home while he was still there. He spent the most time in the bedrooms, dumping clothes out of drawers and scattering them around.

He found and stole an expensive coin collection, and he also took cash from the residence.

At the conclusion of the burglary, the VR left the home through a different window than the one he had used to enter it.

The head of this household was a male – close to fifty years old. He worked in the agriculture industry. Other residents lived in the home as well.

Latent fingerprints were found at the scene, but they didn't match the prints found at the burglary on South Whitney Street in April. Since there was no match in prints, but the crimes were clearly committed by the same person, police assumed that the prints at both scenes belonged to friends or family members of the victims.

This residence was a corner house, situated across the street to the east of Rotary Park and Divisadero Middle School. As the crime spree wore on, it was learned that the Ransacker often burglarized homes near parks and schools, possibly parking transportation on the other side of them or hiding at those locations to watch the neighborhood and to make sure that the coast was clear for him to proceed. Since these areas were bordered by streets that weren't directly connected, he probably also realized that if he were ever pursued from a crime scene, he could shake a vehicle by dashing across one of these lots.

One more advantage to these types of locales – the parks and schools were much darker than the streets during the hours that he ransacked. Operating near them likely afforded him more cover.

VR #015 – *Ransacking*
May 5th, 1974 | W Feemster Ave

On Sunday night, sometime between 7:00 PM and 10:25 PM, the Visalia Ransacker entered a single-story home on West Feemster Avenue while its occupants were away for a few hours. This was the day after VR #014 occurred.

He entered by prying open a sliding glass door. Once inside the house, he went to one of the bedrooms, opened a window, pried the screen out from the inside, and placed the screen on the bed.

He primarily focused on ransacking the bedrooms. He took clothes out of drawers, scattered them around, and rummaged through jewelry boxes extensively. Apparently nothing was to his liking, because he didn't take anything from them, but he did take a piggybank and some money.

The VR exited through the window he had opened earlier. Since this was his "emergency exit," perhaps he'd heard the residents returning and had to dash out.

The head of the household was in his late fifties. He worked as a salesman.

While the home targeted the day before was on a corner, this one was not. He did seem to prefer corner houses in many of his burglaries, but it clearly wasn't a deal-breaker if he found a viable target in the middle of street. In some ways, corner houses possibly posed more risk to him than houses that were deeper inside a neighborhood because they were so much more exposed. They did, however, offer a quicker escape route to a main thoroughfare and *less* risk of being seen or heard by neighbors living adjacent – fewer sides of the house bordered other properties. Houses located further down the street had more places for the offender to disappear to and hide, which may have been one of the reasons that even in the beginning, he didn't *exclusively* target corner houses.

Like the prowling incidents covered earlier in the book, this ransacking occurring on West Feemster Avenue, though the portion of the street it occurred on wasn't connected to the other strip of road that the prowling incidents occurred on. Evan's Ditch was still located nearby. Based on analysis of other crimes in the series, many feel that he might have used the ditch to travel to and from certain homes. It's not known for sure if he did that in this instance though, because it wasn't a *direct* route – there was plenty of open ground between the street and the ditch.

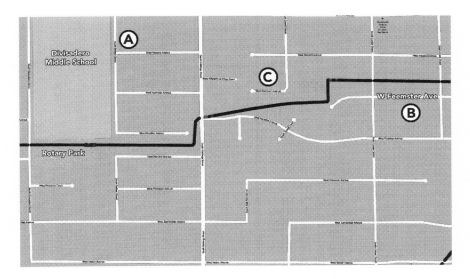

The locations of these two incidents with the park, school, and ditch highlighted. Also noted are the locations of the W Feemster Ave prowling incidents from 1973 and 1974.

A) VR #014 South Dollner Street ransacking

B) VR #015 West Feemster Avenue ransacking

C) The location of the September 1973 and January 1974 prowling incidents on West Feemster Avenue

Second May 1974 Series

To anyone reading about these events for the first time, the Visalia Ransacker may hardly appear worthy of in-depth study. After all, he was simply prowling the streets, occasionally finding a house whose occupants weren't home, and then poking at it until he found an easy way inside. From there he opened some windows, emptied some drawers, stole some coins, and left peacefully without inflicting much damage to the household.

That seems to be how the police felt about the situation at first too, even when it became apparent that the crimes were part of a series. This was understandable, though. They had worse criminals to worry about, and their initial assumption was that these crimes were being perpetrated by young teens who were looking for arcade money and sharing giggles over strangers' panties. Even some of the victims themselves were writing off the incidents, simply feeling relieved that their more valuable items hadn't been taken.

But this story will take several turns. In the second week of May 1974, the first indication of the burglar's capacity for violence was revealed.

VR #016 – *Ransacking*
May 10th or 11th, 1974 | W Tulare Ave

Sometime between 7:30 PM on Friday, May 10th and 10:40 PM on Saturday, May 11th, the VR ransacked a single-story house on West Tulare Avenue while the residents were away for the weekend.

He entered by prying open a window. Once inside, he placed items on the inside of the front and rear doors – items which would make noise if someone tried to enter the residence. He also opened another window, removed the screen from the inside, and placed the screen on the bed. Officers were certain that the window was opened so that he could escape quickly if he had to – if the window were merely opened so that he could hear any activity outside, then there would be no reason to remove the screen.

He ransacked several rooms and dumped clothes out of drawers. He stole a coin bank, money, a .380 Remington automatic pistol, and a clip of ammunition.

He left through a sliding glass door.

The head of the household was about forty years old. He lived alone at the residence.

When the police arrived, they were able to lift several fingerprints. Unfortunately, none of them matched the prints that had been taken at previous scenes, and they were thought to belong to visitors that the resident had entertained.

So much for their nuisance offender – from this point forward, the Ransacker could be considered armed and dangerous. He had probably been thinking about his crimes, thinking about what would happen if he were cornered, and thinking about how a gun might be traced back to him if he were to use one of his own.

West Tulare Avenue was one of the major east/west streets in the VR's typical attack zone. The main east/west thoroughfares in the area of the city where he offended were State Route 198 (and its parallel partner, West Noble Avenue, which effectively formed the northern border of his attack zone), West Tulare Avenue, and West Walnut Avenue. South of that was West Whitendale Avenue, and activity grew more sparse down toward there. Of course, other streets ran east/west in the affected area, but they were usually broken up and didn't span the whole city. When thinking about thoroughfares that the VR could've used to get from one side of Visalia to the other in a hurry, those were his options.

VR #017 – Ransacking
May 11th, 1974 | S Whitney St

Sometime between 7:30 PM and 11:00 PM on Saturday, May 11th, the VR entered a single-story home while the residents were away.

Rather than having to pry at anything, he found an unlocked window. Once inside, he left himself multiple points of escape by opening more windows, and he pried the screen off of one of them and left it on a bed. He engaged the chain lock on the front door, most likely as a trick to slow down the residents if they arrived while he was still on the premises.

The VR spent extra time ransacking the bedrooms, and in one of them, he took the woman's underwear out of drawers and arranged all of it in a deliberate way on and near the bed.

He stole cash from the house, not coins, and he went through wedding cards that he found in one of the drawers. When the homeowners took inventory of them later, they realized that he'd stolen some of them.

The head of the household was in his mid fifties, and he worked in manufacturing. Other family members lived at the residence as well, including a teenage son who attended Mt. Whitney High School.

At this burglary, the VR left noticeable shoe prints for the first time. Since fingerprinting hadn't come up with anything significant at this point, the shoe prints were considered one of the earliest viable pieces of physical evidence in the case.

Because the resident in the other ransacking was away for two nights, the other burglary could've happened on Friday night *or* Saturday night. Since we know *this* one happened on Saturday night, it's possible that the other one did as well. Of course, on the weekend prior, he'd ransacked one house on Saturday night and another house on Sunday night, so there's no way of knowing. One of the difficulties in pinning down his comings and goings from the neighborhoods is that, since he struck while people were gone for the evening or out of town, it was impossible to know when exactly their home was entered. The Ransacker was usually the epitome of a silent and stealthy as criminal, so neighbors rarely noticed anything particularly suspicious in the area to help narrow down the time windows.

The two homes that he hit on this weekend were fairly close together. He probably traveled in between them on foot, so one has to wonder what made these particular houses more inviting to him than the other houses that he must've passed as he traveled between the two locations. While some of his selection methods still remain a mystery, as the book goes on we'll make at least *some* headway in figuring out why he chose some of his targets over others.

45

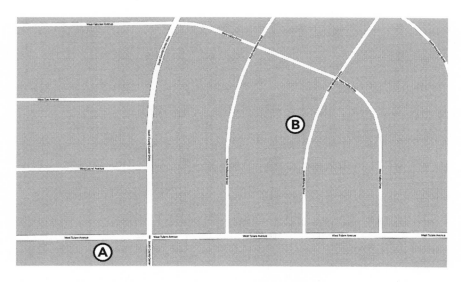

A close-up of the attack area from this weekend of ransacking. The homes were less than a quarter mile away from each other.

A) VR #016 Ransacking on W Tulare Ave
B) VR #017 Ransacking on S Whitney St

This was the first clear example in the reports of the Ransacker taking extra time to arrange women's undergarments in a particular and deliberate way. Whether it happened at the previous scenes and the police didn't take note of it or whether this was truly the first time, this odd activity was a part of the VR M.O. that became an unmistakable element of his crimes. In many scenes, he *only* dumped and arranged women's undergarments, leaving the men's clothes alone. In other scenes, he didn't discriminate as much – there were some ransackings where he rearranged or lined up men's undergarments on the floor. Since this behavior obviously didn't serve a practical purpose, the motivation for it was most likely sexual, psychological, or it was kind of commentary on something known only to the offender.

It's considered a "signature" behavior – something that the offender didn't *have* to do in order to carry out his crime. It's something that he *wanted* to do.

It should be noted that in the previous ransacking we discussed, the victim was a man who lived alone. Perhaps the VR was frustrated that there were no female affects at that location, and his frustration resulted in him taking extra time at *this* ransacking to deliberately rearrange and spend extra effort on the female undergarments. After studying the Visalia Ransacker for so long, we do notice some quirky cause-and-effect behavior like that sometimes.

The manipulation of (and if we're understanding the documentation correctly, the theft of) the wedding cards continues to show that the VR is not a typical thief. These items don't have any financial value – they're purely personal and have sentimental value only to the victims.

Most burglars commit their crimes for financial gain. Not the VR. This action is one of the first ones that speak volumes about the psychology and the motivation of the offender. What could be more important or sentimental than wedding cards? In light of his interest in those, the piggybank thefts start to make more sense. He wasn't fishing for dimes so that he could make phone calls – he was after specific types of items of supposed importance to his victims.

For a teenager or child, those types of items included keepsake piggybanks given to them by doting grandparents. A child or teen would spend a lot of time collecting coins in their piggybanks, and those meager earnings were often being saved over a long period of time for something special. For an older resident, a precious coin collection seemed to be an acceptable substitute, and a coin collection was something that the Visalia Ransacker had also stolen at this point.

It seems that these types of activities might've been a way to hurt or disappoint his victims in a very specific way. A way that he had been hurt or disappointed himself? A substitute for something important that he had lost in his own life? Something that he had worked for a long time to achieve or collect, and then lost?

Whatever the underlying motivation actually was, he seemed interested in the personal and private items of his victims. Aside from the sexual component of these intrusions (which will become more pronounced later on), influencing the personal lives of his victims appeared to be a motivator in some cases. As the East Area Rapist, he may or may not have been pleased to know that his attacks were so traumatic, about 90% of his adult victims ended up divorcing.

Looking at these two ransackings more closely, it's clear that the VR was already escalating. In the first one we discussed, he mixed ransacking with violence – the theft of a gun and ammunition. In the second one, he mixed it with sexual behavior – the laying out of female undergarments.

One final note about the theft of the wedding cards – this will become more apparent as our analysis of the crime spree moves forward, but the offender seemed to have an issue with the idea of marriage and family. In subsequent ransackings, he began to steal wedding rings, destroy wedding photos, and displace family portraits.

Third May 1974 Series

Presenting the case with all of this organization and hindsight is probably making it pretty obvious that this was a man headed down a dangerous path. It wasn't quite as apparent at the time, but one of the red flags that began to emerge was the fact that he began offending on a very regular basis and with a regular routine. Basically, every week in May had Visala Ransacker activity attached to it. Not only were his behaviors escalating and not only were new things being added to the mix (guns, sex), but the unrelenting nature of his offenses were starting to become apparent. This was a man obsessed with his crimes, and he was committing them on a more frequent basis.

VR #018 – *Ransacking*
May 17th, 1974 | S Emerald Ct

Sometime around 10:30 PM on Friday, May 17th, the Ransacker entered a single-story home on South Emerald Court while the victims were away from home.

He entered through an unlocked window, and then he opened additional windows in the home to use as possible escape routes. He pulled some of the screens inside and set them on the beds.

He ransacked every room in the house, spending quite a bit of time taking out and arranging underwear belonging to the two teenage daughters.

He stole coins and a man's ring from the residence.

When they responded, the police looked very thoroughly for fingerprints, but they couldn't find any. They were certain that he was wearing gloves or using something else to keep from leaving evidence. He hadn't slipped up at all yet – nothing could be matched from any scene. This was significant development, because it showed a basic awareness of forensic techniques and a dedication to self-preservation that most burglars did not possess.

The head of the household was a man in his mid forties. He worked as an insurance salesman. The two teenage daughters were both cheerleaders at Mt. Whitney High School.

Note that the VR stole one of the man's rings at this burglary. Much of our time will be spent focused on the violation of the women that occurred during the peepings, prowlings, and ransackings, but it's important to relate that the Ransacker also targeted the men, especially when it came to stealing items of personal significance.

This was one of the first solid indications that the Ransacker was interested in teenage girls. Specifically, teenage girls who attended Mt. Whitney High School. This would become a common theme as the series progressed, and it was one of the reasons that the police initially felt that the crimes were being committed by a team of teenage boys. During the active years of the case, most of the VR suspects identified by police were under twenty. It wasn't until Officer McGowen came face-to-face with the unmasked perpetrator in December 1975 that the VR's probable age range was bumped up to between twenty-five and thirty-five years old.

VR #019 – *Ransacking*
May 17th, 1974 | W Dartmouth Ave

A woman was living alone in a single-story home on West Dartmouth Avenue. She went out on Friday night (May 17th) from 9:30 PM to 1:40 AM and while she was away, the VR burglarized her home.

He made his way in by prying open a door. Once inside, he ransacked her bedroom and scattered her clothing around, particularly her underwear.

He stole a coin bank. It's possible, but not known for sure, if Blue Chip stamps were stolen from the scene. He also stole some cash.

It's not known how he exited the residence.

The woman was in her early fifties. She worked as a bookkeeper.

The two ransackings that we've discussed in the chapter thus far were both committed on Friday night. The next one that we discuss might not have been – the possible timeframe encompassed virtually the entire weekend. The fourth one was definitely committed on another night, making this yet another weekend where the VR was active on more than one evening.

Looking at the location of the two ransackings that definitely happened on the same night reveals some interesting geographical features – the proximity of the school, the park, and Evan's Ditch.

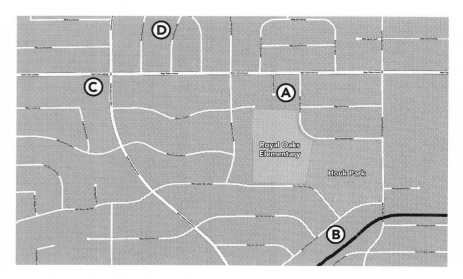

The Ransacker may have traversed the park rather than the street, and he may have arrived at this location via the ditch. Ransackings from May 17th, 1974 and ransackings from May 10th/11th, 1974 are both featured here because of how close they were to each other.

A) *VR #018 May 17th: ransacking on S Emerald Ct*

B) *VR #019 May 17th: ransacking on W Dartmouth Ave*

C) *VR #016 May 10th or 11th: W Tulare Ave ransacking*

D) *VR #017 May 11th: S Whitney St ransacking*

The proximity of parks, schools, and the ditch is a factor that remains fairly constant throughout most of the crimes, but it seems *especially* pronounced in this earlier phase. Perhaps it's coincidence, or perhaps the offender was still learning the area and becoming comfortable with the types of crimes he was committing. It seemed to take time for him to work up the courage to attack further away from these crutches.

It's also possible that he was using old tricks to get the lay of the land. There's work underway to examine early burglaries in Exeter, East

Sacramento, and even the Goleta/Santa Barbara area that may be tied to this offender. None of those crimes are quite as extensive as the Visalia Ransacker series, but the peeping, prowling, and petty theft could've been part of this perpetrator's lifestyle for a long time.

Another geographical crutch that should be mentioned is a footpath at the northern part of his strike zone. It used to run the entire length of the city between West Noble Avenue and State Route 198. He was a bit holder on nights that he seemed to rely on this path. That area, in particular the portion of it near Whitney/Redwood/Linda Vista, was an early comfort zone for him.

Some do argue that geographical features may not have played as much of a role in the series as we think, but it's hard not to visually notice the ditch and the schools being so close to so many of the ransackings. The two that we've discussed in this chapter so far seem especially tied to the topography of the area. The ransackings from the previous weekend were only a thousand feet from these, making the case even stronger.

The mention of "Blue Chip stamps" may have been confusing for anyone who wasn't alive during the era. This was a rewards and redemption program that's mostly disappeared in the modern era. In the "Blue Chip" stamp program, participating stores (like grocery stores) would give customers reward stamps based on how much merchandise they purchased at the store. The stamps would be pasted by the customer into small books specially designed for that purpose, and then the customer would save up their stamps and take them to a redemption center once they had an appropriate amount. The stamps could be traded in for merchandise like housewares, jewelry, toys, or even furniture.

The stamps were mentioned here because in later crimes, it was clear that the Visalia Ransacker took them from a scene anytime he found them. Along with coins, they seemed to be of particular interest to him. They weren't worth very much, but perhaps the ease of carrying them away from a crime scene was attractive to him, along with maybe the satisfaction that he had essentially stolen away the time and care that someone else had spent in collecting them.

VR #020 – *Ransacking*
May 18th, 1974 | W Feemster Ave

Sometime between Friday, May 17th at 4:30 PM and Sunday, May 19th at 5:00 PM, the Ransacker entered a single-story home on West Feemster Avenue while the residents were away for the weekend.

He first attempted to enter by prying on a sliding glass door, but he was unsuccessful. Entry was gained by prying open a window.

Once inside, he opened several other windows to use as possible escape routes, and he placed a bottle of perfume on the doorknob so that he would know if someone else opened the door.

He ransacked the bedrooms, throwing female underclothing onto the floor as he went.

Coins, cash, and some piggybanks were stolen (a total loss of just over fifty dollars). He also stole a broken necklace, some pantyhose, and some cologne.

The VR exited the residence through a sliding glass door.

A man in his mid forties was the head of the household. He worked as an insurance agent. His family included a daughter that was in the band program at Mt. Whitney High School.

The family attended the First Baptist Church of Visalia, located nearby. This is the first in a long string Ransacker connections related to that church. A deacon's home, the pastor's home, and various prominent members all suffered burglaries attributed to the Visalia Ransacker. In one instance, the Ransacker even went out of his way to destroy a Sunday School pin. He also seemed to specifically target young women who sang in the choir, though whether it was because of their church affiliation or because he used his obsession with one of them to discover others is somewhat unknown, and it's a concept we'll explore as we make our way through the series.

In September 1975, he attempted to kidnap one of the young ladies affiliated with the church. This was the incident where her father, Claude Snelling intervened, resulting in the Ransacker shooting him to death. Claude Snelling, too, was very active in the church. Again, we'll explore all of this later on.

This was one of the largest places of worship in Tulare County, and with its relatively high attendance, these things could all be mere coincidence. Like many of the variables related to the case (including any Mt. Whitney High School connection), the church's proximity to the VR's hunting grounds may be the chicken, or it may be the egg.

VR #021 – *Ransacking*
May 18th, 1974 | W Cambridge Ave

Between Saturday, May 18th at 1:00 PM and Sunday, May 19th at 12:25 PM, the VR hit a house on West Cambridge Avenue. The victims weren't home when he committed the burglary.

He gained entry through an open window. Once inside, he opened others.

This was considered a "light ransacking" because for some reason, he left several portions of the rooms alone. Many drawers and other common VR targets were untouched. He did take the time to remove the women's clothing and underwear, and he tossed them onto the floor and the bed. Even though the chaos wasn't as extensive as it had been in other burglaries, there was at least one item disturbed in almost every room.

Sometimes, a house wouldn't be ransacked as extensively if the VR were interrupted in the middle of his activities. That's unlikely to be the case here, though, because the family arrived home in the middle of the day, most likely many hours after the VR had left.

He left through a sliding glass door, stealing nothing from the scene.

The head of the household was a retired man in his mid fifties. He lived there with the rest of his family. His son, who also lived at the residence, was a freshman at Mt. Whitney High School.

Shoe prints were found. It was clear that the offender was careful about not leaving fingerprints, but he didn't seem as cautious about covering up shoe prints. In some cases, of course, leaving them was unavoidable, while in others it did seem that he purposely covered them up. In general, he didn't seem to go out of his way to conceal shoe impressions.

Because of the timeframe that these victims provided about when they left the home and when they returned, we can be certain that the VR made at least two trips out to burglarize over the weekend. The first two ransackings can definitely be tied to Friday night, the third one could fit on either night, and this one can be tied pretty solidly to Saturday night.

For the third burglary, placing it on a map seems to illustrate that it probably did happen on Saturday night. The following is a map that plots these Saturday night burglaries, and also shows one that occurred on May 5th. Its proximity to these other two shows that he was returning to areas that he had already hit, probably because he'd already gained some familiarity with them and he could operate more quickly and more discreetly.

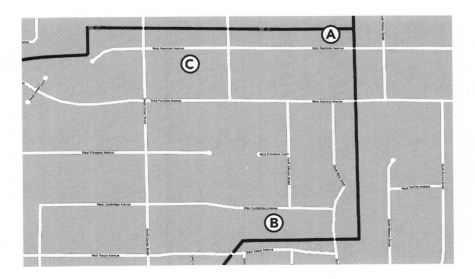

The ransackings that most likely occurred on Saturday, May 18th. 1974. A ransacking from May 5th is also shown to illustrate how close some of these ransackings were to each other, even when they didn't occur on the same night.

A) *VR #020 Ransacking on W Feemster Ave*

B) *VR #021 Ransacking on W Cambridge Ave*

C) *VR #015 May 5th, 1974 ransacking on W Feemster Ave*

One feature stands out – Evan's Ditch, which is represented by the dark lines. Recall the other instances we've studied so far where it seemed to border the houses that he was prowling and ransacking. The vast majority of the homes in Visalia did *not* border the ditch, but a large portion of the homes by the VR *did*. Even at this point in the crime series, it's statistically significant. Perhaps the ditch was used exclusively for covert travel, or perhaps he found it easier to hide there and case homes from a distance. It's likely that he was in the process of building up his confidence as an offender and/or still getting to know the area.

Fourth May 1974 Series

VR #022– *Ransacking*
May 21st, 1974 | W Howard Ave

Most confirmed VR crimes had occurred on weekends, but on Tuesday, May 21st at 7:30 PM, the VR entered a single-story residence on West Howard Avenue while the victims were away.

He entered by prying open a window. Once inside, he set about his usual routine of opening another window to use as an escape route.

He rummaged through the bedrooms, and anytime he came across women's undergarments, they were removed and placed on the floor. He rummaged extensively through the jewelry boxes and left them all turned upside down.

Nothing was stolen during this ransacking. The offender left through a sliding glass door.

The head of the household was a businessman, and he lived at the residence with his family.

Fingerprints were found at the scene. They were lifted carefully and compared to prints from other ransackings. No match. They probably didn't belong to the burglar.

It was rare for a ransacking like this to happen on a Tuesday. It was also odd that there was nothing stolen, although the VR didn't always take something from every scene. It speaks loudly to his motivations, however. Most burglars would ask themselves "why go through the risk of breaking into someone's home if you're not going to steal anything?" But the VR clearly wasn't "most burglars." His focus was elsewhere.

Despite the day of the week being an outlier, the M.O. and behaviors at the scene indicated that the Ransacker was responsible. The geographic location in relation to a ransacking that had occurred just a few days before it deserves to be noted, as well:

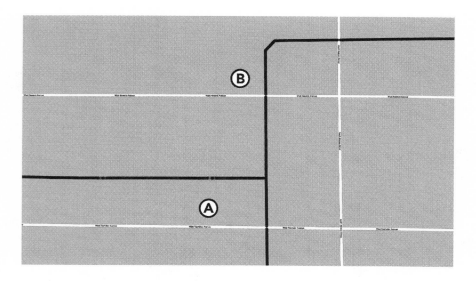

These two ransackings occurred a few days apart, but they practically backed up to each other. Evan's Ditch is represented by the thick lines.

A) VR #020 May 18th, 1974 ransacking on W Feemster Ave
B) VR #022 May 21st, 1974 ransacking on W Howard Ave

Fifth May 1974 Series

The final weekend in May was the VR's most extensive outing yet: six known burglaries occurred.

This weekend shows the Ransacker taking things a step *further* and actually masturbating in one of the homes. It's also the first documented debut of one of his signature moves – stealing a single earring from a pair and leaving the matching earring behind.

It was Memorial Day weekend. For some reason, the Ransacker was often busier on holidays. Perhaps because more people were out of town, because his home situation afforded him more time to commit these crimes, or because holidays themselves were a trigger for him in some unknown way. Regardless, it was a busy end to a busy May, and after it was over, the town wouldn't feel his presence again for nearly a month.

VR #023 – *Ransacking*
May 25th or 26th, 1974 | W Sue Ave

Between Friday, May 25th at 10:30 AM and Sunday, May 26th at 12:05 PM, a single-story residence on West Sue Avenue was ransacked while the family was away.

The Ransacker entered by prying a sliding glass door. Multiple windows and doors were opened as possible escape routes.

He ransacked every room, removing women's undergarments and placing them on the floor and the bed.

A coin collection and some regular coins were stolen from the scene.

He exited through a different sliding glass door than the one he had used to enter the residence. Rather than simply opening the door, for some reason he actually pried it open from the inside. This was behavior he would repeat a couple years later as the East Area Rapist and again as the Golden State Killer.

The head of the household was a businessman in his early/mid sixties.

A sock was found in an odd place, and technicians at the scene theorized that the Ransacker had used it as a glove. Still, some fingerprints were lifted that were initially thought to be the Ransacker's, but they didn't match any other prints on file.

The layout of this home was atypical for the area, and it was located to the west of the College of the Sequoias – a location that would play into the crime series in several different ways as the months went by.

VR #024– *Ransacking*
May 24th through 27th, 1974 | S Redwood St

Sometime between Friday, May 24th at 5:05 PM and Monday, May 27th at 7:29 PM, a single-story residence on South Redwood Street was ransacked while the family was away for the weekend.

He entered the house by prying open a window. Once inside, he opened several more windows, prying off a screen from the inside and leaving it on the bed.

He rummaged through the bedrooms, removing the wife's and the daughter's undergarments. He "arranged them" on the floor, the bed, and in other areas of the house in a very intentional way. The exact details are missing from our documentation.

He broke a piggybank, stole the coins from it, stole cash, and stole single earrings from sets (leaving the matching earrings behind). At the time of the burglary, the victims weren't completely sure if the earrings had been stolen or if they had lost them. Since the Ransacker stole single earrings at many of the burglaries that followed, it's safe to assume that he took them.

He left through a door.

The head of the family was a man in his mid thirties, and he worked as a salesman.

Stealing a single earring from a pair is an odd thing to do. If the thief was interested in the value, he'd take both of them. If he was afraid that the earring would be identified while fencing or pawning it, then he'd also need to take both of them or else one earring could be used to identify the other. If he was interested in having a personal item from the victim, then what would it matter if he stole one earring or both? It's significant that several times over the course of the series, he steals only half of the set. Was there some kind of thrill or illusion of a "bond" between him and his victim by him having one piece of the set and the victim retaining the other? Was this done so that the victim would discover the missing earring later on and feel violated all over again?

This type of behavior is difficult to explain, but so much of what the Ransacker did seems to be aimed at thumbing his nose at victims.

There's also that added layer of "I'm only doing this to piss you off. The value means nothing to me, or I'd take both." Regardless of his actual thought process, it's quite a statement, both in how little he thinks of his victims' possessions and how he might wants *them* to see *him*.

VR #025– *Ransacking*
May 25th or 26th, 1974 | W Cambridge Ave

The family in a single-story residence on West Cambridge Avenue was gone from approximately 6:00 PM on Saturday, May 25th to 8:00 AM on Sunday, May 26th. Sometime overnight, the Ransacker entered their home.

He made his way in through a window. Once inside the residence, he began ransacking the bedrooms and removing underclothing from the wife's and teenage daughter's drawers. He stacked bras and panties on the floor and on the beds. He ransacked every single room in the house.

Before leaving through a sliding glass door, the VR broke a piggy bank apart and took the coins from it.

Fingerprints were found at the scene, but there was no match for any known criminal and they didn't match the prints from the other ransackings. It was assumed that they belonged to friends and family who had visited the residence over the years.

The daughter was a student at Mt. Whitney High School.

Unlike most of the other ransackings that occurred over Memorial Day weekend, this one can be tied to a pretty narrow time window. It helps determine when the other ones were likely to take place. The

South Redwood Street ransacking (VR #024) was only a few houses away from this one, so it's likely that those two occurred on the same night.

VR #026– *Ransacking*
May 26th, 1974 | W Sowell St

Between 7:45 PM and 9:30 PM on Sunday, May 26th, the Ransacker entered a single-story residence while the victim was away.

He entered through an unlocked window. As he often did, he opened multiple exits inside the residence. It's important to note that he didn't close any of these doors or windows before he left – at most scenes, the exits were still open when the homeowner returned.

The intruder ransacked the bedrooms. A woman didn't live at the residence, so there was none of his distinctive behavior related to female underclothing.

Nothing was stolen. The VR left through a different window than the one he'd used to enter the residence.

The man who lived there was in his early sixties and worked as a CPA.

One of the mysteries of the Visalia Ransacker series is his method of selecting targets, especially early on. Investigators eventually determined that he was most likely making "rounds" through select areas of the city and peeping in at certain individuals on a regular basis, and that he would strike their homes and the ones around them when the opportunity presented itself. Even so, it's hard to explain his intrusion into a sixty-year-old man's home. No female undergarments to look at (clearly a primary motivator at this point for entering homes) and there was nothing that interested him enough to steal. We're assuming that this was just a crime of opportunity – "easy-pickings" because a window was unlocked. So was opportunity and availability a big part of his method at this stage? Or even some of the later ones? When he entered a home and went through a victim's personal things, did he always know who lived there beforehand? How many of these were crimes of opportunity, and how many of these were people had he previously observed in some form or fashion? Was there ever any personal connection between him and his victims? In the early crimes, these questions are hard to answer. Later VR crimes weave a few surprising threads.

In this particular case, it seems as simple as this home being located along the path he happened to be taking, and the home being vulnerable because of an unlocked window.

VR #027– Ransacking
May 25th to 27th, 1974 | W Howard Ave

Sometime between 10:30 PM on Saturday, May 25th, and 12:30 PM on Monday, May 27th, a single-story residence on West Howard Avenue was ransacked while the victim was away.

The VR attempted to pry a door and a window to gain entry to the house, but he failed at both. He succeeded in prying open a *different* door.

Once inside, he opened windows. At one of them, he pried off the screen from the inside and placed it on the bed.

He ransacked the bedrooms and forced open strongboxes that contained jewelry. He apparently sifted through all of it, but he didn't take anything. He stole regular coins and a coin collection from the residence.

The victim was a retired man in his mid sixties. No one else lived at the house with him – another possible example of the Ransacker not knowing whose house he was in.

VR #028– *Ransacking*
May 24th through May 27th, 1974 | W Cambridge Ave

Sometime between Friday, May 24th and Monday, May 27th at 3:00 PM, a single-story residence on West Cambridge Avenue was ransacked while no one was home.

He failed at prying open one of the doors, but another one eventually gave way.

Once inside, he ransacked every room.

While rummaging, he came across a Playboy magazine. He moved the magazine to the bed, and at some point put large amounts of lotion on his hands. Gooey palm prints thick with lotion were found at the scene.

He stole a piggybank with coins in it, and he also took cash and some 8-track tapes. He left through the same door he had used to enter the residence.

The head of the household was a man in his mid forties. His wife and daughter also lived there, and the daughter attended Mt. Whitney High School. The family was very active in the First Baptist Church.

Incidentally, this wouldn't be the last time that it appeared that the

Visalia Ransacker masturbated in the home of someone who worked for or volunteered for the church. We'll cover another example of that in 1975.

Technicians looked for fingerprints, but they couldn't find any outside of the palm prints. Apparently the intruder had used gloves when touching everything but himself. None of the palm prints were discrete enough to have any value.

Memorial Day weekend of 1974 had seen quite a bit of activity – based on these locations and the timeframes given by the victims, our best guess is that VR #023 happened either Friday night or Saturday night, #024 and #025 happened Saturday night, and #026, #027, and #028 happened on Sunday night. The locations are mapped:

(map appears on the next page)

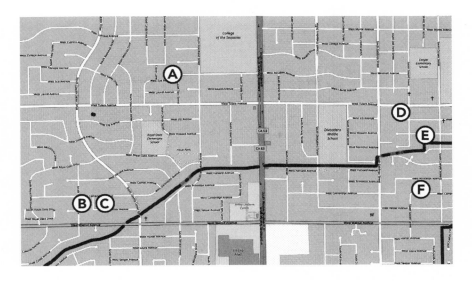

The ransackings that occurred the weekend of May 25th-27th, 1974.

A) VR #023 W Sue Ave

B) VR #024 S Redwood St

C) VR #025 W Cambridge Ave

D) VR #026 S Sowell St

E) VR #027 W Howard Ave

F) VR #028 W Cambridge Ave

After a busy May, the Ransacker would be relatively quiet for most of the summer. Only one known incident was attributed to him.

June 1974 Ransacking

VR #029 – *Ransacking*
June 22nd or June 23rd, 1974 | S Conyer St

Sometime while the residents were away from their home on Saturday, June 22nd, between 8:30 PM and 12:45 AM, the Ransacker entered their single-story residence on South Conyer Street.

He gained entry by prying open a window. Once inside, he opened a few more.

He rummaged through the bedrooms, removing the woman's undergarments as he went and piling them nearby in a deliberate fashion. He also dumped out jewelry boxes and left them upside down.

Nothing was stolen. He left through a different window than the one he'd used to enter.

The head of the household was a man, thirty or so years old, who worked as a surveyor.

Fingerprints were found at the scene, and they were compared to fingerprints found at previous scenes. As usual, no matches. This meant that the fingerprints probably belonged to people who had visited in the past.

It had been roughly twenty-six days since the last ransacking, which was quite a stretch of time given that he had attacked so prolifically in May. Some of the most important and objective facts in this case are the geography and the timing between attacks, so that span might be an important clue as to what the offender might have been doing or thinking during this time. Geographically, this residence was a corner house, located just to the northwest of the Mt. Whitney High School near Myrtle and Kaweah. Definitely a hotspot for Ransacker activity.

When it comes to timing, this one stands out quite a bit – the spring, fall, and winter seasons had so many incidents tied to them and yet the summer had only this. Because this was a one-off in the middle of what became an extended quiet period, what's the significance? The couple living there was a different age range than the typical Visalia Ransacker victim – so far he'd gravitated toward the homes of middle-aged couples with teenage daughters. The occasional older couple was thrown in. The victims in *this* ransacking were only about thirty years old. At the end of the crime spree, the VR was estimated to be in his late twenties or early thirties, so could there have been some kind of connection between the Ransacker and the couple who lived at this house? Was the woman a target from the past or the present? What other reasons would he have had for making this his only stop for the entire summer?

Two other factors also set this one apart from some of the others – nothing was stolen, and there wasn't as much ransacking at this burglary as there'd been with some of the others.

71

September 1974 Ransacking

The Visalia Police Department wasn't sure where their quirky burglar had come from, and as the summer wore on, they weren't sure where he'd gone to, either. On a warm night in September, they learned that the offender hadn't left the area completely – he'd merely been on hiatus.

It's hard to say what could've been responsible for this lull in VR activity. Perhaps the extended daylight hours and blistering heat of the summer months had kept him at bay. When he did start up again, it was for a one-off hit in September before he began ramping back up for a more frenzied October, November, and December.

As the East Area Rapist, summertime breaks were commonplace, and he'd often take about three months off in the middle of the year. It's interesting that this pattern is evident even in 1974 during the Visalia Ransacker series.

The following is a brief chart illustrating the types of breaks he'd in the East Area Rapist series:

(*chart begins on the following page*)

1977
May 17th: Attack #21
May 28th: Attack #22
—3 MONTH BREAK—
September 6th: Attack #23

1978
June 24th: Attack #35
July 6th: Attack #36
—3 MONTH BREAK—
October 7th: Attack #37

1979
June 25th: Attack #47
July 5th: Attack #48
—3 MONTH BREAK—
October 1st: Goleta Attack

In the East Area Rapist series, the breaks often ended with the offender entering a new area and/or attacking a new set of victims. It appeared that some of the "time off" was spent stalking new streets and new targets. It's possible that as the Visalia Ransacker, he was using the summer months of 1974 to gather intel about several areas of town and to gain a comfort level with potential victims and their routines. In later years, this pattern was quite evident and his attacks seemed cyclical. May and October were always months where he seemed to capitalize on all of his stalking in the form of burglaries and attacks, and then it seemed he'd have to pull back and find new victims for a period of time. It's probable that the summer of 1974 was actually the moment in time when the offender was experimenting and discovered that this pattern worked well for him.

VR #030 – *Ransacking*
September 10th to September14th, 1974 | W Princeton Ave

Sometime between Tuesday, September 10th and Saturday, September 14th, the Ransacker entered a single-story residence while the family was away.

He entered by prying open a window. He ransacked all of the bedrooms, and he removed women's undergarments from drawers.

One single earring from a pair was stolen at the scene.

The male victim was about seventy years old, and he was retired. Other family members lived in the home as well.

Latent fingerprints were found, but they didn't match the ransacking from June, nor did they match any of the others. The possibility of getting the Ransacker's prints began to seem unlikely. Aside from the adventure with the Playboy magazine, it seemed he was far too evidence-conscious to remove his gloves or to leave any obvious evidence. There was still the possibility that he would slip up, so they kept trying.

It had been roughly eighty days since the last ransacking. We've discussed how this pattern matched the East Area Rapist series, but it also followed the 1973 pattern almost exactly. There was the inaugural prowling in May, the ransacking in June, and then a break until September before any more activity could possibly be considered in this series. Here again in 1974 there was activity in May (and leading *up* to May, in this case), a single ransacking in June, and then a break in activity until September. Nothing in July or August for either year. The pattern would *not* be repeated in 1975, though he was quiet for most of June and the first few weeks of July of that year.

What's interesting about the *decrease* of activity in the summer is that a lot of case study literature in the criminal justice world typically shows an *increase* in burglaries during the summer for most types of offenders. The VR/EAR series displays an inverse relationship to that. There could be a variety of reasons for this pattern to exist. Perhaps it comes down to the fact he was obviously skilled and adept at what he was doing in some way – whether it be planning, risk aversion, stealth, or other qualities and perhaps the summer added too much risk to the equation for his taste. To commit so many crimes in such a small area and never be caught indicates that, at least at this point, he *was* quite risk-averse. Another theory is that perhaps he had a job or a family that kept him busier during the summer. Maybe it was simply the fact that the extra daylight hours in the evening would've cut down on his prowling time too much.

Another note about the summers – during June, July, and August, some of his neighborhood pathway, like Evan's Ditch, were more crowded with kids out playing. Evan's Ditch also sometimes became less accessible during the summer due to flooding.

Since his primary M.O. was to enter homes while the residents were out, the summer vacation months would seem prime for capitalizing on family trips and other events that would draw families out of their homes for extended periods of time. It's possible, however, that their erratic schedules made it harder for him to figure out when people would be gone and when they would be home.

At this point, Law Enforcement acknowledged the possibility that the VR could be tied to a school schedule. As the series wore on, they no longer believed that to be the case.

This was the only known Ransacker incident in September. It occurred at a house that backed right up to the Evan's Ditch, and it was pretty obvious that he must've used the ditch to come and go from the area. This residence had a much shorter fence than some of the other homes nearby, and if the VR were prowling along the ditch, he would've been able to tell that no one was home simply by observing from a very safe distance. This one, even though it was an isolated incident and those are often looked at as candidates for extended stalking or intentional burglary, actually seems to be a crime of opportunity.

October 4ᵗʰ, 1974 Ransacking

<u>**VR #031**</u> *– Ransacking*
October 4th, 1974 | S Grant St

On Friday, October 4th, between 7:30 PM and 9:00 PM, a single-story residence was hit by the VR while the owner was away.

He entered by prying open a window. Once inside, he opened several additional windows.

He ransacked the house, particularly the bedrooms, but left the clothing in the drawers. There were no women in the house, so no bras, panties, or jewelry were to be found.

The VR stole coins, a Ruger .22 revolver, three boxes of .22 ammunition, and about one and a half boxes of 12-gauge ammunition.

At the end of the burglary, he left through a one of the doors.

The victim was a man, thirty-ish, who worked as a craftsman. He lived at the home by himself.

Latent fingerprints were discovered. The victim gave them a short list of people who had been in the house recently, and the police tried to eliminate them. At the end of their efforts, there were still prints that they couldn't eliminate, but the prints didn't match any of the previous ransackings. They held onto the fingerprint cards just in case a match could be found someday.

This was the second time that the VR had stolen a firearm (the first time was in May, where he stole a .380 Remington automatic pistol and a clip of ammunition), so once again, the offender's activities were hinting at his capacity for violence.

It's certainly worth noting that the VR had again ransacked a home that didn't have a female living in it. It's impossible to know whether or not he knew this beforehand, but it seemed that a few of the Ransacker's crimes during this phase were opportunistic and not based on stalking or peeping at the residents. Perhaps this was a crime of utility, and he knew about the firearm ahead of time and wanted to take it.

One of the big discussions in this case relates to whether the VR would select a group of residences based on geographical criteria and then troll for victims or homes that intrigued him, or whether he gained an interest in certain individuals and then made the most of whatever geography was around him. The police weren't really investigating this series very closely yet and the reports lack a lot of detail that could shed light on this discussion, but as the crimes became more serious later on, more data was captured and we have more to work with.

It had been about twenty days since the last VR crime. This ransacking occurred just a bit south of the Mt. Whitney High School, an area frequently serving as the epicenter of his outings.

October 16ᵗʰ, 1974 Prowler

Throughout the Visalia Ransacker series, there are *a lot* of reports describing prowlers. We've sorted through a lot of them, even those that had been discarded by investigators as unrelated. Some seem integral to the series. Others, not so much. We've included all of the ones that investigators feel are relevant.

The prowling incidents that involved a suspicious man appearing at homes later targeted by the VR are the most compelling. This event on October 16th, 1974 is one of those incidents.

While we do tag this one with a "not confirmed to be related" because there's no physical or M.O. evidence to tie it in, it seems overwhelmingly likely that this was the VR. The residence where the prowler was seen ended up being ransacked in January, and then several months later, someone tried to break into their home in the middle of the night *while they were still in it.* This type of long-term stalking wasn't recognized very often in 1974, but it started to become par for the course later in 1975 and *especially* when he evolved into the East Area Rapist and Golden State Killer.

Side note: In the late 1970s and early 1980s, some of his rape victims were stalked for up to six months, and the husband of a murder victim noticed the offender's shoe prints four months before the homicide. Clearly, the offender stalked some of his targets for quite a long time.

While long-term stalking did occur during the EAR/GSK phases, it also wasn't uncommon for the offender to identify a victim and then attack in a matter of days or weeks. During the Visalia Ransacker phase, he seemed to work a bit more slowly. A few months elapsed between the prowling and the ransacking of this couple, but ten months passed between the ransacking and the apparent home-invasion attempt. Part of this could've been because it seemed he hadn't quite evolved to the stage of actually committing sexually motivated crimes in *occupied* homes yet. His first known attempt was in September 1975 when he attempted to kidnap the Snelling girl, and the home-invasion attempt with this couple was in early October 1975. Later in October 1975, he's suspected of committing a home-invasion rape in Sacramento.

If that seems like a lot of information to keep track of, don't worry – these events will all be discussed in detail later on.

VR #032 – *Prowler*
October 16th, 1974 | S Verde Vista St

-NOT CONFIRMED TO BE RELATED-

At 8:00 PM on Wednesday, October 16th, a prowler was spotted standing in a carport at a house on South Verde Vista Street. When the owner spotted him, he went outside to confront the subject. The prowler took off running, and when he was last seen, he was located south of the residence near West Campus Avenue.

Again, this sighting of a prowler was given quite a bit more weight than some of the others due to the fact that this residence was ransacked by the VR on January 25th, 1975 (VR #076) and because someone tried to enter their home on October 4th, 1975 (VR #119). Either this was a very unlucky family that had two or three different criminals after them, or this family was targeted by the VR for an extended period of time.

A strong geographical case can be made for a tie to the Visalia Ransacker as well – this sighting took place very near the April 6th/April 7th, 1974 ransacking incidents, and this area would see quite a bit more VR activity as time went on.

October 19th, 1974 Ransackings

VR #033 – *Ransacking*
October 19th, 1974 | W Cambridge Ct

On Saturday, October 19th, between 9:30 AM and 8:30 PM, the Ransacker entered a single-story residence on West Cambridge Court while the victims were away.

He entered by prying open a window. Once inside, he opened more windows and removed one of the screens from the inside. It was found later near the bed.

He ransacked the residence, removing women's undergarments from drawers and scattering them around the bedroom.

Nothing was stolen, and he left through a sliding glass door.

The head of the household was a man in his mid forties who worked as a car salesman.

A brief note about the "head of the household" convention that we're using. You've probably noticed how we don't go into too much detail about the rest of the family. One of the interesting quirks of the police reports related to this case is that they usually only list the man of the house as the "victim" and there's very little else about the other residents. It's an interesting sign of the times and perhaps an indication that the nature of the offender was initially misunderstood. It's obvious from this bird's-eye view of the case that the women of the household often seemed to be the primary targets. Of course, we're also using modern sensibilities to look back on the standard operating procedure of days past, as well as hindsight knowledge of the crimes that the VR later committed and the type of criminal that he eventually evolved into. It's just an interesting feature of the documentation on this case that deserved a little bit of clarification.

VR #034 – *Ransacking*
October 19th, 1974 | S Oak Park St

Between 2:00 PM and 9:45 PM on Saturday, October 19th, the Ransacker invaded a single-story residence on South Oak Park Street while the family was away.

He pried open a sliding glass door for entry, then he went through the motions of opening other windows, ransacking the house, and tossing clothing all around the residence.

Surprisingly, during his rummaging he came across a .38 revolver and he opted to leave the weapon behind rather than take it. We can be sure that he did in fact see the weapon because he moved it to another location in the house.

He stole coins from the scene, and at the conclusion of his ransacking, he exited through a different sliding glass door than the one he'd used to enter the residence.

The head of the household was a man, roughly sixty years old, who worked as a chiropractor.

Latent fingerprints were found. As usual, they didn't provide officers with a match to any other ransackings or to any offender known to Law Enforcement. The officers felt that the prints belonged to an extended family member or a friend, not the thief.

The night of the 19th was a busy one, with three confirmed ransackings occurring (we still have one more to discuss). Since the residents were away from all of the homes, it's impossible to know which order they occurred in. This one had the latest time window of all of them (9:45 PM), but given the timeframes of the other two, the ransackings could've all been completed by 8:30 PM.

Did he leave the revolver at the scene because he was already armed? Was there something about it that he was unfamiliar with or didn't care for? Even without that revolver, the police still assumed he was armed due to previous thefts. Since he most likely had guns with him every night, there's no telling what could've happened at this stage had he been confronted or even if he had mistakenly entered a home that was actually occupied. There are a couple examples of these things happening later – with tragic results.

VR #035 – *Ransacking*
October 19th, 1974 | W Cambridge Ave

On Saturday, October 19th, between 7:00 PM and 8:30 PM, the Ransacker entered a single-story residence while the victim was away.

He went in through an unlocked window. Once inside, he opened another window and removed the screen.

All of the rooms were ransacked, and clothing was tossed around. He came across a piggy bank and broke it, stealing the coins that were inside. While rummaging, he came across *another* piggy bank, but rather than breaking it and taking the contents, he stole that particular one. He also stole cash and a pack of unused personal checks.

He didn't steal *all* of the cash that he found, however. He came across some cash that was hidden in a clever spot in the house, and rather than deciding to steal it, he removed it from its hiding place and left it behind in plain sight. It was a "look what I found" kind of a gesture; one of many that he made throughout the series.

He left through a sliding glass door.

The head of the household was a man in his mid thirties who worked in construction.

The VR left behind a shoe print, and police were able to analyze it. It seemed to match others that had been left at Visalia Ransacker scenes. Since fingerprint evidence in the case had not yet panned out, this shoe impression would become a useful physical link.

There was only a window of ninety minutes during which this ransacking could've taken place. That's a much tighter window than most of the other crimes. Because the timing was so tight and there's no direct evidence of him being interrupted, it's worth considering that he didn't come across this empty house by chance – but rather was hiding somewhere nearby and actually saw the residents leave. He clearly spent a lot of time inside the home, so he must've entered it very soon after they'd left. Perhaps he somehow knew their schedule, either by stalking, prowling, or some other means.

It *is* possible that he was interrupted toward the end though – he didn't *always* leave obvious shoe prints (or perhaps the police just weren't always looking for them), so perhaps he'd made a quick escape and didn't have time to cover up them up. We're on the fence as to whether he ever even attempted to do that or not – throughout the East Area Rapist and Golden State Killer series, he *never* seemed to worry about leaving shoe prints. Not even at the murder scenes. Fingerprints were another story, of course. Out of the hundreds of latent prints that were collected in all of these crimes spanning the VR to the EAR to the GSK years, none of them were ever known to match each other.

This was yet another instance of the Ransacker entering the home of someone that was fairly close to what came to be his suspected age of twenty-five to thirty-five years old. It helps make for an interesting cluster of victims in this general phase of his attacks, not only in age but also in profession – one recent victim was a surveyor, another a craftsman, and this one worked in construction. Even today, it's possible that common links can be found among these people (or other groups of victims), which may lead down interesting roads of investigation.

This residence was located a few blocks south of Mt. Whitney High School. For anyone following along on a map, please note that the street this ransacking occurred on, West Cambridge Avenue, shares a similar street name with another ransacking that occurred on this night (which was on West Cambridge *Court*). These two streets aren't connected. Well, unless you're going through backyards, something that police later learned that the Visalia Ransacker was doing quite a bit.

The map on the next page illustrates a few possible scenarios. If the South Oak Park Street crime happened chronologically between the other two, then it seems he walked or used transportation to go east on West Princeton Avenue to arrive at West Cambridge Avenue. Or, it could've happened in the reverse order, with the West Cambridge Court one happening last. There's also a section of yard on either side of 1744 South Oak Park Street that he could've used to emerge in the large backyard of 1801 South Sowell Street – that way, he could've stuck to the shadows better and used a bit more stealth. Note: neither of those addresses are homes of VR victims – they're simply parts of pathways that the offender could've taken. There was plenty of grass, dirt, and debris found on top of fence slats in several VR areas – a fence never stopped him from traveling through.

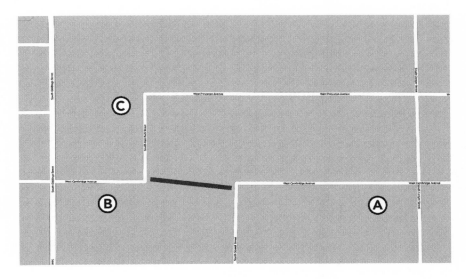

The ransackings that occurred on Saturday, October 19th, 1974. The dark line indicates where the VR may have cut through backyards.

A) *VR #033 W Cambridge Ct*
B) *VR #034 S Oak Park St*
C) *VR #035 W Cambridge Ave*

We assume that VR #035 happened after the West Cambridge Court burglary since the time window for that one is so tight and they both have the same end times.

October 23rd, 1974 Ransackings

With rare exception, the VR's activities up to this point had been restricted to weekends. The burglaries in this chapter, which were obviously the work of the VR because of the matching modus operandi, represent a deviation from that – they both occurred on a Wednesday night. A shift like this wasn't unheard of, but it wasn't common, either.

VR #036 – *Ransacking*
October 23rd, 1974 | S Giddings St

Between 7:15 PM and 10:05 PM on Wednesday, October 23rd, the Ransacker broke into a single-story residence on South Giddings Street while the victim was away.

He entered by prying open a sliding glass door, and then he ransacked several rooms and dumped clothing out of drawers.

At this burglary, he stole a 32-caliber revolver and two low-end Kodak cameras. He didn't steal any cash or coins. He exited through the same door that he had used to enter the residence.

The victim was a retired man in his eighties. It doesn't appear that anyone else was living there at the time.

Law Enforcement dusted for prints, but they didn't find any. They concluded that the burglar had worn gloves.

This is one of ransackings where the information we have is either incomplete or the report was just very brief. Not every responding officer paid attention to the same types of details at every burglary, nor did they transcribe everything the same way.

With less than three dozen incidents under his belt, the Visalia Ransacker had already stolen a handful of firearms. It's odd, though, that he'd stolen one at this ransacking but hadn't taken the .38 that he'd come across a few days prior. One question emerges from that – based on the day of the week that this ransacking occurred (a Wednesday, which was odd for him), was this crime impulsive and not "planned"? Did he have to steal a gun because he didn't have his weapon with him?

This was the first time that he showed any interest in cameras, and it wasn't really something he went out of his way to steal in the Visalia Ransacker series . Throughout the East Area Rapist and Golden State Killer series, however, he was definitely prone to taking camera equipment from time to time. One has to wonder if he actually used the cameras, and what sort of pictures he took if he did. Since the cameras taken at this ransacking were cheap Kodak models, he would've had to get them developed somewhere. It's strange to think that some unsuspecting photo technician could've unknowingly developed the Visalia Ransacker's photos.

Other camera equipment that he stole during his criminal career included items taken at EAR Attack #37 (October 7th, 1978), which was his first assault in Contra Costa County. He also stole a Minolta camera from the scene of the Offerman/Manning murders (December 30th, 1979).

VR #037 – *Ransacking*
October 23rd, 1974 | S Oak Park St

On Wednesday, October 23rd, sometime before midnight, the Ransacker entered a single-story residence on South Oak Park Street while the victims were away. It's unknown whether this home was burglarized before or after the incident we just discussed.

The VR entered by prying open a sliding-glass door. Once inside, he opened a window and removed the screen. He ransacked the bedrooms, stole coins and a piggy bank, then exited through one of the main doors of the house.

The head of the household was a male in his early/mid fifties. He worked as a liquor salesman. There were other victims living there as well.

Dusting for fingerprints at this scene proved fruitful – several were found. They were eventually compared to other prints taken from Ransacker scenes but, predictably, there was no match among any of them.

Geographically, both of the events occurring on Wednesday night were just to the west of Mt. Whitney High School. This ransacking was about half a mile to the north of the one that we discussed first, which was on South Giddings Street. A map featured on the next page gives a zoom on the area:

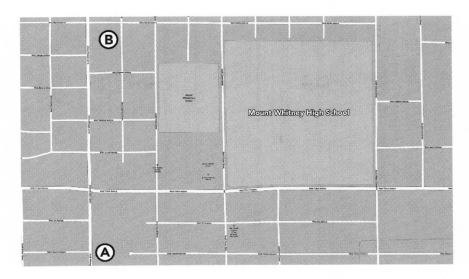

The two ransackings that occurred on October 23rd, 1974.

A)   *VR #036 St Giddings St*
B)   *VR #037 S Oak Park St*

November 1st, 1974 Ransackings

A little less than a week and a half after his previous outing, the VR embarked on one of the busiest weekends of the crime spree. It ended up being merely a prelude – roughly four weeks later, he again set out and committed even *more* crimes than he had on the weekend we're about to discuss. It seemed that he was trying to top himself – testing the limits of what he could get away with and perhaps even trying to get some public attention for his crimes. The newspapers had been slow to pick up the fact that there was a serial burglar on the loose, which obviously worked to his advantage.

But if he were looking to stay under the radar, then he obviously wouldn't have started committing *so many* crimes during November. The sheer scale of his activities caused the local police *and* the local media to finally sit up and really take notice. By the time November was over, the media had latched onto the story and the Visalia Police Department had begun planning concerted, proactive maneuvers to catch him in the act.

The geography of the two weekends we're about to discuss can be difficult to follow, and the timelines can be difficult to untangle. Luckily, fairly good records were kept, and we were able to reconcile most of it.

Five ransackings are attributed to November 1st, and four are attributed to the following day. We split these up into two chapters.

VR #038 – *Ransacking*
November 1st, 1974 | W Vassar Ave

On Friday, November 1st, sometime between 5:30 PM and 8:30 PM, the VR entered a single-story residence on West Vassar Avenue while the victims were away for the evening.

He entered their home through a window. It's not clear whether it was already unlocked or if he had to jimmy it open himself.

Once inside, he opened several potential points of escape, just as he had done at most of the other break-ins. He ransacked every room in the house, and when he came across female undergarments, he threw them onto the floor.

He broke a piggybank and stole the coins from it, and he also stole a collection of valuable collector-grade coins.

He left through the same window that he had used to enter the residence.

The head of the household was a man in his mid thirties who worked as a CPA. He lived there with his family.

There were no latent prints found on items that the VR had handled. One of the theories proposed by officers was that he was using his sleeves as a sort of makeshift glove and also using them to wipe off prints on anything that he touched. If this was the case, he apparently never slipped up, because matching prints could never be found at any of the ransackings in the 1970s.

This residence was located on West Vassar Avenue and in an area of the street located a few blocks south of Rotary Park. Rotary Park seemed to be home base for several of the burglaries as the months went on.

A bit of history: the park was originally gifted to the city by the Rotary Club of Visalia, and in the 1970s it was a very nice neighborhood park. Even today, the Rotary Club continues to look after the property, having established several committees in the 2000s that renovated large areas of it and added several new amenities.

Evan's Ditch runs through the southern portion of the park, making this location ideal for the VR. He could enter and exit the ditch unseen and use the green space as a buffer between himself and any strikes.

VR #039 – *Ransacking*
November 1st, 1974 | W Vassar Ave

On Friday, November 1st, between 7:00 PM to 10:50 PM, the VR entered another single-story residence on West Vassar Avenue while the victim was away. This residence was just two houses to the east of the previous ransacking that we discussed. It's unknown which house was entered first, though it appears that the Ransacker was traveling in a northeast trajectory on this night, making this likely to be his second stop.

He entered through a window. After landing inside, he placed items against the front door – items that would make a loud noise if the door were to be opened. While he would most likely escape if someone were to come home while he was still there, part of us wonders if at this point, as frenetic as his burglaries were, the Ransacker would react by drawing his weapon. Thankfully, we don't know of any events during this time period where anyone had a chance to find out.

He ransacked the bedrooms. As he did, he took the victim's panties and bras and threw them to the floor.

Coins and paper money were stolen, and he took Blue Chip stamps from the residence. He then left through the same window he had used to enter the home.

The victim in this case was a female in her early/mid forties. It seems that she lived alone at this residence, but her occupation is listed as "housewife." This was a common term at the time, so we're not sure if anyone else lived there. Property records from the time period didn't clarify it for us.

The scene was dusted for fingerprints, and some were found in suspicious places. Predictably, later analysis showed that they didn't match any of the previous prints taken from other VR crimes.

There was a ransacking earlier in the series where it was thought that the VR had taken Blue Chip stamps, but the resident at that burglary wasn't sure. This one *was.*

It became clear over time that the Ransacker had a proclivity for taking these whenever he came across them. It would stand to reason that if he stole these, then surely he redeemed them at some point... right?

He very well might have. There was a very promising "person of interest" who frequented a Blue Chip stamp redemption center in Visalia starting in about September 1973 – right around the time that the strange incidents began occurring on West Feemster Avenue and West Kaweah Avenue. A strange man brought in copious amounts of these stamps and usually bought jewelry with them, which at one point he said was for his mother. The workers became suspicious of him because of his demeanor and some of his occasional theatrics, like one instance where he hit the curb with his vehicle and launched into an angry tirade. This individual was never conclusively identified – he refused to leave his name or number when asked.

Nothing ever tied him to this crime series. At one point a composite sketch was made of him, but it was never released.

VR #040 – *Ransacking*
November 1st, 1974 | W Cambridge Ave

On Friday, November 1st, between 7:00 PM and 9:00 PM, a single-story residence on West Cambridge Avenue was burglarized by the VR while the victim was away.

He entered by prying open a sliding glass door. Once inside, he began opening windows, and he removed one of the screens.

He ransacked the bedrooms, then placed the woman's undergarments onto the floor and carefully arranged some of them into a pattern.

The VR stole cash and some coins from the residence before exiting through a window.

The victim was a female, age sixty or so, who worked as a clerk. She apparently lived alone at the residence.

This scene was only a few hundred feet away from the West Vassar Avenue incidents if the VR was traveling by backyard. If he took the street, then it was about a quarter of a mile away (most likely using a route that took him up South Giddings Street). A full map will be included at the end of the chapter.

VR #041 – *Ransacking*
November 1st, 1974 | S Giddings St

On Friday, November 1st, between 6:30 PM and 10:50 PM, a single-story residence was entered while the family was away. It was on South Giddings Street, which runs north/south and has corner houses on both sides for a considerable stretch. This wasn't one of the corner houses, however – it was situated in the middle of a fairly long stretch of homes.

The VR entered by prying open the main door to the house. Once inside, he set about his usual pattern and stole money from a piggybank. He also stole cash that he found in the residence. Every room was ransacked, and he removed underclothing from drawers and carefully laid out all of the daughter's bras and panties on the floor and on the bed.

When he exited the residence, he went out through a window.

The head of the household was a man in his early forties. He worked as a foreman. Other victims lived in the house as well, and the daughter attended Mt. Whitney High School.

Scene technicians were pleased with what they were able to find at this location – not only were there some promising latent fingerprints found, but shoe prints were found too. The fingerprints ended up being insignificant, but the shoe prints were a rough match for other shoe impressions found at previous ransackings.

VR #042 – *Ransacking*
October 30th to November 2nd, 1974 | W Paradise Ave

Sometime between Wednesday, October 30th at 4:00 PM and Saturday, November 2nd at 6:40 PM, the VR ransacked a single-story residence on West Paradise Avenue while the family was away.

He entered by prying open a window. Once inside, he opened another one and removed the screen from the inside.

He ransacked the bedrooms, removing only female underclothing as he went and dropping the items on the floor.

A piggybank was opened, and the coins were taken. The VR also stole cash, a single earring, and an alarm key that the victim used at his place of employment.

The head of the household was a man in his mid/late twenties. He worked as a manager. There were other people living in the household as well.

The family was out of town when this crime occurred, so there was a wide window of time that the Ransacker could've used to enter their home. The probable date is November 1st, the same night as the others that we've discussed in this chapter. It can't be confirmed, of course, but the location of it makes it fairly likely. The next group, which occurred the following day, was clustered together far away from the incidents we're discussing.

Taking South Giddings Street northbound from the other ransackings, he would've arrived at a very interesting part of Evan's Ditch where it runs up along South Giddings Street for a bit, then it curves and runs parallel to West Paradise Avenue. It's possible to hop into the ditch from South Giddings Street and then disappear for quite a while, then end up at Rotary Park. Even though West Paradise

Avenue doesn't connect directly to South Giddings Street, it seems probable that this was what the offender did. The house that was ransacked on West Paradise Avenue sits directly across from the ditch, in a scene very reminiscent of some of the early possible West Feemster Avenue incidents.

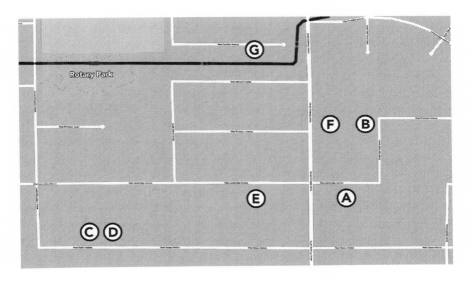

The ransackings that occurred on Friday, November 1st, 1974, and their close proximity to ransackings from October 19th, 1974.

A) *October 19th, 1974: VR #033 on W Cambridge Ct*

B) *October 19th, 1974: VR #034 on S Oak Park St*

C) *VR #038: November 1st on W Vassar Ave*

D) *VR #039: November 1st on W Vassar Ave*

E) *VR #040: November 1st on W Cambridge Ave*

F) *VR #041: November 1st on S Giddings St*

G) *VR #042: ransacking on W Paradise Ave (could've occurred anytime from October 30th to November 2nd)*

November 2nd, 1974 Ransackings

The ransackings from October 19th and November 1st had a lot in common when it came to their location. It seemed that the Ransacker had decided to move on from that area for the time-being though, because the day after the November 1st burglaries, he began operating in a different part of town – an area to the south of the Whitney/Linda Vista zone that he'd targeted before. Four burglaries occurred.

VR #043 – *Ransacking*
November 2nd, 1974 | S Mountain St

On Saturday, November 2nd, between 5:30 PM and 10:20 PM, a single-story residence on South Mountain Street was invaded while the victims were away.

The VR entered through an unlocked window. Once inside, he opened another window to use as a potential escape route.

While he usually focused on the bedrooms, this time he also ransacked the kitchen extensively. It was obvious that he'd focused on the jewelry quite a bit, because all of the jewelry boxes had been dumped out and then picked through. Items were found spread out on flat surfaces and littered across the floor.

The VR pushed over a bookcase inside the residence, a rather destructive action that was somewhat uncharacteristic of him during this particular phase of his evolution. He also opened a piggybank, stole coins, and stole Blue Chip stamps.

He left through a sliding glass door.

The head of the household was a male in his mid thirties. He worked as a car salesman. Other family members were living in the house. It may be worth looking into the people that this man sold a car to in the weeks leading up to this ransacking, given the anger that seemed to be present in the pushing over of his bookcase.

The police found latent prints inside the home. As usual, none of them matched and were assumed to be from friends and visitors.

It's a bit surprising that even after all of the activity on Friday, the Ransacker still went out on Saturday night and hit several *more* homes. The weather conditions were somewhat poor (there was some rainfall), but that didn't seem to deter him. Perhaps the darker night even aided him as he moved about the city.

This incident took place on the part of South Mountain Street that's below West Tulare Avenue, right by Royal Oaks Elementary School. Looking at it from Google Earth today is a bit deceiving. During the time period when the ransackings were occurring, the Houk Park area (which was put together in the 1960s) encompassed more of the land belonging to the elementary school. There was plenty of green space to the east of this crime scene location.

The house was located on a corner, an attribute that showed up quite a bit but didn't appear to be statistically significant.

VR #044 – *Ransacking*
November 2nd, 1974 | W Laurel Ave

On Saturday, November 2nd, between 2:00 PM and 10:15 PM, a single-story residence on West Laurel Avenue was invaded while the victims were away.

The offender gained entry to the home by prying open a door. Once inside, he set about placing items against the front door – items that would crash and make a loud sound if someone tried to enter.

Again, he seemed to pay special attention to the kitchen, rummaging through it quite a bit. He ransacked the bedrooms, taking out whatever women's undergarments he could find from the drawers. At one point, he came across photos of the couple's children. He picked the photos up and threw them to the ground.

He stole coins and a single earring from this scene, and for some reason, also took four tubes of epoxy glue.

The head of the household was a man in his mid thirties. He worked as a financial manager.

Fingerprints were found at the scene, but the story was the same as the others – no match.

The street that this home was on, West Laurel Avenue, initially seems like it would be a difficult area to prowl – almost impossible if the VR were coming and going by car. Despite its proximity to the main road of West Tulare Avenue, it's a seemingly closed loop when looking at it by map. On the ground though, it becomes clear why the VR might've felt comfortable on this street. If he ran into trouble and he was on foot or bike, there were multiple ways to escape – he could go up or down South Linda Vista Street to get to West Tulare Avenue or South Clover Street, or he could double back and take South Terri

Street to the same escape points. He could've also just hopped a few fences and ended up on West Sue Avenue or back over to South Mountain Street, which would've made him almost impossible to catch if he were being pursued by vehicle. Whether any of this factored into his mind or not is unknown. His victim selection process has yet to be fully cracked.

It was probably chilling for the couple to see that the photos of their had been thrown to the ground. They no doubt feared for their children's safety. This action could hint at a lot of things related to the offender's psychological state – a deep-seeded anger for the family unit, some kind of frustration about his personal life, childhood trauma, or something else entirely.

The theft of epoxy glue is kind of strange. The product is often used to glue wood, but it can also be used for general household and even auto repairs. Did he need this for something related to his prowling? Did he use this in his personal life, or even at work? Or did he just take it for jollies and toss it in someone's trashcan or onto a roof later on in the night?

VR #045 – *Ransacking*
November 2nd, 1974 | W Campus Ave

Sometime on Saturday, November 2nd, the Ransacker hit another single-story home while the residents were out of town. A female housekeeper lived at this residence.

He entered by prying open a window, and once inside, he opened four more windows to use as possible escape hatches.

Every room was ransacked. Even though the housekeeper's clothing had clearly been rummaged through by the Ransacker, he didn't remove any of it. That was odd for him. Could her role as a non-family-member in the household be the reason? Did he even *know* that she was the housekeeper? Did he feel that embarrassing a non-family member was, in a sense, a waste of his time?

Nothing was stolen from the scene.

This burglary was reported several months after it happened – the owner didn't feel that it warranted police intervention right away since nothing had been taken. The information about this incident came to light around the time that the area was canvassed after the Claude Snelling homicide.

The resident remembered seeing shoe prints in his yard, primarily near back corner. It's unknown if these were a match for the Visalia Ransacker. The resident recalled there being more than one trail of footprints near the fence that faced the neighbor behind him, and he remembered that the trail faced South Whitney Street. The shoe prints pointed directly at another house that was ransacked by the VR on this date.

The owner seemed sure of the day, but not sure the time, so even though there's no solid information as to what time of day this intrusion occurred, it can be estimated fairly well because of its proximity to the ransacking on South Whitney Street. We'll discuss that one next.

VR #046 – *Ransacking*
November 2nd, 1974 | S Whitney St

On Saturday, November 2nd, between 6:30 PM to 11:40 PM, the Ransacker hit yet another single-story residence. It was essentially across the street from the one on West Campus Avenue. The victims were away at the time of the intrusion.

He entered by prying open the door (and when he left, he left through the same door).

He ransacked the bedrooms and ended up stealing quite a few things from this scene: regular coins, collectible coins, Blue Chip stamps, and an unopened pack of men's t-shirts.

The head of the household was in his mid sixties and owned a brake shop. His family lived with him at the house.

Many researchers and investigators operate under the belief that it was the women who were the primary interests of the VR, not the men. Over the crime spree, there are several clear-cut examples of the Ransacker targeting the wife or the teenage daughter(s) in the household. This incident is actually one of those that might be an exception, and it bends the traditional victim-selection paradigm in an interesting way: not only were this man and his wife a victim of the VR, but this man's *ex-wife* also became a target of the VR over a year later. On December 1st, 1975, the VR attempted to enter the ex-wife's home *while she was in it.* Whether he knew she was there or not is unknown, but the attempted entry occurred during a portion of the crime spree where the Ransacker was behaving in dangerous and unpredictable ways.

Coincidence? Maybe so, but it's fascinating that two people very close to this particular man were given attention by the VR. Granted, the Ransacker targeted a *lot* of homes, and connections like this are bound to come up. It's been theorized that the attempted entry to the ex-wife's home was an attempted home-invasion rape, but there are a few reasons why that might be unlikely (he ran away when he was noticed, she was outside his typical demographic, and he'd burglarized other homes that night). The fact that these incidents occurred over a year apart seems to make it more coincidental as well, but it's still a very intriguing thread. This offender had a long memory and he seemed to gather *a lot* of information that he acted on later. Almost nothing is outside the realm of possibility.

Latent fingerprints were found at this burglary, but they most likely belonged to friends of the family or people who had visited the home. They didn't match any of the other fingerprints collected at Ransacker scenes.

As mentioned, Blue Chip stamps were stolen again. And just like the glue that was stolen at another scene that was hit on this date, the t-shirts seemed to be for personal use. Later on in the crime series, he stole even more unopened packages of t-shirts. It might've given him a kind of twisted thrill to wear these in public as he went about his daily life.

The VR had hit South Whitney Street before, and not too far away from this scene. If this one was the last hit of the night (and we think it probably was, given the timeframe and the fact that he stole a bulkier item), can that tell us something about his comfort zone or where he might've lived? Or at least where he might've parked a car or a bicycle?

Zooming out a bit and looking at the Saturday cluster of ransackings can lead readers to a lot of interesting speculation about what his path through the city might've been that evening, and where his possible origin could've been:

(*map is featured on the following page*)

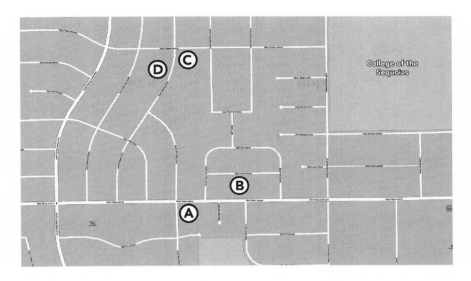

The ransackings that occurred on Saturday, November 2nd, 1974.

- A) VR #043 S Mountain St
- B) VR #044 W Laurel Ave
- C) VR #045 W Campus Ave
- D) VR #046 S Whitney St

These incidents were to the southwest of the College of the Sequoias. The whole area started to see a lot of Visalia Ransacker activity once 1975 was underway.

Thanksgiving Weekend 1974

November 28th, 1974 was Thanksgiving Day – a national holiday in the United States originally held as a traditional celebration of the year's harvest.

The day after Thanksgiving is typically referred to as "Black Friday." This day isn't a holiday – it's actually a commercial term for the beginning of the holiday shopping season. In 1974, "Black Friday" also marked the beginning of the VR/EAR's most active weekend in the entire 12+ year history of offenses.

If not for these crimes having the same self-indulgent M.O., it would almost seem that an entire gang of criminals had descended on Visalia for the weekend. In a period of roughly forty-eight hours, up to eighteen residences were burglarized. About a dozen of them are well known to investigators, and the reports from them were saved, organized, and stored. Of those, they all had the same distinctive entry and ransacking pattern. The others, which we won't discuss in-depth, are given mere mentions in some of the documentation and may not have been the work of the Visalia Ransacker at all.

Because he hit houses where the victims weren't home, and many of the residents were out of town for extended periods due to the holiday season, it's impossible to reconstruct an accurate timeline of his movements throughout the Thanksgiving weekend. We did our best to lay out a logical progression, but there's plenty of room for other researchers to play around with this data. We're not married to any particular interpretation of what his pathway through the city was or what his comings and goings might have looked like. The takeaway is that his crimes had begun to reach a fevered pitch, and he was escalating in a variety of disturbing ways.

VR #047 – *Ransacking*
November 29th, 1974 | W Princeton Ave

On Friday, November 29th, between noon and 6:25 PM, the Visalia Ransacker entered a single-story residence while the victims were away.

He entered the residence through an unlocked window. Once inside, he opened additional windows to use as possible escape routes.

He ransacked all of the rooms, removing women's clothing from drawers and closets as he went.

A piggybank was stolen, one that had about seven dollars in it. Two boxes of .22 rifle shells were taken.

He left the residence through a sliding glass door.

The victim was an adult in his mid thirties who worked as a salesman. He lived there with his family.

This crime, like many of the others before it, offers a strange juxtaposition. On one hand, we have an offender who's exhibiting childlike behavior by stealing piggybanks. On the other hand, we have the intruder showing a deadly tendency with the theft of ammunition. It's no wonder that the police were perplexed by him.

The part of West Princeton Avenue that the Ransacker had hit here was the stretch situated right off of South Giddings Street, located southeast of Rotary Park. He had just attacked this area on November 1st, which was the last weekend he was active. Timeline information puts this one (and the next) squarely at the beginning of the crime frenzy that took place this weekend, so this serves as a probable starting location for the crimes that he committed over the weekend.

VR #048 – *Ransacking*
November 29th or November 30th, 1974 | W Tulare Ave

Between Friday, November 29th at 5:30 PM and Saturday, November 30th at 10:00 AM, the Ransacker entered a single-story home while the victims were away. It's likely that he committed this crime around the same time as the one on West Princeton Avenue that we just discussed.

He entered by prying open a window. The screen to either that window or another one was found inside the residence when the family arrived home.

The VR ransacked the bedrooms and threw female undergarments to the floor, as he usually did. He turned their piggybank upside down, but may or may not have emptied it first.

He stole quite a bit at this burglary. In total, he stole regular coins, collectible coins, some costume jewelry, a bra, a ladies' wallet, a single earring belonging to a pair, and two photos of the victims' children.

The head of the household was a man in his mid thirties. He worked as a probation officer and lived there with his wife and children.

The part of West Tulare Avenue that was hit here was north of the previous ransacking and just a few houses to the east of South Giddings Street. This is the route that he would take if he were heading from the previous scene to Mt. Whitney High School, and it was only a few houses *away* from the school. Perhaps that's where he parked, since it seemed to be a comfort zone of some sort and he had a lot of items with him that he'd taken from this scene. A lot of the paths he took on his burglary nights seemed to lead to or away from Mt. Whitney High School.

The theft of personal items belonging to the lady of the house (her jewelry and bra) adds another dimension to the theory that these crimes were sexually motivated. And if indeed they were, the theft of the children's photos is a terrifying addition to his behaviors. This burglary continued the path of escalation: at one of the recent ransackings he'd merely thrown the children's photos down, and now he was taking them. Another point of escalation: in previous ransackings he'd removed women's undergarments from drawers, and now he'd taken one.

With as much as he'd stolen during this burglary, it's possible that either this was the final one on Friday, or that he lived/parked nearby. It's also possible that he stashed the items in a secure location (near the school, perhaps, if there was nothing going on there) and continued on.

VR #049 – *Ransacking*
November 29th or November 30th, 1974 | W Meadow Ave

Between Friday November 29th at 10:00 AM and Saturday, November 30th at 8:15 PM, the VR entered a single-story residence on West Meadow Avenue while the occupants were gone. Even though Friday is a possible day for this ransacking to have taken place, it's more likely that it occurred on Saturday evening based on the next incident, which happened next-door and was definitely on Saturday.

He entered by prying at the sliding-glass door. Once inside, he removed a window screen and left the window open so that he could make a quick escape if he needed to. He also placed items against the front door so that if anyone tried to open it, he'd hear a crash.

He ransacked the bedrooms, and as he came across the mother's and teenage daughter's undergarments, he threw them to the ground and onto the bed. Some of them were bunched up. According to officers at other scenes, this behavior might indicate that he'd masturbated with those garments.

A strongbox inside the residence was pried open, and he stole coins and cash from it and from other areas in the house. He also came across a photo of the couple's son and for some reason, he tore it to pieces. At this point in the crime spree he'd already knocked a photo of children down, he'd taken a photo, and now he'd torn one up. This was yet another disturbing twist to his behavior.

At the end of the burglary, he exited through a door.

The head of the household was a doctor in his early forties. The couple's daughter attended Mt. Whitney High School, where she played in the band.

VR #050 – Ransacking
November 30th, 1974 | W Meadow Ave

Sometime between 5:30 PM and 10:15 PM, the VR entered another single-story residence on West Meadow Avenue. This residence was situated next-door to the previous one we discussed. The victims were away for the evening.

He entered by prying open a window. Once inside, he opened another window to use as an emergency escape route, and he placed items against the front door to use as a warning system in case someone came home.

He stole some coins from one of the bedrooms.

The head of the household was a retired man in his sixties.

These two incidents happened on the west side of South Giddings Street, just a couple blocks directly above Divisadero Middle School. It's not known which house he ransacked first, but he appeared to spend quite a bit more time at the home next-door. Perhaps that was the one he'd set out to hit, because that one had a woman living in it and this one did not. This house could've been entered simply because it was next-door to one of his targets and it was temporarily unoccupied.

VR #051 – *Ransacking*
November 30th or December 1st, 1974 | S Encina St

Sometime between 7:00 PM on Saturday, November 30th and 1:30 AM on Sunday, December 1st, the VR entered a single-story house while the victim was away from the residence.

He entered by prying a sliding glass door. Once inside, he stacked items against the back door so that if someone entered, he'd be alerted.

He ransacked the bedrooms and threw women's undergarments onto the floor. He dumped out and rummaged through all of the jewelry.

He also opened a piggybank, stole the coins from it, and stole some collectible coins that he found elsewhere inside the residence.

He exited through the front door.

The head of the household was about thirty years old. He worked as a clerk, and he lived in the house with his family.

Police dusted the scene for fingerprints, but it quickly became apparent that the offender had worn gloves or had concealed his prints some other way.

VR #052 – *Ransacking*
November 30th or December 1st, 1974 | W Paradise Ave

Sometime overnight on Saturday (between 11:00 PM November 30th and 6:00 AM on Sunday, December 1st), a single-story house on West Paradise Avenue was broken into by the VR. The occupants were away for the night.

He entered through an unlocked window and opened another window as a possible escape route, removing the screen as well.

He ransacked all of the rooms, throwing women's underclothing to the ground wherever he found some. At this ransacking, he didn't steal anything.

The head of the household was about seventy years old and retired.

Technicians were unable to lift any usable prints, but they did find shoe prints that they were able to catalogue.

The scene of this burglary was located just a few houses to the northwest of the previous one that we discussed (the one on South Encina Street). This can help tighten up the possible timeline between the two, assuming they were ransacked back-to-back.

VR #053 – *Ransacking*
November 27th to December 1st, 1974 | W Paradise Ave

Sometime between Thursday, November 27th at 8:00 AM and Sunday, December 1st at 8:45 PM, the Ransacker entered a single-story home while the victim was away.

He entered by using some kind of flat tool to slip open the lock to the door.

Once inside, he opened another exit so that he could easily escape in a hurry if he had to, and he began ransacking both the kitchen and the bedrooms.

He was probably disappointed by what he found – there were no female undergarments in the house, nor was there any jewelry. He did find some coins to steal.

The victim was a man who lived alone. The demographics here were a little different in the sense that this was one of the Ransacker's only non-white victims.

A matching shoe print was found on the scene, which helped connect it to the other burglaries that were happening throughout the weekend.

Mapping out this location relative to the other one on West Paradise Avenue reveals something interesting: this burglary and the previous one were both located on opposite sides of where a topographical map from the period shows that Evan's Ditch ran at one time (or was planned to run), and they were roughly the same distance away from the ditch marker on either side. Other maps that we've found from the era show that near this point, the ditch ended and the street took over, which was probably the case when the Ransacker was committing his crimes. It's difficult to tell if there was much of a ditch there at the time, but either way, it was clear that he was making his way down West Paradise Avenue as he ransacked on this date. Existing portions of Evan's Ditch were definitely located one block to the north of this ransacking (and the next), so it may have been used for covert transportation in this instance.

VR #054 – *Ransacking*
November 30th to December 1st, 1974 | W Paradise Ave

Sometime between Saturday, November 30th at 10:00 PM and Sunday, December 1st at 11:30 AM, the VR entered a single-story residence while the victims were away. This home was located next-door to the previous ransacking that we covered.

He entered the same way that he had entered the previous house on West Paradise Avenue – by using a flat tool of some kind to force the lock open.

Once inside, he opened another window. He ransacked every room, and anytime he came across female underclothing, it was removed and thrown it onto the floor or the bed.

He stole coins (only thirty cents), two rings, one earring from a set of two, and he stole a check payable to the victim – just one more little "f* you" that he devised.

At the conclusion of his ransacking, he exited through a sliding glass door.

The male victim in this burglary was about fifty years old, and he worked as a health director. There were other victims living in the house as well.

As mentioned, the location of this burglary was next-door to the previous one – situated just one house to the west.

VR #055 – *Ransacking*
November 30th to December 1st, 1974 | W Cambridge Ave

Another burglary occurred during the same rough timeframe as the previous four that we've discussed, and it happened less than ten houses directly to the south.

Sometime between Saturday, November 30th and Sunday, December 1st at 1:45 PM, the VR entered a single-story home on West Cambridge Avenue while the victim was away. The residence was located in a small section of the road between South Johnson Street and South West Street.

The VR first attempted to pry open a door, seemingly using the same technique that he'd used on West Paradise Avenue. He was unsuccessful. Undeterred, he tried prying at another door, and it gave way.

He opened up an escape route in the house and began ransacking every room in the residence. He tossed clothing around as he went.

He came across a piggybank and opened it. There were about five dollars in coins kept inside, and he stole them all.

The Ransacker did something new at this scene – he ate some of the victims' food. When they returned home, it was clear that the VR had helped himself to some bread and a nice cold beverage.

As active as he was on this night, it's not surprising that he stopped for a free meal. It was also another way to rub his victim's nose in the fact that he was in complete control of their domain, if only for a short time. When he became the East Area Rapist, eating at the scene would become commonplace.

When he left, he used a sliding glass door.

The head of the household was a man who was employed as a maintenance worker. He was about sixty years old and lived there with his family.

Because the VR had helped himself to some food, fingerprints were carefully taken from the kitchen. None of them matched any of the other prints that had thus far been collected.

This was the first *known* incidence of the Ransacker eating at the scene. When he burglarized homes, his victims were always away so he could've easily been pilfering food and drinks since the beginning. If he took some crackers or a can of soda from time to time, no one would notice. But when the Ransacker did something, it seemed that he wanted the residents to *know* that he did it. In future scenes where it was clear that he ate and drank, he would leave half-finished beverages on the floor near the refrigerator, or he would take food from the pantry and throw it into a nearby yard or leave a cupboard door open and leave the items arranged in such a way as to make it obvious that he had taken something. This behavior would continue into his East Area Rapist phase – he'd usually sexually assault a victim several times, and in between he'd often stop and eat loudly in a nearby room. He'd eat so loudly that even if they were on the other side of the house, they'd know what he was doing. He *wanted* them to know. He would also discard boxes of crackers, empty beer or soda cans, and food wrappers in their yards just to show them that he'd helped himself. When he ate in homes as the Visalia Ransacker, it was no different.

Geographically, this burglary helped make a little box with the previous four, though we're missing a southeast corner. It's hard to figure out the paths that he took throughout this particular weekend, but it's somewhat clear that these five were grouped together. He either hit them in the order we've laid out here, or in reverse order because of the logical way that they're arranged. A map at the end of the chapter will help bring it into focus.

The next ransacking we discuss happened about a mile and a half away.

VR #056 – *Ransacking*
November 29th to December 1st, 1974 | S Sowell St

Sometime between Friday, November 29th at 3:00 PM and Sunday, December 1st at noon, the VR entered the first part of a duplex on South Sowell Street while the victim was away for the weekend. This was the first known time that the VR entered a duplex (or any similar type of residence).

He entered by prying open a sliding glass door. Once he gained entry, he went through his usual routine of opening a window and leaving the screen on the bed.

He primarily ransacked the living room and the bedroom. There weren't any items of women's clothing in the house, but the Ransacker still took clothing out of drawers and scattered it on the bed and the floor.

He stole money from this scene, and he took one ring. The VR then left the residence through the same sliding glass door that he'd used to enter it.

The male victim was in his early forties and worked as a librarian. He lived in the house alone.

This was the first unit of the duplex. The second unit was also hit – we'll describe that burglary next.

This residence was located just a couple blocks northwest of Mt. Whitney High School.

VR #057 – *Ransacking*
November 29th to December 1st, 1974 | S Sowell St

Between 9:00 PM on Friday, November 29th and sometime on Sunday, December 1st, the VR entered the second unit of a duplex. The victim was away from the residence.

He entered by prying open a sliding glass door. The offender went through his usual routine and tossed women's undergarments around different places of the bedrooms.

While inside the residence, he came across a bottle of Sine-Off pills (a brand of cold and allergy medication). He dumped the entire bottle of pills into the sink. Just one more way to inconvenience his victims and just one more outlet for his anger, perhaps.

He stole regular coins and some collector coins from the scene. One report mentions him stealing alcohol, but we were unable to corroborate that information. Given that he had eaten at a previous scene and that he was known to steal small amounts of alcohol during the East Area Rapist phase, this would not be out of character.

The head of the household was a man in his early/mid thirties who worked as a serviceman.

With this particular ransacking occurring adjacent to the previous one, it seems very likely that they were done consecutively. So despite the wide timeframes given by these two victims, it helps us make some progress in figuring out when he hit certain homes during this busy weekend.

VR #058 – *Ransacking*
November 30th or December 1st, 1974 | W Kaweah Ave

Taking South Sowell Street northward, the next street is West Kaweah Avenue. Two more ransacking incidents occurred here.

Sometime between Saturday, November 30th at 10:30 AM and Sunday, December 1st at 5:30 PM, the VR entered a single-story house on West Kaweah Avenue while the victims were away.

He entered by prying open a window. As usual, he opened an additional escape window for himself, he ransacked every room, and he threw female underclothing onto the floor and the bed when he came across it.

He didn't steal any coins or cash, but he did steal 20-gauge shotgun shells and a box of .22 ammunition. Once again the offender showed his propensity for violence.

He exited through one of the main doors of the house.

The head of the household was a man in his early fifties. He was self-employed.

It's noted offhand in one piece of case documentation that the residents in this house had received phone calls that investigators thought might have been from the Ransacker. One of the jurisdictions in charge of this case looked through every case file that was available and they couldn't find any additional details on what may or may not have transpired, and it's possible that such calls didn't even occur or that they were unrelated to the VR. Without any additional information to confirm or corroborate the info, it remains merely an interesting footnote. The VR didn't seem to start calling his victims until nearly a year later, so it very well could be nothing. But once he became the East Area Rapist, phone calls to his victims (most of them the silent, hang-up type) were a regular occurrence. And the documentation isn't clear about when the calls occurred at this home that we just discussed, so they could've occurred months later when the Visalia Ransacker *did* start harassing former and future victims by telephone. The residents of West Kaweah Avenue, like the residents on and near South Whitney Street, were generally targeted and harassed far more than other Visalia Ransacker victims.

VR #059 – *Ransacking*
November 30th or December 1st, 1974 | W Kaweah Ave

Sometime between Saturday, November 30th at 9:50 PM and Sunday, December 1st at 9:10 PM, the VR broke into a single-story home while the victim was away. This residence was located on West Kaweah Avenue, situated directly across the street from the other West Kaweah Avenue ransacking that occurred on this particular weekend.

The VR entered by prying open a window. Once inside, he opened an additional window to use as a quick escape route, removed the screen, and began ransacking the bedrooms.

Not only did the Visalia Ransacker steal coins at this burglary, but he stole a bookshelf stereo as well. He left through the same window that he had used to enter the residence.

The head of the household was a man in his mid fifties. Like the previous victim, he was also self-employed, and he was two years older than that victim. He lived in the house with his family.

This man *also* seems to have reported suspicious phone calls at one point. Someone somewhere must've thought they were related to the Ransacker, because that's what was written – but just on one piece of documentation and nothing else. We have yet to come across anything to confirm this or to provide additional details, and one of the jurisdictions working the case has nothing additional for us. Again, the idea of victims on this street receiving phone calls, even this early, wouldn't completely be outside the realm of possibility. This was a street that the Ransacker ended up spending a *long* time on – he was stalking, burglarizing, and peeping here on a regular basis. In fact, this street would also be the scene of his last stand with Law Enforcement – an event we'll discuss much later. But to be clear, nothing available confirms that the calls took place.

The crime scene was dusted for prints, but it was clear that the intruder had covered his hands somehow or had worn gloves. There was a complete lack of prints on areas that the VR surely would have touched.

The VR had stolen quite a few things throughout the weekend, and a stereo couldn't have been easy to carry around if he had broken into more homes after this one and was traveling solely on foot. For this reason (plus the assumed path, geography, and general timeline), we put this incident as most likely being the last crime that he committed on Thanksgiving weekend. No matter what time of the day or night that the burglary happened, the thief would've looked fairly suspicious walking around the residential streets of Visalia with overloaded pockets (or a big bag) and a desktop stereo. It's likely that this location gives us some sort of clue as to where he parked or where he originated from that weekend.

Other Possible Ransackings

In addition to the marathon session of burglaries described in this chapter, there's information available indicating that even *more* burglaries could've occurred on that weekend. Up to five additional incidents have been identified through a throwaway comment in documentation, some old newspaper articles, and tips that have been sent into our website.

The jurisdictions in charge of the case don't have information or files on any of these five incidents, so they're being excluded from the narrative until more can be determined. If anything changes, we'll provide an update at visaliaransacker.com.

Geography

It's difficult to determine when, and in what order, the ransackings occurred over this weekend. But when plotting out the locations of these incidents, some clear clusters and pathways do start to form.

Evan's Ditch was clearly a safe-zone of some sort – a pathway he stuck to and struck from. Some of the other ransackings could've seen him emerging from Divisadero Middle School, and the ones in the northwest seem to rely on him striking from the pathway that ran from east to west along the northern border of the strike zone. A footpath existed there, relatively untraveled and difficult to traverse in the dark. It made for a perfect way to navigate this quadrant of the city unseen and observe certain areas from a distance.

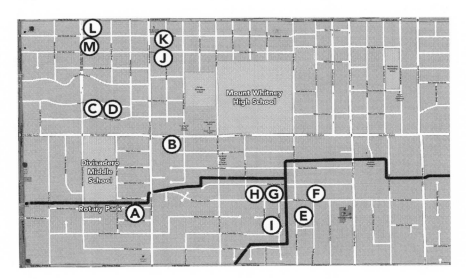

The ransackings that occurred between November 29th and December 1st, 1974. Evan's Ditch is highlighted.

A) VR #047: W Princeton Ave

B) VR #048: W Tulare Ave

C) VR #049: W Meadow Ave

D) VR #050: W Meadow Ave

E) VR #051: S Encina St

F) VR #052: W Paradise Ave

G) VR #053: W Paradise Ave

H) VR #054: W Paradise Ave

I) VR #055: W Cambridge Ave

J) VR #056: S Sowell St

K) VR #057: S Sowell St

L) VR #058: W Kaweah Ave

M) VR #059: W Kaweah Ave

The footpath that runs between West Noble Avenue and State Route 198. It's believed that the Ransacker used this area to travel the city unseen, and it also factored into some of his escape routes when sought by the police in 1975. Photo by Bill Harticon.

December 14th, 1974 Ransackings

Police Stakeouts
December 13th through December 15th, 1974

Up until this point, very few people in the general public were aware of the Visalia Ransacker's existence. The newspapers hadn't done much with him, and neighbors didn't often discuss the crimes with each other. The burglaries were odd, but they didn't result in much damage or financial loss. Since they were "merely" personal and unsettling, most people had been content to do what they could to shrug off the events and continue on with their lives.

November had changed all of that, however. The sheer scale of the VR activity from Thanksgiving weekend had finally made the case too big to ignore. The police were shaken, and the media had begun to realize that there was a story afoot. Victims began to talk to their neighbors, and the community as a whole gained some awareness. It wasn't exactly the most talked-about story in town, but conversation about the crimes had finally bubbled to the surface. The Visalia Times-Delta (the local paper) even ran a story about the series.

The police decided that they needed to cut this criminal down to size before things got out of hand. They began organizing special patrols and stakeouts that were specifically designed to catch the Visalia Ransacker.

As part of this special detail, officers were paired up and given sections of the city to patrol. Their locations were based on areas that the VR had targeted before, and the days were chosen based on the days when he was most likely to offend – Fridays, Saturdays, and Sundays.

Friday December 13th, Saturday the 14th, and Sunday the 15th were chosen as the first dates to start looking for him. It had been a couple weeks since there had been a fresh report, so based on past patterns (especially from October), they were banking on him making an appearance sooner rather than later.

And he *did*.

But not in the areas where the patrols were looking for him. Somehow, he managed to avoid detection and amazingly, despite the police being out in force, he was still able to commit *four ransackings* on Saturday night.

The officers were good at what they did, and the teams had spent hours sweeping the town on patrol. So how could he have accomplished this?

Did he spot them while he was prowling or driving around? Did he have inside information about their locations? Or was he completely unaware and he simply got lucky?

One of the ways he avoided detection (unknowingly or not) was by committing the four burglaries in a very small area of the city away from the police dragnet. He offended in a part of town that he'd never hit before. Moreover, he cut down on the amount of time that he was out and about – he seemed to rush through the ransackings and he didn't spend nearly as much time in the residences as he *had been* spending. It's likely that all four of the ransackings occurred between 7:30 PM and 9:15 PM, which is a really fast given the fact that investigators believed that he was spending up to an hour working each individual home during some of his previous outings. Of course, he hadn't spent as much time in each residence during the Thanksgiving weekend either, so perhaps he was getting "better" or more efficient at committing his particular type of crime. Perhaps he was getting the satisfaction he needed from each one more quickly.

If he was attacking so many homes in such a short amount of time on this weekend *and* Thanksgiving weekend, did that mean that he was becoming more brazen in his approach? In other words, was a lot of his time in the past spent observing the home, the neighbors, and the street and looking for any possible signs of people who could spot him or report him? And was he now simply casing them faster? Was the offender becoming a little more reckless or overconfident, and had he abandoned some of the attack-night reconnaissance that he might've done in the past?

One possible explanation is that he was needing to commit more and more of his crimes in a shorter period of time to get the same rush that he'd been getting in the beginning from fewer burglaries. He seemed to be upping the ante the only way he was comfortable to at this point – by offending *more*. Before long, the Ransacker would start finding new and more frightening ways to escalate.

VR #060 – *Ransacking*
December 14th, 1974 | W Vassar Ave

On Saturday, December 14th, sometime between 4:30 PM and 9:18 PM, the VR ransacked a single-story residence on West Vassar Avenue while the residents were away.

He entered through an unlocked sliding glass door. Once inside, he opened a window to allow himself a quick escape if he needed it, and he also removed the screen and left it in the bedroom.

Most of the rooms in the house were ransacked (including all of the bedrooms, where he removed a lot of their clothing and tossed it all around the room). He came across a piggybank, broke it, and stole the coins that were inside.

He exited the house through one of the main doors.

The head of the household was about fifty years old and worked as a minister. He lived in the home with the rest of his family.

Shoe prints were found at this scene, and they roughly matched other shoe prints that had been found at Visalia Ransacker crimes.

VR #061 – *Ransacking*
December 14th, 1974 | S University St

On Saturday, December 14th, sometime between 7:30 PM and 11:15 PM, the VR entered a single-story residence while the victims were away.

He entered by prying open a sliding glass door, opened a window from the inside, and then removed the screen.

He ransacked the bedrooms, throwing women's clothing and women's undergarments onto the floor and the bed as he went.

Cash from the scene was taken, along with two rings. When he exited, he left through a different sliding glass door than the one he had used to enter the residence.

The head of the household was a man in his mid thirties. His job title was "director." There were other victims living there as well.

This crime scene was located fairly close to the one we just described. A map plotting all four ransackings will be shown at the end of the chapter.

VR #062 – *Ransacking*
December 14th, 1974 | W Cambridge Ave

Just over a hundred feet away from the previous break-in, the VR entered another home. It happened between 4:00 PM and 11:20 PM.

He entered through an unlocked sliding glass door. Again, he opened an additional window, removed the screen, and ransacked every bedroom (tossing copious amounts of clothing from the drawers onto the floor).

He also went through all of the valuables, dumping out jewelry boxes as he found them. He found a piggybank and opened it, but there was nothing inside to steal.

He left without taking anything, making his exit through a different sliding glass door than the one he'd used to enter the house.

The male victim was about thirty years old and worked as a teacher.

A partial shoe print was found at this scene, which appeared to match some of the other shoe prints found at other Visalia Ransacker crimes. Since it was only a partial print, the exact size was impossible to determine.

VR #063 – *Ransacking*
December 13th to December 15th, 1974 | W Cambridge Ave

The VR entered another home on West Cambridge Avenue sometime between Friday, December 13th and Sunday, December 15th while the victims were away for the weekend. Police assumed that this crime occurred on the same night as the other three due to its location.

He entered by prying open a sliding glass door. Once inside, he began ransacking bedrooms. He spent a lot of extra time in the daughter's room, rummaging through every drawer and handling most of her clothing. Almost everything was taken out of her drawers and closet.

He also stole coins and cash from the daughter's bedroom, and then left through the same sliding glass door that he'd used to enter the residence.

One of the benefits of looking at the VR crimes night by night (or weekend by weekend) is that sometimes, something in a cluster stands out a bit and possibly gives us a glimpse into how his mind was working. When looking at these four, they all seem pretty homogenous – except for this one. With as quickly as he was hitting homes on this particular night, he spent a disproportionate amount of his time in this girl's room and closet. It seemed more significant or more "enjoyable" to him than his other activities of the night. We've wondered if she was the main, preplanned target of the night, and if the other three homes that he hit were simply opportunistic burglaries that took place because, as he made his way from his origin point to the home where this girl lived, he noticed that these residents weren't home.

There are several nights where it seems like the Ransacker had one target in mind, but decided to help himself to empty homes along the way to and from. If true, was he trying to hide which target was the "real" target because there was perhaps a personal connection or a clear sighting that he could've been identified from? Or was he burglarizing other homes as he went simply to satisfy his desire to commit these types of offenses? Was he gathering more intelligence on families or potential targets that he might've intended to revisit or begin stalking? Later on in the crime spree, he ransacked a home on West Royal Oaks Drive, stole some photos of the daughter, and *then* began stalking the family. It's possible that he sometimes entered homes out of curiosity, hoping to find information about someone who could fit his victim profile.

The police were ready for him on this night, so it's a shame that the Ransacker restricted himself to such a small geographic area. Apparently he didn't offend at all on the 13th or 15th, which were also nights that the stakeouts and patrols were out looking for him. The activity on the 14th was too far to the southwest of where he'd been hitting in recent months, so the police had no idea to look for him there. By keeping his activities to a tight time window and to a small geographic area that he hadn't struck before, he knowingly or unknowingly evaded capture.

(map featured on the following page)

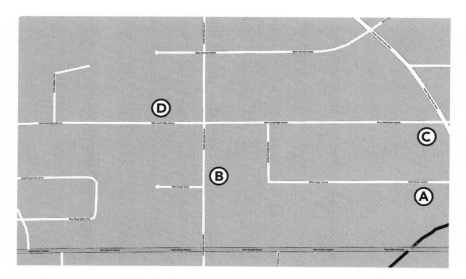

The ransackings that occurred on December 14th, 1974. We can't be sure about the order he committed all of these in, so it's possible that the order is incorrect.

A) VR #060 W Vassar Ave

B) VR #061 S University St

C) VR #062 W Cambridge Ave

D) VR #063 W Cambridge Ave

Note the proximity of Evan's Ditch to the first mark on the map. This was the ransacking that Law Enforcement felt that he committed first. It's not known, of course, if he used the ditch to traverse the area, but entering the ditch there and taking it northeast (back toward the heart of his comfort zone) would've taken him straight to the Houk Park area, a place near where he'd offended before and possibly a good spot to park a vehicle. Again, it's possible that he didn't use the ditch on this night, but it's interesting how it crops up so often in close proximity to many of his crimes. Later on in the crime spree, the police *did* find his shoe prints in and near the ditch, indicating that at least on occasion, he definitely did take it.

December 16th, 1974 Ransacking

The specialized police patrols ran from Friday to Sunday. It was a logical time to pick – almost all of the Ransacker's crimes had occurred on a Friday, Saturday, or Sunday. And they were right, he struck on a Saturday. Bu then he went on to hit on a *Monday*, which was an odd date for him.

Coincidentally (or perhaps not), this was the day after the special stakeouts ended. Did the Visalia Ransacker know that the patrols would not be out that night? Had he been aware of them, and had he modulated his urges long enough to wait until they stopped looking for him? He'd offended on Saturday, right in the middle of their operations, so it's not known *what* he might've known or not known.

His ransacking on Monday again saw him choosing a different type of area than he'd been offending in. This could be read one of two ways – the first is that perhaps he *was* aware of the increased police presence and he was trying to throw them off. Surely he knew that the papers had started writing about. Another way it could be read is that he was completely ignorant of the police patrols and he was simply looking for new areas – he'd hit a new area on Saturday while they were looking for him, and now he'd hit one on Monday while they weren't. Perhaps he was just proceeding with more caution than he'd exercised in the past due to the new media attention.

VR #064 – *Ransacking*
December 16th, 1974 | W Seeger Ave

On Monday, December 16th, between 8:00 PM and 11:20 PM, the VR entered a single-story residence on West Seeger Avenue while the victims were away for the evening.

He entered through an unlocked window. For some reason, he decided to take a window screen from this residence and throw it into the pool. The homeowners found it settled at the bottom when they returned. They also found that two fence boards had been removed or broken off by the Ransacker.

He opened a few different windows inside the residence, ransacked the bedrooms, and threw female undergarments onto the floor and the bed.

According to one report, nothing was stolen, but according to another, some money was taken.

He left through a sliding glass door.

The head of the household was a man in his mid thirties who worked as a grocery store clerk.

Technicians dusted the scene for fingerprints, but it became clear to them that the offender had used gloves while handling the drawers and windows.

This location was odd for the VR, even *further* south from the areas he'd been frequenting throughout 1974. As mentioned before, the day of the week was also atypical.

As far as location goes, Evan's Ditch is a few blocks to the north, but there's nothing to indicate that he used it. Other than possibly a desire to explore different areas of town or avoid some of the heat his crimes had generated, there's no solid clue as to what could've led the VR to West Seeger Avenue.

Timing and geography are, of course, important variables to look at in all of these instances. But the Ransacker likely considered many things when he went prowling, and sometimes it's beneficial to try to see things from his point of view. It's likely that he did quite a bit more prowling and peeping that anyone realizes, and this could've easily been a simple crime of opportunity that he came upon while he was out scouting for new victims. Since their window was unlocked, he might've been in the "right place" at the "right time" and simply decided to help himself.

The main reason that we think he was there to peep is that the VR broke into this very same property again nearly a year later. On November 6th, 1975, the Ransacker entered this home on a Thursday afternoon. This is significant, because this property is located in a part of town where the Ransacker rarely hit, and it was hit *twice* by him, which was fairly rare. Both burglaries were done at odd times (Mondays and Thursdays, which were uncommon days for him to be active). Additionally, the ransacking on November 6th, 1975 occurred in the *afternoon*, which was virtually unheard of in all of the Visalia Ransacker crimes. It's possible that this couple was a long-term target of the Ransacker – but did his infatuation start *before* this ransacking, or was it the result of him being in their home and noticing something that caused them to stay on his radar?

With so many outliers present, this is one of the more interesting burglaries in the series. There had to be *something* that drew him to this house, and it could be as simple as him possibly living or visiting nearby.

One last point – the fence boards and the screen ending up at the bottom of the pool again showed a destructive streak. Anger had started to emerge in his recent crimes. He seemed to be intensifying, not just in the scale of the crimes but with more fetish-type behavior and more rage shown toward his victims.

December 21st, 1974 Ransackings

Police Stakeouts
December 21st, 1974

The VR's activities in December had not quite reached the same level as the onslaught of November, but he certainly wasn't showing any signs of slowing down or going away, either. The Visalia Police Department was understandably frustrated at missing their slim opportunity to catch him on the 14th, and they were quite insulted that he'd gone on to offend the day after they'd stopped their patrols. Remembering how active he'd been around the Thanksgiving holiday, they wondered if they could nab him with a focus of efforts around the Christmas season. Since he'd offended on Saturday the 14th, they marked Saturday, December 21st as a good day to give it another shot.

Amazingly, it happened again! The Visalia Ransacker was active at the exact same moments and on the exact same night that the police were staking out the town looking for him. While he had flown under the radar last time by hitting a new area and staying in a confined location, this time it seemed that he took the opposite approach – he covered a very large area, hitting sporadically throughout the night an in an unpredictable pattern. They never spotted him and when burglary reports came in, they couldn't keep up with him.

The calls started at around 8:00 PM. Another after 10:00 PM. By the time anyone responded, the VR was long-gone from the area.

After 11:00 PM, things had grown quiet, and they were forced to call it a night.

Again they had come up empty-handed, and this time was far more maddening than the last. The Visalia Ransacker, perhaps knowing full-well what he was doing and perhaps accomplishing this feat by listening to police-band radio or stealthily observing his surroundings before making any moves, had eluded the police once more.

VR #065 – *Ransacking*
December 21st, 1974 | W College Ave

Sometime on Saturday, December 21st, between 6:00 PM and 8:00 PM, the VR entered a single-story house on West College Avenue while the victims were away for the evening.

He entered through an unlocked window. Once inside, he placed items against the front door of the house so that he would hear a loud crash if someone came home unexpectedly. He closed the master bedroom curtains so that no one from outside could see him burglarizing the house – perhaps an indication that he knew there were extra patrols on the streets that night.

He ransacked the home. He pushed over a dresser, stole a small amount of cash from the victims, and stole a coin collection. He took a shaving kit as well.

At the end of the burglary, the VR left the residence through a sliding glass door.

The head of the household was a man, about sixty years old. He worked as a real estate broker.

This ransacking took place just a few blocks to the west of the Mt. Whitney High School.

VR #066 – *Ransacking*
December 21st, 1974 | W Meadow Ave

Sometime on Saturday, December 21st, between 6:00 PM and 7:55 PM, the VR entered a single-story residence while the victim was away.

He entered by prying open a window. Once inside, he began ransacking the house, spending most of his time in the bedrooms. He threw women's undergarments to the floor and the bed.

Quite a bit was stolen from this scene: he broke a piggybank and stole its contents, he stole a coin collection from the house, he took four single earrings (but left behind the matching earring to each of the four sets), he stole Blue Chip stamps, and then he stole a pair of binoculars.

The information listed for the victim in this case says that a woman in her mid/late fifties lived in the home. Her occupation was listed as "housewife." There's no other information given about any other residents.

A shoe print was found, and it appeared to be a match for some of the other Visalia Ransacker crime scenes.

That's not all that was found nearby. The shaving kit that was taken from the previous burglary (the one on West College Avenue) was found on the roof of the next-door neighbor's house. Either the Ransacker decided that he didn't want it anymore, decided that his hands or his bag was full and he needed to get rid of something to lighten the load, or he wanted to leave some kind of calling card / display of disinterest in the victim's belongings.

The house that was burglarized was fairly large, and it had a unique layout. It was located about a dozen houses to the southwest of the house that the shaving kit had been stolen from.

VR #067 – Ransacking
December 20th to December 27th, 1974 | S Divisadero St

Sometime between Friday, December 20th at 6:00 AM and Friday, December 27th at 11:45 AM, the Ransacker entered a single-story home on South Divisadero Street while the family was away from the residence for an extended period of time. Even though the timeframe given was quite wide due to the family being out of town, it's likely that this burglary occurred on Saturday night (the 21st, the same night as the other ones we've been discussing) between 6:00 PM and 10:30 PM.

The point of entry was a main door to the house, which he was able to open by forcing through the lock. Once inside, he placed items against the front door as a rudimentary alarm system. He also opened a window and pushed the window screen out from the inside of the house.

He engaged in his usual behavior of ransacking almost every room in the home and removing items of female underclothing from drawers whenever he came across them.

He stole a lot from this scene, including collectible coins, two rings, two earrings (each from a set), and a small transistor radio. For those unfamiliar with the term "transistor radio," these were small, portable radios designed to allow people to listen to local stations. They were quite popular during the 1970s.

The adult female who lived in the house was in her fifties.

Latent fingerprints were found, as well as shoe impressions. They were cataloged by crime scene technicians. The fingerprints came up with no matches.

This location was a straight shot south of the burglary on West Meadow Avenue, located only a few houses away, which made it likely that they both happened back-to-back.

Looking at just these three burglaries alone, the Ransacker had stolen quite a few more items than usual. To be able to steal this many items, the Ransacker probably had some kind of bag with him, a vehicle nearby, or somewhere to stash things as he went. It's riskier to carry so many stolen items around on a night when police were out looking for him, so it may be an indication that he didn't know about the patrols.

VR #068 – *Ransacking*
December 21st, 1974 | S Fairway St

On Saturday, December 21st, sometime between 8:00 PM and 10:30 PM, the VR entered a single-story residence on South Fairway Street while the victims were away.

He entered by prying open a door. Once inside, he opened a window and removed the screen so that he'd have a clear path to the outside if he needed to escape. Then he began ransacking.

Most of the rummaging took place in the bedrooms. When he came across women's underwear, he removed it from the drawers and put it on the beds or the floor. He picked up some photographs of the family and threw them to the ground.

Before leaving, he stole ten-cent postage stamps and some Blue Chip stamps.

He exited the residence through a window.

The female in the household was in her mid sixties. Her profession was listed as "housewife." There were other people living at the residence as well.

The police seemed to be catching on to the idea that the women of the house were probably the target or the "victim" rather than the men. It was *their* unmentionables being tossed all over the place, after all. There was more of an emphasis on the demographic information of the women in some of the police reports during this phase of the attacks, which seems to be a result of this shift in thinking. The term "housewife" seems a bit antiquated, but that was the term they used.

This ransacking was located to the south (and a bit to the west) of the other ransackings that occurred on December 21st. It was just a few houses to the west of Rotary Park. A map showing this (and the other burglaries) will be featured at the end of the chapter.

VR #069 – *Ransacking*
December 21st, 1974 | W Iris Ct

On the evening of Saturday, December 21st, between 7:00 PM and 10:12 PM, the VR entered a single-story home on West Iris Court while the victims were away.

He entered by prying open a door. He engaged in his usual routine of opening escape routes, and he actually pried one of the windows open from the inside.

He ransacked the bedrooms, removing the woman's undergarments and rearranging them carefully on the floor and bed.

The Ransacker opened a bottle of Jergens body lotion that he found in the residence and used some of it. Lotion was found on the wall and on the floor of one of the bedrooms, and officers assumed that he had used it to masturbate with. They couldn't tell if there was any masturbation emission in the lotion smears.

The Ransacker came across photos of the couple's young children and he threw them onto the floor. He also broke a piggybank in the residence, stole the coins from it, stole cash, and stole some of their keys. He then exited the residence through the window that he'd pried open from the inside.

The head of the household was a male in his mid twenties who worked as an electrician. He lived there with his wife and kids.

A shoe print was found at this scene, which apparently matched some of the other scenes and helped tie some of the Visalia Ransacker incidents together through physical evidence.

The anger or disgust shown toward the photos of the children was a disturbing behavior. The indication that he'd masturbated at the scene was even *more* disturbing. This was one of those crimes where the full spectrum of his neuroses was present.

The information available to us doesn't indicate what kind of keys the Ransacker stole from this residence. It's not known if they were house keys or keys to something else. No doubt a locksmith was called immediately.

The potential timeframes for most of the attacks that we've covered on this date were so wide that they could've happened in almost any order. We *do* know that the one on West Meadow Avenue was earlier than two of the others, and because of the location of the one on South Divisadero Street, it seemed he was initially traveling from north to south that night. That makes it likely that this ransacking was the last one of the night. If officers were correct about him masturbating at the scene, that detail might *also* point to this being the last house he visited.

What's interesting about this location, whether it was the final ransacking of the night or not, is its proximity to Mt. Whitney High School. If West College Avenue was the first one of the night, and this one was his last one, then it appears that his origin may have been from the general location of the school. We have an attack near the western side of the northern half of the property, and then this attack on the western side of the southern half of the property. He could've committed most of these in almost any order, but looping back makes sense given some of the other paths he'd taken on nights that he'd offended.

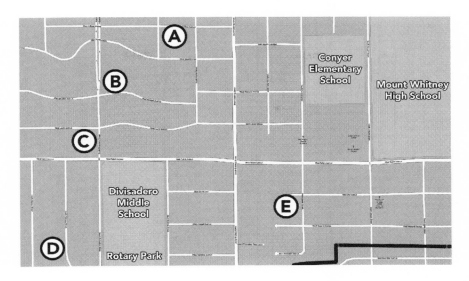

The ransackings that occurred on December 21st, 1974.

A)   VR #065 W College Ave

B)   VR #066 W Meadow Ave

C)   VR #067 (occurred between Dec 20th-Dec 27th on S Divisadero St)

D)   VR #068 S Fairway St

E)   VR #069 W Iris Ct

Also notice the proximity of these to Rotary Park. Looking at the map, it would also make sense if the West Iris Court ransacking wasn't the last one after all, and he might've ended his night by ransacking on South Fairway Street and then escaping into the park. Recall that Evan's Ditch runs through the southern portion of Rotary Park. He could've also caught the ditch simply by heading south on South Sowell Street, if he used that pathway at all that night. The ditch ran fairly close to West Iris Court as well – and he could've entered it from that point.

December 22nd, 1974 Incidents

Police Stakeouts
December 22nd through December 30th, 1974

Frustrated by their lack of success and the audacity that the VR had shown by offending right under their noses, the police put even *more* officers on Visalia Ransacker detail. They committed themselves to working through the Christmas holiday and almost all the way up to News Year's Eve, still feeling strongly that holidays were either a trigger for their offender or a prime opportunity that he was exploiting to find empty homes.

You guessed it – he struck again. And again, he evaded detection and capture. But they were getting closer – they were able to respond quickly and also able to gather intel on prowling incidents that otherwise might not have been noticed. It's also believed that their presence and actions prevented more burglaries from occurring.

In fact, at the rate he'd been offending, they may have prevented *many* more burglaries. Their concerted efforts and the patrols nipping at his heels are probably what shut down the VR for the rest of the year. He offended on the first night of these expanded patrols, but operated on none of the others. It seemed to be an indication that the police presence was indeed working as a preventative measure, at least. It's even possible that he had a close call with police – at one of the incidents described toward the end of this chapter, it's likely that he was still in the vicinity when the police responded.

After the burglaries discussed here, he wasn't heard from again for over a month.

VR #070 – Ransacking
December 21st to December 29th, 1974 | W Fairview Ave

Sometime between Saturday, December 21st at noon and Sunday, December 29th at 5:00 PM, the Ransacker entered a single-story house on West Fairview Avenue while the residents were away for an extended period. It's assumed that this ransacking took place on Sunday night (December 22nd) because there were two other ransackings that occurred about five hundred feet away on the same evening.

He broke a window to gain entry.

Once inside, he opened up another window and began rummaging through the house. He ransacked every room, pulling several articles of clothing out of drawers and tossing them to the floor.

He found a can of shaving cream in the house and began spraying it on the floor (including the carpet), the furniture, and onto the walls. This was somewhat reminiscent of the mess he'd made with the lotion at the previous scene that we discussed, but the activity was far more extensive.

He also took their three-panel tri-fold dressing mirror and laid it on the bed.

The VR stole coins and a piggybank at this scene. To exit, he went through one of the main doors of the house.

149

The head of the household was a male adult in his mid twenties that worked as a Navy pilot. Demographically, the couple was similar to the victims of the previous ransacking that we described (the one on West Iris Court).

This was one of the most extensive ransackings, and the police dusted the area for prints. They were able to find some but after processing them, they determined that there was no match between the prints found at this burglary and prints found at any other VR scene.

This ransacking was located in between South Whitney Street and the College of the Sequoias – certainly prime VR "hunting grounds" and an area that he returned to time and time again throughout 1975.

VR #071 – *Ransacking*
December 22nd, 1974 | S Terri St

Sometime on Sunday, December 22nd, between 2:00 PM and 8:45 PM, the Ransacker entered a single-story home on South Terri Street while the victims were away for the afternoon and evening.

He entered by prying open a door. Once inside, he ransacked several rooms, paying particular attention to the jewelry. While he rummaged through most of the pieces, it didn't appear that he had stolen any of them.

He did steal a piggybank from the scene though, and he stole several coins. He found cash hidden in the residence, but rather than taking it, he deliberately left it out in plain view. It was almost on display, like a kind of a taunt or message – the kind he sometimes left as the East Area Rapist when he found someone's hidden stash of money.

The woman who lived there was retired and was in her mid eighties.

Shoe prints were found by scene technicians. They were a basic match for other Visalia Ransacker scenes.

VR #072 – *Ransacking*
December 22nd, 1974 | W Laurel Ave

Sometime on Sunday, December 22nd, between 5:00 PM and 8:00 PM, the Ransacker entered a single-story residence on West Laurel Avenue while the victims were away.

He entered by prying open a main door. Once inside, he went through his usual routine.

What sets this incident apart from many of the other ransackings is the number of items that he stole. From this scene alone, he took a coin collection, a silver bracelet, two rings, two transistor radios, a pair of men's pajamas, and an unopened package of men's t-shirts. He also stole a suitcase, possibly out of necessity to help him transport all of those items.

The male head of the household was retired and about seventy years old. Other members of his family lived with him at the home.

The police were a bit surprised at how extensive the burglary was. They dusted for prints. Latent fingerprints were found, but none of them matched any of the prints that they'd collected thus far.

The Visalia Ransacker had hit this street before, just six weeks prior, on November 2nd (VR #044). It's a very small stretch of pavement, but the layout of the street loops around, which might've made the area more conducive to prowling (or escaping from). The map shown at the end of the chapter illustrates this.

VR #073 – *Prowler*
December 22nd, 1974 | W Beverly Dr

-NOT CONFIRMED TO BE RELATED-

Sometime between 8:00 PM and 11:00 PM, a prowler was spotted at a residence on West Beverly Drive. Because the timeframe given is fairly wide (and it overlaps with the next two prowling incidents), it's possible that it actually occurred *after* the next two. Investigators feel that it happened before them, however.

The residence that experienced the prowler wasn't broken into or ransacked, but a house on the same street would be ransacked by the VR a year later in December 1975.

This home was located a couple blocks to the east of the College of the Sequoias, which is interesting to note because the ransackings that occurred on the same night occurred to the *west* of the college. It was fairly rare for the VR to appear on both sides of South Mooney Boulevard in a single night, but it wasn't completely unheard of. For those unfamiliar with the area, South Mooney Boulevard is a major street in the area that basically bisects the two halves of the southern part of the city, and it also borders the college.

As with many of the prowling incidents, it's not known for sure if this was related to the Visalia Ransacker. Investigators believed at the time that it was.

VR #074 – *Prowler*
December 22nd, 1974 | S Oak Park St

-NOT CONFIRMED TO BE RELATED-

Sometime between 8:00 PM and 11:00 PM, a prowler was spotted at a residence on South Oak Park Street. No ransacking or burglary is associated with this event.

This location is over half a mile to the northeast of the prowler activity on West Beverly Drive. If the prowler was the VR and the VR was on foot, that's a bit of a hike considering that the police were out looking for him. It's thought that he may have had a method of transportation.

VR #075 – *Prowler*
December 22nd, 1974 | S Oak Park St

-NOT CONFIRMED TO BE RELATED-

There was another sighting of a prowler on South Oak Park Street. This event occurred at 10:30 PM, and it was reported from the house next-door.

The part of town where these prowlings occurred was no stranger to VR crime. On October 23rd, 1974, the VR had ransacked a residence located on the same street – just a few houses down from these events. On November 6th, 1975, he would return once more and ransack the house next-door to the one he'd ransacked on October 23rd, 1974.

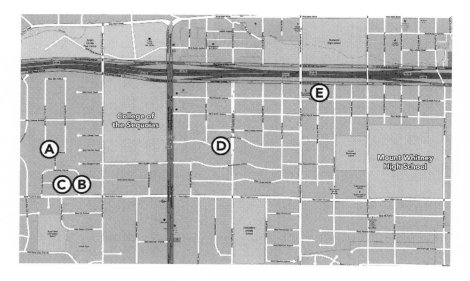

The general locations of the ransackings and the prowling incidents from December 22nd, 1974.

A) *VR #070 ransacking on W Fairview Ave*

B) *VR #071 ransacking on S Terri St*

C) *VR #072 ransacking on W Laurel Ave*

D) *Prowler (VR #073) on W Beverly Dr*

E) *Two prowling incidents on S Oak Park St (VR #074 and #075) occurred next-door to each other*

It's hard not to notice geographic similarity and other parallels between this group of ransackings and the group that had occurred on Saturday, December 21st. In both of these instances, he attacked to the west of a big campus and he stole quite a few items throughout the night.

It's likely that the College of the Sequoias had plenty of areas where the offender could park a vehicle or stash transportation without drawing too much attention. The added benefit of a college campus would be that if he walked around with a backpack or even a suitcase, it wouldn't raise as many suspicions as it would if he were walking down a residential street. Of course, not many students would be hanging around the area on a Sunday evening like that, but it wouldn't be unheard of for people to drift in and out unchallenged on almost any college campus during the era.

January 25th, 1975 Ransackings

A lot of resources were spent by the police on those December patrols, and they hadn't netted the VR. But as the weeks went by and there were no additional incidents tied to him, they began to wonder if their expanded presence had somehow driven him out of town (or had at least convinced him to stop offending). Whatever the reason, it seemed that he *was* gone. At least, for a while.

Then came a pair of ransackings in late January. He'd returned, and the two homes that he hit were so close that they practically shared a backyard.

VR #076 – *Ransacking*
January 25th, 1975 | S Verde Vista St

On Saturday, January 25th, between 11:30 AM and 6:30 PM, the VR entered a single-story home on South Verde Vista Street while the victims were away from the residence.

The timeframe given for this one is fairly early in the day. Was the Ransacker nearby, watching them? Did he know when they would be out? There was a little over an hour of darkness available to him during this window of time – was that when he struck? Did he set up in the empty house behind them and stage his operations from there? That house, which we'll talk about next, was also ransacked.

He entered by prying open a window. Once inside, he ransacked the bedrooms and removed women's undergarments from the drawers. He placed them on the floor and the bed.

He stole regular coins, a coin collection, and Blue Chip stamps from the residence. When he left, he exited through a different window than the one he had used to enter.

The head of the household was a man in his mid thirties. He lived there with his wife.

This house and these particular residents appeared to be specifically targeted by the VR over a long period of time. It seems he visited their home three times that they know of, with each visit an escalation from the previous one:

- VR #032: October 16th, 1974: Prowler spotted in their carport.
- VR #076: January 25th, 1975 (this incident): Their home was ransacked.
- VR #119: October 4th, 1975: The VR attempted to enter their home in the early morning hours while they were inside of it.

More details related to his stalking methods and methods of operation will become clearer as the rest of the book unfolds, but this is one of the victim patterns that makes it clear that the VR was a dangerous offender with a long memory. The attempt to enter the victims' home while they were still inside is part of a terrifying turn that the Ransacker began to exhibit in the fall of 1975.

While it had been roughly a month since the VR's last strike, that wasn't really a very unusual period of time between flurries of VR activity. He'd been so active at the end of November and throughout December that it *did* represent a slowdown, though. The reason for the slowdown could've been personal, or he could've been gathering more intel on potential victims through peeping and prowling.

VR #077 – *Ransacking*
January 24th to January 27th, 1975 | W Pecan Ct

Sometime between Friday, January 24th at 5:00 PM and Monday, January 27th at 9:30 AM, the Ransacker entered a single-story residence on West Pecan Court while the residents were away.

He entered by prying open a door. As was typical for him, he ransacked the bedrooms and tossed women's undergarments to the floor. Cash and coins were stolen.

The head of the household was a man in his mid seventies. He was retired. Other family members lived at the house with him.

The scene was dusted for fingerprints, and some latent prints were found. These were eventually compared to prints found at other scenes, but there were no matches among any of them.

It's assumed that this house was hit around the same time as the one on South Verde Vista Street. The homes backed up to each other.

It's possible that these victims were simply casualties of his interest in the people that lived behind them. The Ransacker probably noticed that they were gone as he was lying in wait, making sure that his primary targets had left for the afternoon, and he simply took advantage of the situation.

These two locations were just to the west of the College of the Sequoias. It was an area he'd hit a few times before.

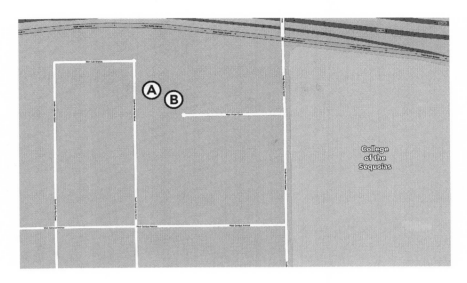

Ransackings on January 25th, 1975.

A) *VR #076 S Verde Vista St*
B) *VR #077 S Pecan Ct*

He struck the first house before 6:30 PM. During the winter months he seemed to get an earlier start – this is important to note because it seems to imply that he based his ransacking times around how dark it was and *not* by the clock. If he were basing his crimes around a personal schedule or around work/family obligations, then the general timeframes of his ransackings wouldn't be affected by seasonality or how dark it was. Since he was offending earlier in the evening during the months when it got dark earlier, it appears that nothing in his personal or professional life was keeping him from starting his activities at the hour of his choosing.

February 2ⁿᵈ, 1975 Ransackings

The burglary on South Verde Vista Street on January 25th was one of the first indications that the Visalia Ransacker had a very specific kind of memory and a long timetable for some of his targets. While some officers believed that the burglaries were more or less random and that they were the work of a teen, the VR being interested in one home for a period of time was a major red flag.

The same thing happened once more on February 2nd. A home on South Whitney Street that had been ransacked in April 1974 was again hit by the VR, and at this burglary, he even had the forethought to bring his own lotion with him so that he could masturbate while inside the residence.

There was no doubt about it – this was not the work of mere teens. There was twisted and complex thinking at work in these crimes, and these first few days of February would lay even *more* groundwork to show that this was a dangerous, sophisticated, sexually motivated offender who had started to formulate long-term plans for many of the families he was targeting. Some of the ransackings that occurred on February 2nd certainly had elements of that, and the peeping incident we'll discuss from February 5th helped solidify the idea. Through the luxury of hindsight, his evolution is quite clear, and the types of offenses that he was capable of committing are very apparent.

VR #078 – *Ransacking*
Feburary 2nd, 1975 | S Whitney St

On Sunday, February 2nd, between 4:30 PM and 7:50 PM, the Ransacker entered a single-story house on South Whitney Street while the residents were away.

He removed the screen to a window and placed it by the back gate, and then he pried at the window but was unable to get through it. He tried a different point of entry, prying at a sliding glass door until it gave way.

Once inside, he ransacked every room in the house, paying special attention to the bedrooms. When he came across articles of women's underwear in the drawers, he took them out.

He'd brought a bottle of Jergens hand lotion to the scene, which he apparently used on himself – copious amounts of lotion had apparently been applied to his hands. Smears of it were found in various places, especially at the sliding glass door.

He left the bottle in their dining room.

Jewelry and a purse were stolen from the scene, as well as a razor, twenty books of Blue Chip stamps (which were in the purse), and a box of 22-gauge ammunition. Only the Visalia Ransacker would steal a purse *and* ammunition from the same crime scene.

The head of the household was a retired male in his mid sixties. Other family members lived with him at the residence.

When police processed the scene, they noticed that the Ransacker had somehow broken a main support beam off of the victims' redwood fence. It didn't appear to be a malicious action – it had been broken off when he tried to climb it.

The police learned that this wasn't the first time that this residence had been ransacked in this manner – as we mentioned in the intro, he had broken in and ransacked this residence in April 1974 during his first wave of known crimes in the area. South Whitney Street was always an epicenter of Visalia Ransacker activity – he had many long-term victims in and around this particular street. Since he had gone back and revisited a home on South Verde Vista Street on January 25th and *now* had revisited a home on South Whitney Street that he had already entered, it appeared that the Ransacker had started the year off by focusing on prior victims. It can't be coincidence that on two consecutive outings, he'd revisited two different scenes. It was a sign that he was escalating even further.

VR #079 – *Ransacking*
Feburary 2nd, 1975 | W Whitney Dr

Sometime on Sunday, February 2nd, between 4:30 PM and 9:50 PM, the VR broke into a single-story house on West Whitney Drive while the residents were out. This home was only three houses away from the burglary we just discussed.

Based on tracks found at the scene, it seems the VR explored the perimeter of the house a bit, looking for an easy way to enter. Using a wooden bench to give himself a boost, he found an unlocked window.

Once inside, he opened another window and removed the screen.

He ransacked every room, rifling through drawers and moving all of the items sitting on shelves. There were no women living at the house, so he didn't come across any jewelry or female undergarments.

He didn't steal anything from the scene. When he left, he exited through a sliding glass door.

The head of the household was a man in his mid thirties who worked as a clerk. Other people lived at the house with him.

The police examined the scene for fingerprints and shoe impressions, and they found both. The fingerprints didn't lead anywhere, but the shoe prints, of which there were several, were a rough match for other Visalia Ransacker burglaries.

This home had no women living in it and nothing interesting enough for him to steal. The story would be the same at the *next* ransacking of the night. These types of hits lend credence to the theory that he could've had one or two targets in mind for a particular outing, and that he would hit empty homes along the way in a more or less random fashion. It helped disguise his true intentions for the evening *and* it made his crimes seem a little more randomized and less sinister. Obviously, on this night, the South Whitney Street home would've been the target and the other two would be the randoms.

VR #080 – *Ransacking*
Feburary 2nd, 1975 | W Gist Ave

Sometime between 9:15 AM and 10:50 PM on Sunday, February 2nd, the Visalia Ransacker entered a single-story residence on West Gist Avenue while the victim was away.

He entered by prying open the main door to the house.

Once inside, he ransacked the residence, but not very extensively. There were no women's clothing or women's undergarments in the house. The victim was a retired man in his early seventies.

The VR stole coins from the scene before making his exit.

Police examined the perimeter of the residence, and they found shoe prints made by the offender. They appeared to match the shoe impressions found on West Whitney Drive.

The Ransacker may have had a close call at this one – the owner felt that he'd scared off the burglar when he arrived home. If true, that probably puts his activity on West Whitney Drive closer to 9:50 PM rather than earlier in the evening.

West Gist Avenue is a little strip of five or six houses that connects South Linda Vista Street and South Verde Vista Street. This general location had seen plenty of Visalia Ransacker activity, and it would continue to be hit and prowled as the rest of the year went on.

This whole area, which you're no doubt familiar with by now if you've been studying this case chronologically, was located a couple blocks to the west of the College of the Sequoias.

(map featured on the next page)

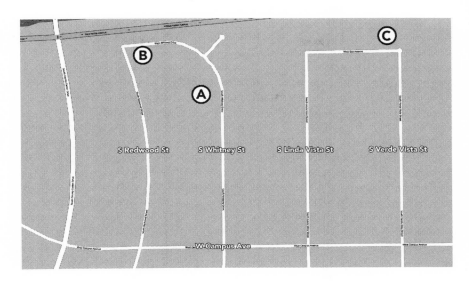

Ransackings on February 2nd, 1975.

A) *VR #078 S Whitney St*
B) *VR #079 W Whitney Dr*
C) *VR #080 W Gist Ave*

February 5th, 1975 Prowler

South Whitney Street was one of the Visalia Ransacker's favorite haunts. One of the residents on that street, a journalism professor at the College of the Sequoias named Claude Snelling, had lived there with his family for several years. A deeply religious man, Claude was a devoted husband and a father to three children.

On the night of February 5th, Claude would have an encounter in the darkness with a man prowling around near his carport. Little did he know, this wouldn't be the last time that the two of them would encounter each other. Later that same year, Snelling would be shot to death by that very same man and from that very same carport.

VR #081 – *Prowler*
February 5th, 1975 | S Whitney St

At 10:00 PM on Wednesday, February 5th, Claude Snelling returned to his home on South Whitney Street. As he pulled into his driveway, he spotted a subject crouched at his teenage daughter's window. The man was peeping into it.

Claude immediately got out of the car and began chasing the prowler. In mere moments, the subject ran under the carport, rounded the side of the house, and was swallowed up by the darkness of the street.

The police checked the perimeter of the home. They focused their attention under the window, where they noticed clear shoe prints.

The shoe prints were a match for the Visalia Ransacker.

Claude described the Ransacker as a white male, 5'10" to 6', with collar-length hair. He was wearing a plaid long-sleeve shirt.

This residence was located virtually across the street from the ransacking on South Whitney Street that had occurred three days prior.

And as we mentioned, this wouldn't be the Ransacker's last visit to this residence – more activity occurred in August and September. We'll discuss those incidents later.

February 16th, 1975 Ransackings

We've discussed how South Whitney Street (and the entire area west of the College of the Sequoias) was a hotspot for VR activity. The same geographical pattern seemed to repeat itself in the area to the west of Mt. Whitney High School – namely, on a street called West Kaweah Avenue.

The VR's stalking behavior was still at its embryotic stages at this point, but this was one of the streets where he began ramping up quite a bit.

The previous chapter introduced the Snelling family. They would become Ransacker victims in September. At the end of this chapter, we introduce *another* significant part of the VR saga – a home on West Kaweah Avenue that would later become the scene of a Ransacker confrontation that ended in gunfire.

VR #082 – *Ransacking*
February 16th, 1975 | S Sowell St

On Sunday, February 16th, between 6:00 PM and 7:00 PM, the VR entered a single-story residence on South Sowell Street while the victims were away.

He had a hard time entering this home, as evidenced by the pry marks found on multiple doors and windows. Apparently he was very determined, because he eventually did get a door to give way.

Once inside, he opened several potential escape routes. He went through his usual routine, removing every female undergarment that he could find from the drawers and putting all of them on the floor or bed. He seemed to spend a considerable amount of time in the teenage daughter's room.

He stole coins and cash from the household, along with one single earring from a pair.

The teenager went to Mt. Whitney High School. This was a common thread among several of the ransackings. This home's location was just to the west of the Mt. Whitney High School area.

VR #083 – *Ransacking*
February 16th, 1975 | W Meadow Ave

On Sunday, February 16th, between 6:00 PM and 8:45 PM, the VR entered a single-story residence on West Meadow Avenue while the victims were away.

The methods of entry and exit seem to be unknown – the information used to determine this isn't in any of the materials that we have access to.

Inside the residence, he placed items against the front door. He took the women's undergarments out of drawers and placed them carefully on the floor and the bed. This was done with the two daughters' things *and* the mother's.

He stole coins and cash from the scene.

As we just mentioned, this couple had daughters. Every home hit on this particular evening had at least one teenage girl living at the house.

VR #084 – *Ransacking*
February 16th, 1975 | W Kaweah Ave

On Sunday, February 16th, sometime between 6:00 PM to 11:00 PM, the VR entered a single-story residence on West Kaweah Avenue while the victims were out for the evening.

His entry and exit methods aren't known, but he attempted to pry open several windows unsuccessfully.

He ransacked bedrooms, again taking the women's panties, bras, and underclothing out of drawers and arranging them on or near the bed.

He picked up one of the daughter's wedding photos and threw it to the floor. He picked up a picture of the couple's son and did the same.

Coins and cash were stolen from the scene, just like at every burglary on this particular night.

A daughter who lived with them at the house attended College of the Sequoias, and their son attended Divisadero Middle School.

The scene was dusted for fingerprints, and some latent prints were found. None of them matched any of the previous ransackings, nor did they match any known criminals.

The burglaries on this particular night were somewhat spread out, but that offers us a bit of a clue and perhaps a bit of insight into what his M.O. was at this point. For one thing, none of the ransackings seem extraneous or opportunistic. He spent a significant amount of time focused on teenage girls' underclothing during this outing, and if these particular girls weren't specifically, then he had an uncanny knack for finding homes with teenage girls who were about the same age and shared several things in common. And again, they were all geographically spaced out, and it's very possible that he'd been peeping for a period of time before selecting this night to ransack some of their homes. He was probably peeping on more homes than these three – these were probably the only ones empty during the time he was out.

Evan's Ditch wasn't there to use as a crutch or to peek through backyards and find empty homes, and it seemed he'd evolved past having to use it. These burglaries seemed carefully planned and quite deliberate – the sign of an offender with more confidence and more of a strategy.

The police were becoming interested in the Ransacker again, and after this burglary, they began finding shoe prints in places where the VR hadn't offended. It's not known if these were made on the same night or on nights before or after these ransackings. It seems to add to the idea that he might've been out prowling on nights where he didn't attack and that he was engaging in peeping activities just as much or even more often than he engaged in burglaries. The spread-out nature of these particular ransackings, plus being caught peeping on February 5th, also helped make it apparent that the VR was covering quite a bit of ground and probably looking into quite a few windows. And on some of those nights, for reasons unknown, he crossed that threshold and burglarized one or more of them. A combination of the victims already being in his sights and the opportunity of them being away on a night where he hoped to peep at them perhaps nudged him in that direction. And once he burglarized one home, he might've felt compelled to hit more of them.

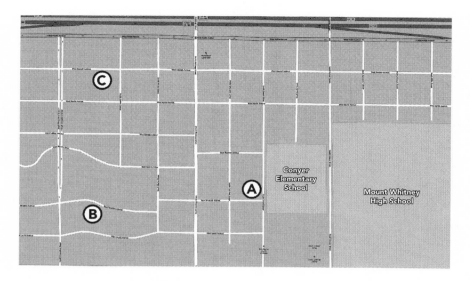

Ransackings on February 16th, 1975.

A)   *VR #082 S Sowell St*
B)   *VR #083 W Meadow Ave*
C)   *VR #084 W Kaweah Ave*

There's something else notable about the geography of these attacks, and really any of the attacks that happened near West Kaweah Avenue. As he began to target this area more and more, it started to seem likely that he was using the dark, overgrown fenced-in path between Noble Avenue and State Route 198 that we've mentioned before. This was the northern border of his attack zone, and it's the northernmost street visible on the above map. His shoe prints were found there, and they seemed to be heading east toward the Mt. Whitney High School area. If he began his night near there, he'd probably have to end it near there, too. He could've lived near the school, or he could've parked a form of transportation nearby.

It's often wondered if he had a sort of affinity or history with the Mt. Whitney High School, since so many of the people he targeted had daughters who went there. Most believe that he just liked targeting high school girls, and that's where the girls on the south side of town went. None of the teenage girls he targeted went to nearby Redwood High School, because that was situated across the highway on the north side of town and the Ransacker was never known to hit there.

We should point out the significance of this home on West Kaweah Avenue that was ransacked. In December 1975, a police officer was informed that the Ransacker had been peeping at the next-door neighbor on a regular basis. The officer hid in this home's garage and waited for the Ransacker to come by again. The night ended with the officer seeing the Ransacker's face clearly, the Ransacker firing at him, seventy officers being called in, and the Ransacker escaping. We'll cover the details later in the book.

It's not known if the girl who lived next-door was on the VR's radar yet, but perhaps that was one of the reasons that the Ransacker visited this area on February 16th. If she wasn't on his radar yet, she certainly would be by July when part of her home was ransacked. She was clearly another one of the VR's long-term targets.

March 1ˢᵗ, 1975 Ransacking

As he sometimes did, the Ransacker disappeared for a couple of weeks. It's seemed probable that he'd been keeping his eye on a few girls around the area to the west of Mt. Whitney High School, and that in February he'd finally ransacked their homes and thus was out of targets for a little while. March, April, and several weeks in May represented a big slowdown for him in 1975.

VR #085 – *Ransacking*
March 1st, 1975 | W Howard Ave

On Saturday, March 1st, between 6:10 PM and 11:00 PM, the VR entered a single-story residence on West Howard Avenue while the victims were away.

This ransacking was pretty much textbook for the VR. He opened some windows to be used as a quick escape route, he ransacked the house (particularly the bedrooms), and he took female underclothing out of the drawers and arranged it nearby. He also took a bunch of shirts, pants, and other types of clothing out and tossed them nearby.

He stole cash, some coins, and some rings. The rings that he took weren't particularly valuable – as usual, he left the valuable jewelry behind. It wasn't that he didn't *see* the valuables – he'd left all of it a disorganized mess. The Ransacker had stolen only some small personal items.

He took a revolver from this scene, but the revolver didn't work. Whether he knew enough about guns to realize that when he took it is unknown.

The house was dusted for fingerprints. Several were found, but none of them matched any of the previous scenes. The fingerprints most likely belonged to friends of the victim.

April 1975 Prowler

VR #086 – *Prowler*

April 1975 | S Redwood St

-NOT CONFIRMED TO BE RELATED-

A prowler was spotted near a house on South Redwood Street. A description isn't available.

This particular incident was reported later on in the crime spree, not right after it happened, so it was impossible to pin down an exact date. Only the address and the month are known.

This area of South Redwood Street would be close to the epicenter of the Claude Snelling homicide. In fact, the prowler was spotted only 150 feet to the west of where Claude Snelling was actually shot and killed later that fall. With as much VR-related activity as this area had experienced and would *still* experience, it really is quite probable that this prowler was the VR. If so, he was most likely scouting out new victims, peeping at them, and prowling/peeping at ones he had already been keeping his eye on. Perhaps he even visited the Snelling household, since he was spotted so close to it on this date and had been seen there in February.

Since there was no physical evidence at the scene and no available description, it's impossible to know if this was truly the VR.

May 24th, 1975 Ransackings

The last ransacking had been on March 1st. Of course, with such a long period of quiet, it once again seemed that the VR was gone. He wasn't. In fact, he was just getting started.

The Visalia Ransacker returned to form on Saturday, May 24th, for an outing that had all of the geographical and behavioral elements that the police had come to associate with his crimes. By now, it was clear that he was a seasoned burglar and he knew exactly what he was doing. The first ransacking we examine was adjacent to the Royal Oaks Elementary School and Houk Park area – like so many nights, he seemed to strike opportunistically from the school or park – which seemed to indicate his origin point. He then went up to the Whitney/Redwood area, where he had been prowling and offending since the very beginning.

As midnight approached, he went all the way over to West Kaweah Avenue, an area that he seemed to be giving more and more attention. He had clusters of victims and potential targets picked out all around the Verde Vista / Whitney / Redwood area *and* the West Kaweah Avenue area, and he wasn't shy about making his presence known.

At the beginning, it had seemed that the offender was meandering the creek and getting the lay of the land. Not anymore. He was comfortable striking from schools and parks, and then covering quite a bit of distance to prowl and strike some more. All of this despite the fact that the police would be alerted to his activity from earlier in the night and could be out in force looking for him.

VR #087 – *Ransacking*
May 24th, 1975 | S Mountain St

On Saturday, May 24th, sometime in the evening, the Ransacker entered a single-story house on South Mountain Street while the victims were away.

He had to work hard to get into this residence – two of the doors failed to open despite extensive efforts to pry at them. The third door that he tried finally gave way.

He ransacked every room in the house. There weren't any women living at this residence, so most likely, he didn't find what he was looking for. No female clothing, no female undergarments, no jewelry, and there weren't even any coins or Blue Chip stamps for him to steal.

He did, however, find a 38-caliber Taurus revolver at the scene. He took it.

This location was immediately to the west of the Houk Park area, and the backyard of the residence was situated against the Royal Oaks Elementary School. The geography of the house was similar to several of the other houses he had broken into, especially the way it was situated – he could walk behind the house and peer through the fence to determine if anyone was at home or not. This was most likely a hit that was done simply because he was on his way to a specific target area and he happened to notice that the house was empty.

VR #088 – *Ransacking*
May 24th, 1975 | S Mountain St

On Saturday, May 24th, sometime in the evening, the VR entered another single-story residence on South Mountain Street while the victims were away.

He opened a couple of windows to use as a quick escape, and he ransacked every room in the residence. He took women's panties, bras, and undergarments out and put them on the floor and on the bed. He also took some other types of clothing out of drawers.

He stole coins and cash from the residence.

This location was on the opposite side of the street from the other South Mountain Street residence that was ransacked, and it was located several houses to the north.

It's always hard to determine why the VR would enter certain homes but would leave others alone. On most nights, he passed several houses that were empty, and for some reason he'd burglarize some but not the others. In this case, the way that the garage was situated might have been a factor – the garage juts out quite a bit from the residence and provides a lot of cover and shadow. In the present day, there are tall hedges that, if they existed at the time, would've provided the VR with plenty of room to work in the side yard without attracting any attention.

VR #089 – *Ransacking*
May 24th, 1975 | S Redwood St

On Saturday, May 24th, between 8:00 PM and 11:00 PM, the Ransacker entered a single-story home on South Redwood Street while the victim was away.

As usual, he opened some of the windows in the residence while he was inside, and he even pulled the screens into the home so that he could escape as quickly as possible if he were interrupted.

He ransacked every room in the house, taking women's undergarments out of drawers and arranging them near the bed. While rummaging through the residence, he found and stole some Blue Chip stamps.

This home was situated on the portion of South Redwood Street just above West Valley Drive, and located several houses south of West Campus Avenue. The yard backed up to South County Center Drive. Later on in the crime series, he would begin traveling to South County Center Drive by way of backyards on South Redwood Street. It's possible that he even did it on *this* night, traveling north on South County Center Drive and then taking the footpath along State Route 198 / West Noble Avenue to the West Kaweah Avenue location that he hit next. The distance was between a mile or a mile and a half depending on which route he took through the city – not insurmountable but definitely much further than he was prone to travel at the beginning of the crime series.

The following is a map of all four incidents from this night, including the one on West Kaweah Avenue that we haven't discussed yet:

(*map featured on the next page*)

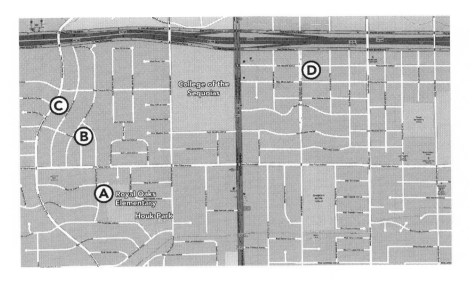

Ransackings on May 24th, 1975.

A) *VR #087 S Mountain St*

B) *VR #088 S Mountain St*

C) *VR #089 S Redwood St*

D) *VR #090 W Kaweah Ave*

VR #090 – *Ransacking*
May 24th, 1975 | W Kaweah Ave

On Saturday, May 24th, sometime between 11:00 PM and midnight, the VR entered a single-story house on West Kaweah Avenue while the victims were away.

The full VR modus operandi was on display at this ransacking, including the placement of items against the door.

He ransacked every room, taking women's undergarments out of drawers and placing them nearby. He stole cash and some coins.

The police dusted the residence for fingerprints, and they did find a few. The prints weren't matched to any family members, but they also weren't matched to any known offenders or to any of the other Ransacker prints that had been taken from previous scenes.

As mentioned earlier, this location was a bit of a distance from the other ransackings that had occurred on the night of May 24th, 1975. It was also just a few houses away from the ransacking that had taken place on February 16th, 1975, which was the last date that the VR had hit multiple homes in one night. It's possible that the VR was ending his night on May 24th by going around and peeping at women that he'd previously identified and kept tabs on, and just through serendipity he'd found one of the nearby homes empty and had simply helped himself. The fact that he ended in the same place as he did on February 16th certainly suggests something like that.

This street was a favorite haunt of the Ransacker's. By the end of 1975, roughly half of the houses in this small segment of the street had been part of incidents that can be tied to the VR. The following map shows the general locations of these events:

(map featured on the next page)

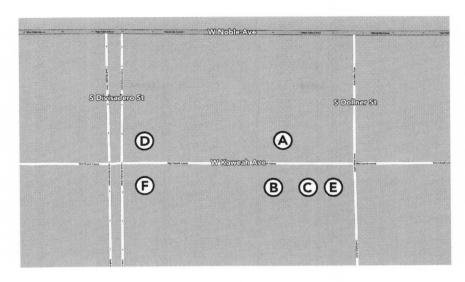

*A map of the incidents that occurred on a small stretch of West Kaweah Avenue. Only six houses on this segment of the street were **not** burglarized.*

(Not pictured)   The prowling incidents from VR #003 and #004, which were a few blocks to the east.

A)   VR #058: November 30th 1974 Ransacking

B)   VR #059: November 30th 1974 Ransacking

C)   VR #084 February 16th, 1975 Ransacking

D)   VR #090 May 24th, 1975 Ransacking

E)   VR #094 July 24th, 1975 Ransacking

F)   VR #131 October 29th, 1975 Ransacking

(Not pictured)   VR #146 attempted entry on December 1st, 1975, located a block to the west

E)   Shoe prints found on December 9th, 1975

E) and C)   Location of the McGowen shooting on December 10th, 1975

E)   VR #151 October 24th, 1976 Burglary

When it comes to the motivation and makeup of the offender, it's important to note what a long and detailed history he had with some of these small areas of the city. He'd been drawn to the Verde Vista / Whitney / Redwood area since the very beginning, and his tendency to prowl and hit this part of West Kaweah Avenue bordered on obsessive. What we have at this point is a peeper, burglar, and stalker who was already committing burglaries of a sexual nature and escalating his activities. Profilers assert that offenders like this, at this stage in their evolution, have rich fantasy lives and begin to be dissatisfied with merely watching or interacting with their fantasy objects from a distance. It's imperative that these types of offenders be identified and stopped before they try to turn their fantasies into realities.

May 31st, 1975 Ransacking

One of the most frustrating aspects of the Visalia Ransacker / East Area Rapist / Golden State Killer canon of crimes is that there's very little evidence or theory on how the offender selected his victims. In the EAR/GSK phase, there are roughly seventy known victims and potential victims from 1976 to 1986, and no solid connection can be made among any of them.

Did he know any of them personally? Did he come across them in his daily life? Did he live near any of them? Or were they all selected through random peeping and stalking?

Several *hints* at connections come up in the EAR/GSK crimes – there were several victims in the education field, the medical field, the military, utility companies, and victims who had connections to the local government. But nothing *specific* ever really materialized.

When examining the Visalia Ransacker case, since we're looking at an early version of that offender, we're also essentially looking at an early version of his stalking methods as well. Some of the same patterns crop up – people related to local government, the medical field, teachers, school administrators, and the like. Clearly, there's still a lot of randomness and there were a lot of people who seemed to be victims of random circumstance in the VR case, just like in the EAR/GSK series. But in some of these burglaries, there was more going on – and a few connections can be made if we dig deeply enough. With the EAR/GSK series, the victimology code hasn't been cracked. With the VR series, some of it *has.*

On Saturday, May 31st and Sunday, June 1st, the Ransacker hit two homes – one on each night. These were the only residences that were targeted over the weekend. They were located half a mile away from each other and had nothing in common – at first glance. But through the victimology research conducted in the process of compiling this book (much of it spearheaded by our friend and fellow researcher Mason Tierney), one of the strongest connections between Visalia Ransacker victims was discovered.

VR #091 – *Ransacking*
May 31st, 1975 | S Sowell St

On Saturday, May 31st, between 7:00 PM and 11:00 PM, the VR entered a single-story house on South Sowell Street while the residents were away.

Once inside the home, he began ransacking most of the rooms. In the bedrooms, he opened several drawers and removed the women's undergarments. He arranged them on and near the bed.

The VR ransacked the kitchen, which was something he'd done before on several occasions. This time, however, he added a twist. For reasons known only to the offender, he removed some orange juice from the refrigerator and poured it all over the residents' clothing.

He stole coins from a piggy bank and took a total of sixteen rings from the scene.

This ransacking was located across the street from Visalia's First Baptist Church, a location that, as we've mentioned, plays into this crime spree in a variety of ways. In addition to the other connections we've discussed, the location of the church seems significant – it's located right on the southwestern edge of Mt. Whitney High School. The rear of it backs up to the Tulare/Conyer intersection. For those matching old locations to current ones, the church is now called Gateway Church of Visalia, and it's located at 1100 South Sowell Street.

We promised you an interesting connection between victims – but it doesn't have anything to do with the church. The connection is that the man who was victimized in this incident worked at the Kaweah Delta Hospital as a doctor. The victim of the *next* ransacking, a young woman living with her parents, was this doctor's *assistant.*

These two consecutive victims worked together, and that's as direct a connection as can be found in virtually all of the Golden State Killer canon of attacks – a series that spans at least twelve years. These were the only two homes that the Ransacker hit during this weekend, and it should be noted that the connection seems even more intentional considering that these homes weren't located very close to each other. They were about half a mile apart.

Did the Visalia Ransacker visit this doctor? Could his identity have been found on the doctor's patient list? Or was the assistant the target all along, and the burglary of the doctor was merely part of his process when it came to gathering intelligence on the assistant, which he obviously would've known quite a bit about already? Did the Ransacker somehow learn about the existence of the assistant during the ransacking at the doctor's house? Or could all of this have somehow been a big coincidence? Did the Visalia Ransacker continue to stalk and choose victims in this manner, even into the East Area Rapist and Golden State Killer phases of his attacks?

We may not be able to answer these questions definitively yet, but there are more connections between victims and more apparent methods that the Ransacker used for selection that we'll dive into as we continue on.

One aspect of the burglary that we need to look at is the orange juice. Pouring orange juice onto the clothing is an odd thing to do. It can leave a mean stain, not only because of the color but also because of the high acidity, which creates a strong bond between the stain color and the fabrics. Many fabric dyes are manufactured to be highly acidic in order to take advantage of that bonding property, but it's not very pretty when it's applied *after* the fact. Whether he did this to be destructive or whether there's some sort of psychological or sexual reason for doing it, we don't know. Law Enforcement officers felt that he was masturbating at the crime scenes, so one theory was that he used the orange juice to try cover up any emission that he wasn't able to clean up well enough with whatever else was available.

June 1975 Incidents

The first incident we discuss is the ransacking of the doctor's assistant, which occurred the day after the doctor's house was ransacked. After that, the Ransacker fell silent for a good six or seven weeks – similar to the "summer break" that he took in 1974 and would continue to take throughout most the East Area Rapist crime series. There was one sighting of a suspicious person that police felt was related, which we'll discuss briefly.

VR #092 – *Ransacking*
June 1st, 1975 | W Harvard Ave

A ransacking occurred on West Harvard Avenue. Unfortunately, the report is gone – investigators know the date, the location, the owner's name, and that's about it. It was recognized at the time as a VR crime because of a matching modus operandi. No other information is available to us – it was through backtracking and research that the rest of the picture was filled in. As we mentioned earlier, the young lady who lived at this address worked for the man whose home was ransacked the previous day.

Since there had been two weekends in a row with VR crimes, police felt that the Ransacker was going back to a regular pattern of offending on every weekends. That ended up not being the case, however. But when he returned to form in late July, he began escalating at an alarming rate.

VR #093 – *Suspicious Person*
June 1975 | S Verde Vista St

-NOT CONFIRMED TO BE RELATED-

A suspicious person was spotted at the corner of South Verde Vista Street and West Campus Avenue. This location is a couple blocks to the west of the College of the Sequoias.

The incident wasn't reported at the time that it happened – it came out later. Like the previous entry, no other details are available to us, but Law Enforcement at the time had reason to believe that this was a sighting of the Visalia Ransacker. It's unknown whether this is the case or not, but we included it here because the date and the location seemed like important data points to capture.

This corner ends up being one of the most heavily stalked areas in the entire VR series. In a later chapter titled "Prowling Incidents on West Campus Avenue," we attempt to review the dozens of noises, sightings, phone calls, and prowlers that were reported in this area.

July 24ᵗʰ, 1975 Ransacking

The next time that the Ransacker hit, he was back on that same small segment of West Kaweah Avenue that seemed to enchant him so much throughout 1975. This first crime after his return from hiatus was a significant one – a resident actually encountered him while he was still inside the home. Her brush with the Ransacker, which was scary enough on its own, was made even more frightening by the fact that sometime afterward, it seems he began peeping at her on a regular basis.

VR #094 – *Ransacking*
July 24th, 1975 | W Kaweah Ave

On Thursday, July 24th, there was a ransacking at a residence on West Kaweah Avenue. This ransacking had three details that made it different from other VR crimes:

The first was that the layout of this home was different – it had a second-story apartment over the garage. The VR had hit single-story homes and he'd ransacked a duplex up to this point, but not a residence quite like this. It's even more notable because he *only* ransacked the second-story apartment.

The second thing that made this unique was that the crime occurred on a Thursday. The VR would hit the next day also, so perhaps he was easing back into his routine.

The final detail that made this one different was that he actually ran into a person from the main house as he was leaving. Confrontation with homeowners was generally something that he'd been able to avoid up to this point.

The usual documents and reports on this ransacking don't exist because apparently the incident wasn't reported right away. Police interviews with the woman who encountered the burglar *do* exist in full, though. The victim, a nineteen-year-old woman who lived in the main house, explained that on the evening of the burglary, she encountered a man in a ski mask as he came down the steps from the upstairs apartment. By his reaction, she could tell that he hadn't anticipated the run-in. Without saying anything, he grabbed her, pushed her down, and then ran away. She told officers that he didn't say anything to her, and he didn't touch her in a sexual way.

The person living in the upstairs apartment found that his items had been rummaged through. Clothing had been pulled out and tossed around. A door had been left unlocked – it was assumed to be the intruder's entry point.

Nothing was stolen, which was the why they delayed their report to the police.

The intruder was described as a white male, 5'10" or 5'11", with a heavy build. The witness could see his arms, and they appeared to be strong and muscular. He was wearing a black ski mask with light-colored eye, nose, and mouth holes.

It wasn't long after this that the woman's mother, who also lived at the residence, began to notice shoe prints in the yard under the nineteen-year-old's bedroom and bathroom windows. Someone had started peeping in at her during the night.

While investigating the case, an interesting connection was found between this victim and some of the others: the woman worked at the First Baptist Church of Visalia.

The ski mask was important – when the VR attempted to abduct a different girl in September, she clearly saw that he was wearing a ski mask. When the VR was encountered by police in December 1975 (next-door to this home, as a matter of fact), he was wearing a ski mask rolled up on his head. Furthermore, a ski mask was the costume of choice for the offender later on when he became the notorious East Area Rapist.

This was the woman's initial brush with evil. As the VR continued to stalk her, her mother took notice and contacted the police. While officers were staking out this residence in December, the VR appeared once again to peep at this young woman. The full story of what happened will be told in a later chapter.

July 25th, 1975 Incidents

The burglary on West Kaweah Avenue must've been a warmup, because the next day he was back in the swing of things. Two ransackings and one attempt occurred on Friday. Being seen by the girl the day before didn't seem to deter him – he must've felt that his mask was adequate in concealing his identity.

VR #095 – *Ransacking*
July 25th, 1975 | W Fairview Ct

On Friday, July 25th, between 7:30 PM and 11:50 PM, the VR entered a single-story home on West Fairview Court while the residents were away.

He entered through a door on the side of the house and, once inside, he set about opening windows to use in case he needed to leave in a hurry.

The bedrooms were ransacked, as usual, with female undergarments being removed and placed on the floor and the bed.

He stole quite a bit from the scene – he took cash, regular coins, a large coin collection, a ring, and 20-gauge shotgun shells. The theft of ammunition was a grim reminder of his potential for violence.

The man of the house worked in the car business, and his wife worked for a bank. Incidentally, it was the same bank that the woman in VR #029 worked at. Both of them were clerks/bank tellers. Perhaps the bank unknowingly had an account registered to the Ransacker, and he had spotted both of them while doing business there.

This house was situated in a cul-de-sac directly to the west of the College of the Sequoias. The layout was unique, as was his point of entry – a non-descript side door.

This Friday night was a little different for the Ransacker. He attempted to hit three homes that we know of, but he only succeeded at two of them. While we list this one as the first of the three, they could've easily occurred in a different order. Investigators have listed this one as occurring first, and if they had a reason for doing so, it wasn't noted. The weight of the coins and the difficulty in transporting loose shotgun shells might point to this one occurring later in the night.

VR #096 – *Ransacking*
July 25th, 1975 | W Campus Ave

On Friday, July 25th, between 7:00 PM and 10:00 PM, the VR entered a single-story residence on West Campus Avenue while the victim was away.

He entered the home by prying open a window. He then opened a few additional windows and removed one of the screens from the inside.

He ransacked the bedrooms and stole coins, cash, stamps (not necessarily Blue Chip stamps – the report isn't clear), and a credit card belonging to the victim. There's no report of him ever using the credit card, but we can't be sure that he didn't.

The man of the house was a director at the Fresno Department of Education.

Police on the scene were able to determine, based on what had and hadn't been disturbed, that he'd exited through the same window used to enter the residence.

With these two burglaries, plus the attempted one on South Whitney Street that we'll discuss in a moment, the classic pattern begins to emerge. He hit both near a school *and* near State Route 198, just as he had done on May 24th, which was the last night that he'd committed multiple burglaries in one night. Which direction he started in and which direction he ended in, we don't know for sure, but he was clearly traveling between the two on several of his active nights. At the risk of being repetitive, gone were the days where he seemed to rely on Evan's Ditch to maneuver – now he was apparently using a dark footpath that ran between Noble and 198 for cover and originating at or ending near the schools and parks.

This residence was located on the corner of West Campus Avenue and South Linda Vista Street – right in the heart of where he'd operated before. It was very close to where the suspicious person had been spotted in June 1975 – probably a factor in helping to make that sighting more official.

This area, as well as the homes near West Kaweah Avenue, seemed to be a peeping or casing route that he'd been following for quite some time. His activity during this portion of the crime spree seemed to revolve around these two epicenters, with other clusters occasionally thrown in from time to time. As noted earlier, residents and police began to notice his shoe prints even on nights when no burglaries were reported. It's very likely that he was out prowling and peeping far more than anyone realized at the time. In 1974 and the first nine or ten months of 1975, this part of his M.O. didn't seem to be well understood by police, which probably accounted for a few of the missed opportunities to catch him in the act.

VR #097 – *Attempted Break-in*
July 25th, 1975 | S Whitney St

-NOT CONFIRMED TO BE RELATED-

During the evening of July 25th, someone pried at a residence on South Whitney Street. The would-be intruder failed to gain entry.

This resident had already suffered her fair share of odd activity – she had even called the police about a suspicious person near her residence back in October. Police believed that sighting in October was almost certainly the VR, and they also believed that it was the Ransacker who had attempted to enter her home on this July night.

The location of this residence is notable – the home was located next-door to the Snellings on South Whitney Street. A prowler had been spotted at the Snelling home in February, he'd be spotted again, in August, and he'd attempt a kidnapping and commit murder there in September. This woman was most likely an additional or alternate target that he had selected, or she was a casualty of his frequent peeping of the Snellings. It stands to reason that he was paying the Snelling residence a visit on this July evening when he noticed that her house was empty and decided to pry at it.

This entire weekend had an undertone of foreshadowing – on July 24th we had the burglary of the residence where the Ransacker would later be confronted by police, and on the 25th we had him trying to enter the home next to the residence where he would later attempt a kidnapping and commit murder. The stolen shotgun shells spoke more loudly than the stolen coins.

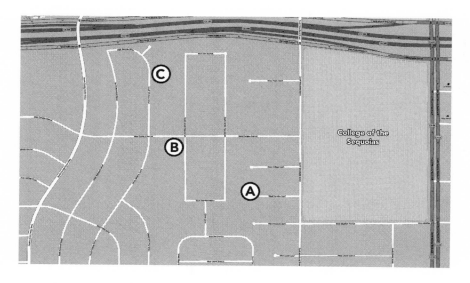

Ransackings on July 25th, 1975.

A) *VR #095 W Fairview Ct*

B) *VR #096: W Campus Ave*

C) *VR #097: Failed attempt on S Whitney St*

August 1ˢᵗ, 1975 Ransacking

<u>VR #098</u> – *Ransacking*
August 1st, 1975 | W Campus Ave

On Friday, August 1st, sometime in the evening before 11:00 PM, a single-story home on West Campus Avenue was ransacked while the residents were away.

The intruder gained entry by prying open a window.

Inside the residence, he opened a few escape windows, and at one of them, he pulled the screen in from the inside and left it in the bedroom.

He ransacked every room in the house, and he took out women's bras, panties, and lingerie from the drawers. Rather than simply arrange them on the floor near the bed or stack them on the covers and pillows like he usually did, he brought the undergarments (especially the lingerie) into the hallway and carefully lined them up in an arrangement on the floor.

He dumped out a piggybank and stole the coins from it. He also took cash, Blue Chip stamps, and two single earrings from a pair.

The husband worked for a large company, and the wife was an instructor at the College of the Sequoias. The man that the Ransacker killed just five weeks after this ransacking was *also* an instructor at the same college. There's no direct evidence that either this victim or Claude Snelling were targeted specifically because of that connection, but it's important to point out.

This home was located near the corner of West Campus Avenue and South Redwood Street, not far at all from much of the recent Ransacker activity.

This was the second weekend in a row where he'd offended on a Friday but not on a Saturday or Sunday... a little bit of a deviation from the norm. Perhaps it meant that he was busy with something else on the weekends during this time period, or perhaps it meant nothing at all.

He wouldn't offend again for a few weeks, and the next time he did, it was south of Mt. Whitney High School – essentially the opposite side of his most frequent target areas of late.

August 23rd, 1975 Ransackings

The next two chapters describe the last batch of ransackings that the VR committed before things really started popping.

The possible church connection is very apparent in this chapter. We've asked before if the VR was purposely targeting prominent members of the First Baptist Church of Visalia, or if the connections were simply there due to random chance or because church attendance was high in the area. At the first ransacking on August 23rd, more than any of the other burglaries we've covered so far, the various possibilities are brought into focus.

VR #099 – *Ransacking*
August 23rd, 1975 | W Howard Ave

On Saturday, August 23rd, sometime in the evening, a single-story home on West Howard Avenue was ransacked while the victims were away. The burglar was probably on the premises sometime around 10:30 PM. That was when the neighbor's dog began an uncharacteristic barking fit.

Once the VR broke into the residence, he opened a window and pulled the screen inside. He left it in the room.

This burglary was similar to many of the others, but it contained a few unique elements of its own. He still ransacked every room, but there was more activity in the kitchen than usual. In fact, when he took the women's undergarments and lingerie out of the drawers, he didn't put all of it on the bed – he actually took several of the garments to the kitchen and spread them out on the floor. There was another burglary where he'd left the clothing lined up in the hallway, so it seemed to be an extension of that.

He found several piggybanks, emptied them, and stole their contents. Cash and Blue Chip stamps were also stolen.

Two personal items were stolen as well, and both of the thefts disturbed the homeowners greatly. One of the items was a photo of the couple's daughter. The other was an engraved gold locket (about the size of a half-dollar) that contained a photo of the couple's baby granddaughter.

The VR also picked up a pin that had been left on the piano, and he moved it to the mantel where the photo of the daughter had been before he'd stolen it. The pin said "Sunday School – First Baptist Church." He smashed it to bits on the mantel with some kind of blunt object.

A jar of cherries, taken from the kitchen of this residence, was found in the yard next-door to this house on the west side. The home next-door on the *east* side also happened to be burglarized by the VR on this same night.

The police found latent fingerprints at the scene. They were processed fully. Unfortunately, even though there were prints that couldn't be identified as belonging to a family member or a close friend, none of the prints matched any previous ransackings. The prints weren't believed to belong to the VR.

Here's the strongest church connection of all: the male victim at this ransacking was the pastor of the First Baptist Church. And of course, a Mt. Whitney High School connection too: the daughter was a student there.

The smashing of the Sunday School pin could be read a few different ways. Was his beef with the church itself? Is that why so many people associated with the church were being targeted? Or did the Ransacker operate in a particular way – victimizing one person, finding intelligence on someone else in their circle, then moving on to *that* person, then finding someone in *their* circle, then moving on to *them*, and so forth? As we re-examine the evidence, we can find several examples of him actually doing this. The doctor and then his assistant, a couple and then much later, the ex-wife. A teenage girl, and then the teenage girl's friend, and then *that* teenage girl's friends. A grown-up son, and then shortly afterward, his mother. Most of these haven't been discussed yet, but the Ransacker's victims could sometimes be chained together. There were associations, and there were sometimes obvious cause and effect scenarios. This was lacking in the East Area Rapist and Golden State Killer phases, at least in an obvious way, so it's very interesting to find these types of relationships in the Visalia Ransacker series.

Perhaps the Ransacker was simply destroying the Sunday School pin to piss off these victims, since he knew or probably found out that the man was the minister of the church. He seemed to enjoy hurting his victims in specific, personal ways.

Not only was a photo of the daughter stolen (perhaps even more than one photo – the documentation isn't clear), but when he smashed that Sunday School pin, he did it in the exact same spot on the mantel where the photo had been. There could be symbolism in this action, just as there seems to be symbolism in the way that he often arranged female undergarments on the beds and in the house. The deliberate display and arrangement of undergarments could be a way to embarrass the residents or "expose" them, or perhaps he simply fetishized these types of clothing items. Studies show that many sexually motivated burglars spend time with their victims' underwear.

Whatever the true motivation for the pin smashing, it's clear that his anger was on the rise. His crimes in general had started out with very few instances of intentional destruction and outright malice, but he'd escalated to pushing nightstands and bookshelves over, dumping medication down the drain, dousing carpet with shaving cream, pouring orange juice on clothes, and other fits of destruction.

The Ransacker hit three homes on the night of August 23rd, 1975. It's impossible to know which order they were hit in, and it's actually probable that this was the second one to be ransacked. The house to the east was hit that night as well, and since the jar of cherries was found near the house to the west, he might have simply been traveling east to west. The third ransacking we'll discuss was also located in a westerly direction. The police generally put this one before the other two on their list, though, possibly because it seems that these victims were specifically targeted. The other two seem to be casualties of him roaming the town.

VR #100 – *Ransacking*
August 23rd, 1975 | W Howard Ave

On Saturday, August 23rd, sometime in the evening, a single-story residence on West Howard Avenue was invaded by the VR while the residents were away.

The VR attempted to pry open a couple of entry points, but he was unsuccessful. Third try was the charm – a window gave way.

Inside, he opened another window and pulled the screen inside. Then he set about ransacking every room in the house.

He took out all of the female undergarments that he could find and placed them nearby. Jewelry boxes were also dumped out and rummaged through.

He opened a piggybank and stole the coins that were inside. Nothing else in the house seemed to be missing.

When the police arrived, the residence was dusted for fingerprints, but nothing useful was found. A few prints were lifted that couldn't be immediately matched to anyone, but those leads didn't go anywhere.

The man of the house was employed by the Tulare County Public Works. A similar employment profile is found in a few of the East Area Rapist cases.

As we mentioned earlier, this one was next-door to the minister's house that had been ransacked. Did the VR just enter this home because he was targeting the one next-door and this one *also* seemed to be ripe for the taking? Had he been stalking or peeping at both of these families and had decided to ransack both of them because they both happened to be empty? Did he not know these families at all and simply burglarized these homes because he was in the area and he could tell that they weren't home? Even over forty years later, we have more questions than answers.

VR #101 – *Ransacking*
August 23rd, 1975 | W Feemster Ave

On Saturday, August 23rd, sometime in the evening, the Ransacker entered a single-story residence on West Feemster Avenue while the family was away.

He pried at several entrances unsuccessfully, but apparently he remained determined. A door, extensively and forcefully pried at, finally gave way.

Once inside, he opened a window to use as a potential escape hatch. He ransacked every room in the house, dumped jewelry out, and took items of women's underclothing out of the drawers. They were placed on the floor and on the bed.

He stole about a hundred dollars in coins and cash from the scene. He also took a ring and Blue Chip stamps. He didn't steal all that he could have though, intentionally leaving cash behind in a prominent place so that the homeowners would know that he had found it.

The Ransacker discovered 22-gauge ammunition in the home. Rather than stealing it, he carefully arranged the bullets carefully on one of the beds. Whether it was meant as a warning to the residents, or if it was just one of his quirks, only the offender knows for sure.

The male victim here was a lawyer, and he was a partner at the law firm he worked for.

The location of this ransacking is significant. The other two we've discussed were directly south of Mt. Whitney High School, and this one was near another feature that hasn't come up in a while: it was situated against Evan's Ditch. They all were during this outing, actually. And not only was this home directly across from a portion of the ditch that the VR had probably used before, but it was next-door to the two houses that had been the scene of that interesting prowler way back in September 1973 and January 1974. While those incidents aren't necessarily believed to be related to the series, *this* particular event was definitely the work of the Visalia Ransacker. It was either his first stop or final stop of August 23rd, 1975.

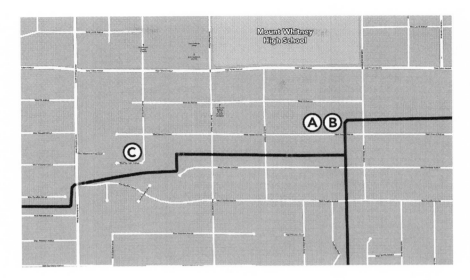

Ransackings on August 23rd, 1975. Evan's Ditch is in bold.

A)   *VR #099 W Howard Ave*

B)   *VR #100 W Howard Ave*

C)   *VR #101 W Feemster Ave*

August 24th, 1975 Ransackings

VR #102 – *Ransacking*
August 24th, 1975 | W Princeton Ave

On Sunday, August 24th, sometime in the evening, the Ransacker entered a single-story residence on West Princeton Avenue while the family was away.

The scene was familiar. He opened a window, ransacked most of the rooms, and removed some of the clothing from the drawers. He also broke open a piggybank and stole the contents.

The husband in this case was a high-level manager at a utility company. It wasn't the same utility company that the victim from the previous night worked for, but it's an interesting parallel.

Nothing particularly unique strikes us from the abbreviated report that exists for this ransacking, other than the day – he was back to offending on a Sunday. This home and the one he hit next were both located southeast of Rotary Park. Evan's Ditch was about five hundred feet to the north – perhaps he was using it again, as evidenced by the locations of the ransackings that had occurred the previous night.

VR #103 – *Ransacking*
August 24th, 1975 | W Cambridge Ave

On Sunday, August 24th, sometime between 8:00 PM and 11:00 PM, the VR entered a single-story residence on West Cambridge Avenue while the victims were away. This residence was located less than a hundred feet from the other burglary he committed that night.

He entered the residence by prying open a door. Once inside, he opened multiple windows to use as potential escape routes. One of them was pried open from the inside.

He rifled through all of the drawers, ransacked most of the rooms, and tossed clothing about as he had done at many of the other scenes.

He found a piggybank, opened it, and stole the contents.

The scene was dusted for fingerprints, and a few promising ones were found. These, however, didn't match any of the other scenes, so they were believed to belong to family and friends.

The male victim at this residence was in the homebuilding business, and the female victim was in the real estate business. These connections come up in the East Area Rapist series a lot, but not as much in the VR crimes.

The two locations that he burglarized on this evening were less than a thousand feet to the southwest of where he'd hit on West Feemster Avenue the previous night. Rotary Park and Evan's Ditch could've been used for cover and travel.

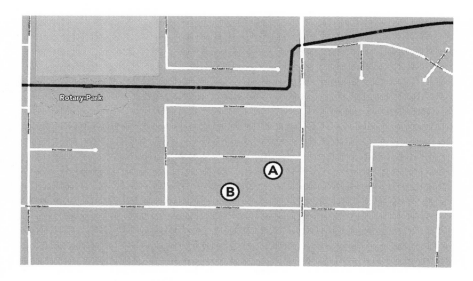

Ransackings on August 24th, 1975.

A) *VR #102 W Princeton Ave*
B) *VR #103 W Cambridge Ave*

August 29th, 1975 Ransacking

One of the most fateful weekends in the Visalia Ransacker series was underway as the sun set on Friday, August 29th. At the rate of one ransacking per night, the VR was preparing his transformation from burglar to kidnapper.

Friday started out with a fairly standard ransacking, and then an analysis of Saturday will give us another glimpse into how the VR was selecting his targets. Finally, Sunday was the last time the VR burglarized a home before becoming a very different beast. He stole a firearm at that ransacking, something that he had done before, but this time was different – the VR would actually go on to *use* this one.

VR #104 – *Ransacking*
August 29th, 1975 | W Dartmouth Ave

On Friday, August 29th, sometime between 8:00 PM and 9:45 PM, the Ransacker entered a single-story house on West Dartmouth Avenue while the family was away.

He had a little trouble getting into the residence, having to pry at a few windows before finding one that would give way.

Once inside, he opened more windows and began ransacking the bedrooms. Jewelry boxes were emptied, women's clothing was removed from drawers, and undergarments were removed. They were either stacked nearby or posed on the beds and the floor. The undergarments belonged to the wife and the two daughters who lived in the home. Both daughters were students at Mt. Whitney High School.

The Ransacker stole cash, coins, some of the girls' rings, and a total of nine single earrings (each from a pair... he left the matching earrings behind).

If you've been paying close attention, you've probably noticed that the Ransacker often failed at prying open one or more entrances to a home. He was many things, but a master at breaking and entering was not one of them. Even all the way up to the double homicide that he committed in Goleta in late 1979, he was still routinely failing at opening many windows and doors. After over a hundred burglaries as the VR, over a hundred burglaries and nearly fifty known home-invasion rapes as the EAR, and everything else that we probably don't know about yet, it's a little telling that he never improved at breaking and entering very much. His skill level at forcing his way into a home remained mediocre throughout his criminal career. His methods usually worked eventually, so he must've seen no reason to increase his skill level. Or perhaps he was being sloppy on purpose to throw authorities off of his trail.

It's often difficult to tell why the Ransacker chose a certain residence over another, and sometimes a certain geographical feature or a characteristic of a residents seems to be the obvious reason. In this instance, it was a near-perfect alignment of geography *and* victimology – classic VR in every sense. The residence was located at the southwest corner of Houk Park, which would've afforded him a way to approach the home without leaving an obvious mode of transportation nearby. It also backed up to Evan's Ditch, and this particular stretch of the canal was particularly easy to traverse. The home was near the street's intersection with West Harvard Avenue, and the Ransacker seemed to prefer corner houses or homes that were situated near an intersection. The street basically ran east-to-west, which he preferred over north-to-south.

Both of the teenage girls living at the residence had characteristics and extracurricular activities that many of the other Visalia Ransacker targets shared. In retrospect, knowing what we know about the Ransacker now, the home was an obvious target.

August 30th, 1975 Ransacking

VR #105 – *Ransacking*
August 30th, 1975 | S Redwood St

On Saturday, August 30th, sometime between 6:24 PM and 9:39 PM, a single-story house on South Redwood Street was entered by the VR while the residents were away.

He opened a few windows to use as emergency exits, and then he set about ransacking the home. The bedrooms were all rummaged through, and jewelry boxes were dumped out as he encountered them.

He removed several items of women's clothing from drawers, but he only focused on removing the daughter's clothing. The daughter was a teenager and attended Mt. Whitney High School.

He found a collection of photos in the daughter's room and took some of them out. None of the photos appeared to have been stolen, but based on the way the scene was arranged (particularly one photo and some panties that were wadded up nearby), investigators felt that he had masturbated while handling one particular picture.

There weren't any Blue Chip stamps in the house for the Ransacker to steal, but he did steal a flashlight. The very same flashlight would be found a few weeks later in a yard two houses away, and investigators felt that he might've dropped it there soon after killing Claude Snelling on September 11th.

This residence was at the northernmost portion of the Ransacker's known attack area, practically bordering the trail between West Noble Avenue and State Route 198 that the Ransacker probably used on a regular basis to escape the area.

The daughter whose undergarments were handled at this crime shared several characteristics with other potential Ransacker targets, including the fact that she was active at Mt. Whitney High School sporting events. She may have been what initially drew the Ransacker to this house, but it wasn't her photo that the Ransacker had singled out.

The photo that the Ransacker had pulled out was of a very young teen who lived a few streets away. This young lady occasionally spent time with the daughter of Claude Snelling – the girl that the Ransacker would attempt to kidnap a week and a half after this ransacking took place.

Not only that, but shortly after the Ransacker found the photo of the young teen, the girl began to experience prowling incidents at her *own* home. Knocking noises, strange phone calls, and even an incident where she spotted a prowler on the premises.

Did the Ransacker learn about her from the photo he found at this ransacking? Did he go through the photo albums, spot her in a picture, and then find where she lived using her name and begin to stalk her? Was she a potential assault or kidnapping victim, since he seemed to begin stalking her so aggressively? And is it significant that he targeted girls who were so young? Several of them, including this one, were barely teenagers.

It's generally difficult to determine how the VR/EAR/GSK selected his victims, which makes connections like this quite significant – a rare insight to a world that seems impossible to understand.

This residence was located on a street that the VR seemed to prowl frequently, and since it was near the Noble footpath, it's possible that he had discovered this family while making his way up to his escape route at the conclusion of *other* nights that he'd spent ransacking or peeping. Or perhaps it was the other way around – he may have chosen that footpath so that he could go by these particular houses along the way.

August 31ˢᵗ, 1975 Ransacking

VR #106 – *Ransacking*
August 31st, 1975 | W Royal Oaks Dr

On Sunday, August 31st, between 6:00 PM and 10:45 PM, a single-story house on West Royal Oaks Drive was entered by the VR while the residents were away.

He entered by prying open a window. Once inside, he opened another window, and he set about his usual routine of ransacking all of the rooms in the house and taking out women's undergarments.

This time he added a twist to the scenario and also took out the man's underwear. He carefully lined the male undergarments down the hallway from the bedroom to the bathroom. Officers familiar with VR scenes were a little perplexed by this, but not entirely surprised. He had done other types of odd things before, including a similar display with women's undergarments earlier in the month.

He stole quite a few items from this residence, including one item in particular that would be talked about for decades to come – the .38 Miroku revolver that was used to kill Claude Snelling. The theft of this particular revolver at this particular scene (which had the obvious Visalia Ransacker M.O.) would eventually provide physical evidence that it was indeed the Visalia Ransacker who murdered Claude Snelling.

The VR also took a small coin collection, a necklace, two boxes of 12-gauge ammunition, and three hundred rounds of 38-caliber ammunition.

The male victim in this ransacking was the manager of a car dealership. His wife, who also lived at the house, worked for the county's Department of Education.

We've already discussed the education link, which seems to come up a lot, but we haven't spent any time looking at the fairly high number of victims that were related to the car business. The victims linked to this industry include VR #40, 43, 46, 92, 95, 106, and a man who had Ransacker footprints in his yard but was never victimized. That's quite a few connections. During the East Area Rapist series of crimes, the offender was potentially linked to several different types of vehicles, and it's even possible that he frequently traded or bought different cars or trucks. Perhaps he was doing this as the Visalia Ransacker, too, but was more careful about hiding his transportation.

This family's trouble didn't end with the burglary on August 31st. A few weeks later, the homeowner assisted the police in tying the Snelling murder to the Visalia Ransacker by leading them to a place where he'd done target practice with the gun before it was stolen. Officers recovered bullets, and they matched the ballistics to the gun used to kill Claude Snelling, proving that the murder weapon had been stolen at this ransacking. Because of this, it could be argued that this man played a big part in helping the police work up a homicide case against the VR. Somewhere in that timeframe, this family received a death threat – the woman of the house answered the phone, and the unknown man on the other end threatened to kill her and her family. Her husband saw that she was distressed, so he picked up the phone. The man on the other end repeated his threats – something to the effect of "I'm going to kill you, your wife, and your daughter." The homeowner, assuming it was the person who had burglarized his house, reacted defiantly. "Well, you know who I am and you know where I live, so come on. I'll be waiting for you."

The caller hung up.

The location of this residence is a bit of an outlier. It's situated in a deep part of town, away from any noticeable geographical crutches like creeks or schools. Despite the lack of cover, West Royal Oaks Drive would become a favorite haunt of the Visalia Ransacker during October, with him committing a fairly brazen prowling or two during that time period and an additional ransacking. Looking at the map, it doesn't seem like an area that would attract him, but it certainly did. What that might mean as far as where the VR's actual base of operations was, or whether he had a tie or a familiarity with the neighborhood in his daily life, is impossible to know at this point.

This ransacking was a good mile from the South Redwood Street location that had been hit the previous day. The following map shows where the three ransackings that took place over the weekend:

(map featured on the next page)

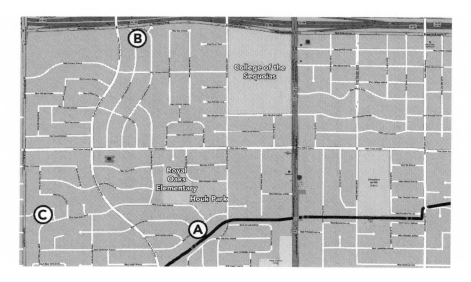

Ransackings from August 29th to August 31st, 1975.

A) *VR #104 August 29th. 1975: W Dartmouth Ave*

B) *VR #105 August 30th, 1975: S Redwood St*

C) *VR #106 August 31st, 1975: W Royal Oaks Dr*

Leading up to the Homicide

He was armed, he was dangerous, and he was looking for ways to take his crimes to the next level.

No ransackings were reported for several days after that gun was stolen from West Royal Oaks Drive. But even though the town was getting a reprieve from the burglaries, all was not quiet in Visalia. There were prowling incidents, sightings of suspicious persons, and odd events leading up to and immediately following September 11th – the murder of Claude Snelling.

It's unlikely that *all* of these suspicious persons or prowlers were related to the Snelling homicide case or to the Visalia Ransacker series, but some of them probably are. It's also possible that these types of suspicious events had been happening in town all along, and that they came to light simply because the police were finally starting to figure out the offender and had started to ask the right questions.

It may be determined someday soon that the Visalia Ransacker / Golden State Killer was responsible for other kidnapping crimes and other murders that occurred before the incident that we'll discuss in the next chapter. In fact, a few crimes are already looking possible, like the Jennifer Armour case (which we'll discuss toward the end of the book). But until more can be learned, the Snelling homicide is the first violent crime we have for him on record.

These are the sightings and events that led up to it:

VR #107 – *Prowler*
September 1975 | W Myrtle Ave

-NOT CONFIRMED TO BE RELATED-

A prowler was caught urinating in a yard on West Myrtle Street. In a scene strangely reminiscent of the late 1973 and early 1974 incidents, the man began talking to himself and to an imaginary partner upon being discovered. He was heard saying "Can't a guy take a leak? Come out and help me, Jim. This guy won't leave me alone!"

The location of this incident was close to West Kaweah Avenue, where the VR had been prowling intently.

VR #108 – *Prowler*
September 6th, 1975 | S Whitney St

-NOT CONFIRMED TO BE RELATED-

A prowler was spotted on South Whitney Street only two houses away from the Snelling residence. The same man was seen multiple times.

He was described as a white male, mid twenties, 5'7" or 5'8", 180 lbs, with brown, collar-length hair. He had a beard, and he wore a dark green army-style cap. Later, a witness saw the exact same man at the Royal Liquor Store, only he *didn't* have a beard.

Was the beard and longer hair part of a disguise? Or had the subject simply shaved the beard off? During the East Area Rapist phase of attacks, the offender sometimes wore a disguise while he prowled.

VR #109 – *Prowler*
September 9th, 1975 | S Whitney St

-NOT CONFIRMED TO BE RELATED-

On Tuesday, September 9th, between 6:30 AM and 7:15 AM, a prowler was spotted clearly at a residence on South Whitney Street. This home was located two houses south of the residence where a trespasser had been spotted three days before.

The subject was described as 5'7" or 5'8", in his late twenties, over 180 lbs, with brown hair worn collar-length. The witness noted that the subject had an unusually round face.

This description matched most witness descriptions of the Visalia Ransacker. Like most of the sightings of suspicious persons, however, it's unknown if the sighting was related to the crimes.

VR #110 – *Prowler*
September 9th, 1975 | S Redwood St

-NOT CONFIRMED TO BE RELATED-

A prowler was spotted on South Redwood Street. This home was located south of West Campus Avenue, roughly eight hundred feet from the Snelling residence. The sighting occurred on the same night as the other suspicious activity on South Whitney Street – the incident where the witness got a good look at the subject.

VR #111 – *Prowler*
September 10th, 1975 | W Cornell Ave

-NOT CONFIRMED TO BE RELATED-

A suspicious person was spotted between 10:30 PM and 11:00 PM on West Cornell Avenue. This sighting, taking place near Houk Park, was roughly a mile south of the Snelling residence.

The subject was described as a white man, late twenties, six feet tall, 175 lbs, with a thin build. He had brown hair, and was wearing dark clothing and white tennis shoes. He was carrying a shoebox.

This sighting occurred less than four hours before the VR woke up the Snellings' teenage daughter. It's unknown whether this sighting was related to the crime or not, but aside from the higher weight estimate and slightly higher height estimate, the description reads very similar to the possible sightings of the offender during his East Area Rapist phase where he was committing home-invasion rapes in Sacramento and beyond.

VR #112 – *Prowler*
September 10th, 1975 | W Whitney Dr

-NOT CONFIRMED TO BE RELATED-

At 11:00 PM, a prowler was spotted in a garage. This sighting took place fairly close to the Snelling residence.

It was later learned that someone had "borrowed" a ladder from a backyard next-door to this home. It was initially theorized that the Ransacker had used it to scale a nearby wall.

Another theory emerged, based on the missing ladder being found one house away. It seemed possible that the Ransacker may have used the ladder to climb up onto a nearby roof to survey the attack area, either before closing in on the Snelling residence (to make sure the coast was clear) or shortly after the murder (so that he could monitor police response).

VR #113 – *Suspicious Person*
September 11th, 1975 | W Campus Ave

-NOT CONFIRMED TO BE RELATED-

There are two sightings worth discussing that occurred in the hours following the murder.

At 8:30 AM (the murder had occurred about six hours before), a suspicious person was spotted at the intersection of South Whitney Street and West Campus Avenue. This location was five or six homes to the south of the crime scene.

The subject was described as a white male, early twenties, between 5'9" and 6', with a stocky build. He had light brown hair and was wearing a brown jacket and blue pants. The subject wasn't wearing any shoes. Aside from the missing shoes, this sighting was consistent with other sightings of the Visalia Ransacker.

Like some of the other reports of prowlers and suspicious persons, it's unknown whether this has anything to do with the murder or not. The reason that it may be more likely to be related is the belief that the Ransacker did *not* leave the vicinity entirely after the murder occurred. A threatening message purportedly from the Ransacker was left on a truck window sometime between 8:00 AM and 12:35 PM that morning. The murder had occurred sometime after 2:00 AM

– which left a period of several hours where he could've been nearby. It's believed that he escaped the immediate area, but he may have hung around to watch the aftermath and to leave the threatening note. During the East Area Rapist series from 1976 to 1979, it's also believed that he often stayed close by for a period of time.

VR #114 – *Prowler*
September 11th, 1975 | S Locust St

-NOT CONFIRMED TO BE RELATED-

A prowler was spotted somewhere on South Locust Street. It appears that this report was taken at 10:30 PM on September 11th, 1975. It's not clear if that's when the actual sighting occurred or if it had occurred earlier.

This particular prowling incident, which is quite a geographical outlier, is nonetheless included in the official timelines generated by Law Enforcement personnel. One interesting note about the geography is that this location was in the general direction where a weapon was found in the days that followed the murder. The weapon was later tied to the Visalia Ransacker.

But ultimately, whether this prowler has anything to do with the VR or not is unknown.

The following is a map that shows a close-up of the suspicious persons and prowling incidents that were reported in the days leading up to the murder. Only the incidents that took place close to the location of the Snelling residence are included in this particular map:

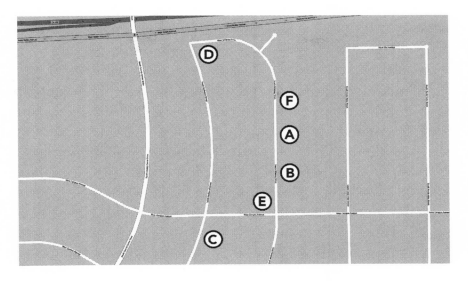

Close-up of the prowling incidents and suspicious persons sighted around the time of the Snelling homicide. While it's impossible to know for sure if any of them were connected, investigators believe that many of them could be. All events took place in the first half of September 1975.

A) VR #108 September 6th on S Whitney St

B) VR #109 September 9th on S Whitney St

C) VR #110 September 9th on S Redwood St

D) VR #112 September 10th on W Whitney Dr

E) VR #113 September 11th on W Campus Ave

F) Snelling homicide location (September 11th)

This next map shows *all* of the prowling/suspicious persons incidents that occurred in the days around the murder. There are a few obvious outliers, but that doesn't discount them from possibly being connected.

A map of all of the prowling incidents and suspicious persons sighted in the general timeframe (days, not hours) of the Snelling homicide. It's impossible to know for sure if any or all of them are connected. All events took place in the first half of September 1975.

A) VR #107 on W Myrtle Ave

B) VR #108 September 6th on S Whitney St

C) VR #109 September 9th on S Whitney St

D) VR #110 September 9th on S Redwood St

E) VR #111 September 10th on W Cornell Ave

F) VR #112 September 10th on W Whitney Dr

C) VR #113 September 11th on W Campus Ave

G) VR #114 September 11th on S Locust St

H) Snelling homicide location (September 11th)

As we dive into the case information related to the homicide itself, it'll become obvious that some of the locations where evidence was found match up perfectly to some of these points.

The Claude Snelling Murder

VR #115 – *Homicide*
September 11th, 1975 | S Whitney St

Background

Claude Snelling, a forty-five-year-old journalism professor, lived on South Whitney Street with his wife, teenage daughter, and two sons. He was a devoted family man, well liked by everyone who knew him, and very active in his church – the First Baptist Church of Visalia. Very little had happened to make him feel unsafe in his home during the seventeen years that he'd been working at the College of the Sequoias. Even the prowler that he'd spotted at his daughter's window in February hadn't shaken him too badly.

The night of September 10th, 1975 was a fairly normal one. It was a fairly warm night. The air conditioner had stopped working earlier in the evening, so several of the windows in the house were open. Claude had just returned home with one of his sons, and his daughter was sitting on the porch with her boyfriend enjoying the breezy night air. Shortly after Claude arrived, his wife also returned home from school. She'd attended classes in Fresno – something she always did on Wednesday night.

Seven months had passed since he'd chased the prowler away from the side of the house. A man had appeared again at his daughter's window in August, but Claude hadn't seen him and still, the family didn't seem to be in any mortal danger. Recently someone had broken into his cars and had rifled through his glove boxes, but it was a petty crime and not much harm had been done.

When he went to bed after 10:00 PM with an upset stomach, his family was tucked away safely inside the house. Claude Snelling had no reason to suspect that anything could happen to any of them.

Pre-Attack Events

Note: Several of the relevant timeline events have been discussed in other chapters. The basics of these events are included here again to provide a comprehensive rundown of all relevant information pertaining to the homicide.

February 5th, 1975 10:00 PM: Prowler

On this date, Claude Snelling arrived home to find a prowler outside his home. As he pulled the car into the driveway, his headlights illuminated a crouched figured peering into his daughter's window. Claude immediately jumped out of the car and chased the man around the corner of his house, but the prowler took off into the darkness and evaded him.

The only description that he was able to give was that the prowler was a white male between 5'10" and 6' tall, had collar-length hair, and that he was wearing a dark plaid long-sleeve shirt.

The police checked the yard and examined the area under the girl's window, and they were able to identify shoe prints. The prints matched those found at Visalia Ransacker burglaries, indicating that the peeper was the VR.

May 24th, 1975: Taurus Revolver Stolen
A Taurus revolver was stolen during a ransacking committed by the VR. It was later found twelve miles away during the course of the Snelling homicide investigation.

Approximately August 15th, 1975: Miroku Fired
The owner of a Miroku revolver went to a secluded area of the St. John's River to do target practice. He discharged the weapon over a hundred times.

Late August 1975: Peeper
The Snellings' teenage daughter was spending time in her room with her boyfriend. They were discussing the peeper that her father had seen in February, and the girl jokingly suggested that he could be peeping again at that very moment. She threw open her blinds. To her surprise, a man was on the other side of her window, looking in at them. He took off.

August 31st, 1975: Miroku Stolen
The Miroku revolver used for target practice at the St. John's River was stolen during a ransacking committed by the VR. This weapon would later be used to kill Claude Snelling.

Late August or Early September 1975: Cars Broken Into
A couple of weeks before the murder, Claude Snelling went outside in the morning to discover that both of his vehicles had been broken into. The thief had rifled through the glove boxes.

September 6th, 1975: Prowler on Whitney
On the Saturday before the murder, a prowler was spotted several times at a home two houses to the south of the Snelling residence. The prowler was described as a white male, mid twenties, 5'7" or 5'8", 180 lbs, with brown collar-length hair. He had a beard, and had on a dark green army-style cap. Later, a witness saw the exact same man at the Royal Liquor Store, but the beard was gone.

September 9th, 1975 Between 6:30 and 7:15 AM: Prowler

A different homeowner spotted a trespasser a few houses to the south of the Snelling residence. The subject was seen clearly, and described as 5'7" or 5'8", in his late twenties, 180 lbs or more, with brown hair worn collar-length. He had a very round face.

September 9th, 1975: Prowler on Redwood

A prowler was spotted at a residence on South Redwood Street. This home was located south of West Campus Avenue.

Night Leading up to the Attack

September 10th, 1975 6:00 PM

The Snellings' air conditioner went out, so they opened windows to keep the house cool.

September 10th, 1975 Approximately 7:30 PM

The teenage daughter heard a noise outside her bedroom window. She looked outside, but it was too dark to see anything.

September 10th, 1975 Approximately 7:45 PM

The boyfriend arrived at the Snelling residence. He and the teenage daughter sat outside on the porch for a while.

September 10th, 1975 Approximately 8:15 PM

Claude Snelling and one of his sons arrived home from a church meeting that they had attended.

September 10th, 1975 8:30 PM

Mrs. Snelling arrived home from school in Fresno. Her husband, daughter, two sons, and her daughter's boyfriend were all at the residence. She set her purse down on the kitchen counter.

September 10th, 1975 9:30 PM
The two sons went to bed.

September 10th, 1975 Shortly before 10:00 PM
The boyfriend left.

September 10th, 1975 10:00 PM
Claude Snelling, suffering from an upset stomach, went to bed.

September 10th, 1975 Approximately 10:15 PM
The teenage daughter went to bed. She checked the back door before going to sleep, and she couldn't remember if it was already locked or if she had to lock it. The screen on the window next to the back door was still there – it would later be removed by the Ransacker. She thought the window might've been open, but she remembered that the curtains were closed.

September 10th, 1975 10:30 PM
Mrs. Snelling checked the back door to make sure it was locked. When she did, she too noticed that the back window screen was still in place. The rear porch light was on, and she left it that way. She turned off all of the inside lights except the kids' bathroom light, and then she went to bed.

September 10th, 1975 Between 10:30 PM and 11:00 PM: Prowler
A prowler was spotted at a home near the corner of South County Center Drive and West Cornell Avenue. This location is about a mile to the south of the Snelling residence and the sighting occurred roughly four hours before the Ransacker attempted to kidnap the Snellings' daughter. The subject was described as a white male, late twenties, six feet tall, 175 lbs, with a thin build. He had brown hair, and was wearing dark clothing and white tennis shoes. He was carrying a shoebox.

September 10th, 1975 11:00 PM: Prowler

A resident living in one of the northernmost houses on Whitney noticed a prowler in his garage. Another nearby resident heard a prowler in his own garage as well.

September 10th, 1975 11:30 PM: Car

Fire trucks went by the intersection of West Campus Avenue and South Verde Vista Street. A couple living nearby walked across West Campus Avenue to see if they could figure out where the fire trucks were headed. As they crossed the street back over to their home, a small car swerved across the road and attempted to hit them. Luckily, they were able to get out of the way, and they escaped from the encounter unharmed.

This couple had a connection to the VR – their daughter was the girl in the photo that had been singled out by the Ransacker at the burglary on August 30th, 1975 on South Redwood Street. Investigators felt that the VR had masturbated to the photo, and the girl had subsequently noticed that she had a stalker. At one point, she spotted her stalker clearly while he was prowling outside of her home. She described the subject as a white male, between sixteen and eighteen years old, 5'7", with a stocky build. He had brown shoulder-length hair.

She'd also been chased by someone the previous fall. That incident had occurred during a slumber party – the girls in attendance had gone outside for a bit, and a white male had appeared from the shadows and he'd chased them home. They felt that this person had been identified. The police had his name, and he seemed to have been cleared from any possible Ransacker involvement.

September 11th, 1975 2:10 AM

A resident on South Redwood Street thought that he heard someone inside his home. He spotted an intruder, and the intruder quickly left after being noticed. The only sign that someone had entered the home was the front door, which was open.

According to reports, this man would hear noises outside his residence roughly twenty minutes later, after the confrontation had occurred at the Snelling house. A stolen bicycle was found outside the next morning.

Reports give the time of the noises as 2:30 AM. Since the intruder and the bicycle noise events are contained on two different reports, and due to some of the inconsistencies that some of the reports contain, it's possible that the intruder and the sounds outside the residence both happened at 2:10 AM (which would put them both before the murder), or that they both happened at 2:30 AM (which would put them both after the murder). For the purposes of this chapter, we're notating the events as they appear in the police files.

The Homicide

September 11th, 1975 2:17 AM

The Snellings' teenage daughter woke up from a sound sleep to the feeling of suffocation. There was immense pressure on her body, and she realized that someone was laying flat on top of her. The person's right hand was covering her nose and her mouth, and his left hand was holding down her right arm. Her brother had done this to her before as a joke, and she assumed that it was him – until she noticed the eyes blazing with hatred just inches away from her face.

She struggled to remove the assailant's hand so that she could breathe. As she struggled with her attacker, one of the braces that held up her bed snapped.

"Don't scream or I'll stab you," the man growled. She didn't see a knife, but she believed his threat. He removed his hand from her face.

"You're coming with me."

With his left hand, he reached back and removed a gun from a back pocket on his left. Then he got off of the bed, grabbed her left arm with his right hand, and pulled her up.

"Why are you doing this? Where are you taking me?" the girl asked. He didn't answer, but simply forced her out of the bedroom and into the dining room area. She began pulling against him, trying to slow him down and hoping to break free. She jerked back violently in an attempt to break his grip, but his hold was too strong. She started crying.

Undeterred by the extra noise, he held the gun tightly in his left hand and continued dragging her through the house and toward the back door. Afraid of being shot but even more afraid of being taken away, she dug her heels into the floor as hard as she could. It made a loud noise – a noise loud enough to wake up her father and one of her brothers.

Not knowing that anyone else in the house had been awakened, the kidnapper and his victim arrived at the back door. The door was already open, apparently having been left ajar by the offender when he'd made entry. The girl noticed that the porch light was still on.

They exited the residence. "Don't scream or I'll shoot you," he warned her.

Her crying intensified as she was led through the yard, through the back gate (which the kidnapper had also left open), and into the carport area. At that moment, she heard her father's voice.

"Hey! What's going on? What are you doing? Where are you going with my daughter?"

She could see her father running through the house. He paused for a moment and their eyes met through a window.

The kidnapper immediately let go of the girl and she fell to the ground, exhausted from the struggle. Rather than attempting to flee the scene, the kidnapper waited for Claude to come outside.

"Hey! What do you want? Where are you going with my daughter?" Mr. Snelling asked as he stepped out onto the patio. He began walking down the steps and toward the short fence. He raised his arms as he got closer, clearly intending to climb over.

The masked man raised his gun and fired.

Claude was hit in the shoulder, and the force of the blast spun him around. Another shot was fired quickly. It hit its mark.

Snelling staggered backward, his pajamas soaked with blood. Mustering whatever strength he could, he purposefully made his way to the back door and into the house.

The shooter then trained his gun directly at the teenage girl's face. Crying, she turned away – but as she did, she caught a glimpse of him lowering his weapon. Rather than kill her, he kicked her squarely in the mouth two or three times and then took off down the driveway at a jogging pace.

The girl got up and ran to the back door.

Immediate Aftermath

September 11th, 1975 2:21 AM
Mrs. Snelling was awakened to the sound of one of her sons screaming. Shortly afterward, she heard gunshots.

September 11th, 1975 2:22 AM
Mrs. Snelling ran into the family room, where she saw Claude enter from the rear of the residence. His clothes were covered in blood, and he began staggering through the house. "I've been shot, I've been shot," he said. She went to help him, but he brushed past her and made his way to the front door. There, he collapsed. She ran over to him and found that he was unconscious. His breathing was slow and labored.

September 11th, 1975 Approximately 2:24 AM
Mrs. Snelling called for police and paramedics. Her daughter had reentered the residence by this time, and she spotted her father near the front door. Mrs. Snelling handed her the phone and then went back to tend to her husband. Claude never regained consciousness.

September 11th, 1975 2:24 AM
An ambulance and a police officer were dispatched to the Snelling home.

September 11th, 1975 2:26 AM
An officer arrived and was led straight to Mr. Snelling. The officer treated him while they waited for the ambulance to arrive.

September 11th, 1975 Approximately 2:30 AM
The ambulance pulled up. Medical personnel began treating Mr. Snelling and preparing him for transport. They also tended to the teenage daughter, whose face was swollen. There was a cut on her lip.

Claude was transported to Kaweah Delta Medical Center, where tragically, he was pronounced dead on arrival.

His bullet wounds were examined. The first shot had entered his left arm, and there it remained lodged inside of his body. The second shot had entered the right side of his chest and had gone clear through his torso. Officers at the scene found that the bullet had then gone on to shatter part of the window that the killer had used to break into the residence.

Post-Attack Events

September 11th, 1975 2:30 AM
The resident on South Redwood Street (the one who had found his front door open and had seen an intruder in his home) heard clicking and creaking sounds outside. When he checked his yard in the morning, he saw that a yellow Schwinns women's bicycle had been abandoned on his property. He called the police, and they determined that the bicycle had been stolen from a residence on West Tulare Avenue sometime after the evening of September 9th.

It was later learned that two different witnesses had seen a prowler in this area, though the documentation available to us doesn't divulge anything else. Shoe impressions matching previous Visalia Ransacker castings were found in the area of the home.

September 11th, 1975 Early Morning
Mrs. Snelling's purse was located on a brick planter in the backyard of her residence. The only items stolen from it was a couple of one-dollar bills. A ten-dollar bill was still inside of the purse and may not have been seen by the offender. Small bits of paper were found nearby, both by the planter and near the window / back door where the killer had gained entry.

The window screen to the back window was missing and couldn't be located on the premises.

September 11th, 1975 Early Morning
A clear bottle of liquid, determined to be alcohol, was found outside the home next-door to the south of the Snellings. It appeared to be partially consumed, and if it was related to the homicide, it had

probably been abandoned prior to the VR making entry. It was believed that he was in the area for quite a while before attempting the kidnapping, based on noises that the teenager had heard outside of her bedroom window shortly after dusk.

September 11th, 1975 7:00 AM

The residents of a house on Gist Drive noticed that a badminton net that they'd set up in their backyard had been knocked down sometime overnight. Responding officers felt that because of the height of the net and its position in the yard, it had probably been knocked down by someone running quickly through their property in the dark – possibly the killer.

September 11th, 1975 8:30 AM: Suspicious Person

A suspicious person was spotted at an address located to the west of the Snelling residence. He was described as a white male, early twenties, between 5'9" and 6', with a stocky build. He had light brown hair and was wearing a brown jacket and blue pants. The subject wasn't wearing any shoes. Since the killer could basically only be identified by his shoe prints, this was an interesting sighting.

September 11th, 1975 Between 8:00 AM and 12:37 PM: Note

A suspicious message was found at Mt. Whitney High School, the school that the victim attended. Hours after the attempted kidnapping, a teacher parked his truck in the parking lot, and a young lady parked next to him. This young lady, incidentally, was friends with one of the girls who had started to experience prowling and stalking issues near her home. This girl had even experienced some incidents *herself*, the most recent one on September 9th, 1975 at 11:35 PM – she'd seen the shadow of a man outside her bedroom window. The police believed that the Visalia Ransacker was most likely the person stalking her, stalking the Snelling girl, *and* stalking several of her friends.

Sometime after the teacher parked his truck, but before the girl went to lunch at 12:37 PM, someone put a note on the mirror of the teacher's truck. The note said the name of Claude Snelling's daughter, (the kidnapping victim) and then said, "I'll get the rest." News of the Snelling homicide had not traveled very far yet, and the police felt that the note was probably the work of the killer. The mirror and writing were taken into evidence.

September 11th, 2:30 PM to 4:00 PM
Claude Snelling's daughter was interviewed by police. This was her second interview – the first one took place shortly after the crime occurred.

September 11th, 1975 Night: Prowler
A prowler was spotted at a home on South Locust Street. This location was roughly five miles to the southeast of the Snelling residence, so it may not be related. However, it *is* in the general direction that a weapon stolen from a previous ransacking was later found.

September 12th, 1975: Window Screen Found
In order to help visualize and plot out the crime scene (and to help uncover any evidence that may have been missed), an aerial photograph was taken of the area around the Snelling house. The photo was developed immediately, and technicians were able to finally spot the missing window screen – the one that the killer had removed from the back window before gaining entry. It had been placed on top of the travel-trailer parked in a driveway across the street.

September 12th, 1975 4:00 PM
Claude's wife was interviewed by police.

September 12th, 1975
A resident living on the northernmost portion of Whitney contacted the police and told them that someone had stolen an aluminum

ladder from his backyard. The ladder was typically kept on their back fence, but it had gone missing on the night of the murder. Responding officers found the ladder a short distance away. It had been moved to another yard closer to the highway.

September 20th, 1975
A flashlight was found in the backyard of a residence on South Redwood Street. It was determined to be the flashlight that had been stolen by the Visalia Ransacker on August 30th, 1975, from a residence two doors down. It had possibly been used on the night of the murder.

September 20th, 1975
A gun was found abandoned in a ditch just north of the intersection of Road 164 and Oakdale Avenue/Avenue 256. This location was almost twelve miles to the southeast of the Snelling murder location and was fairly close to the nearby town of Exeter.

The weapon was analyzed and was determined to be a 38-caliber Taurus revolver. While it was ruled out as being the murder weapon, it was positively identified as a gun that the Visalia Ransacker had stolen during a burglary on South Mountain Street that took place on May 24th, 1975.

This finding was significant because it showed that the Ransacker was ditching some of the weapons he'd stolen, and it also seemed to tenuously tie him to Exeter. Whether this was a route that he traveled frequently, or whether he made a special trip out to this location simply to drop the weapon, is unknown.

September 22nd, 1975
A screwdriver wrapped in a clear plastic raincoat was found in a nearby ditch. It's unknown if this find was related to the Visalia Ransacker or not.

October 10th, 1975, 3:00 PM to 3:30 PM
Claude Snelling's daughter was interviewed by police again.

October 15th, 1975 4:30 PM
The daughter was interviewed by police for a fourth time.

October 23rd 1975 6:00 AM
The police took the Snellings' daughter to Los Angeles for a hypnosis session at the Parker Center, hoping that the latest hypnosis techniques could provide additional details about the murder that the girl may have forgotten. She underwent hypnosis and provided some additional information about the killer, including the observation that his fingers were "short and stubby." She offered a bit more about his clothing – he was wearing a windbreaker and slacks. She also recalled that his jaw seemed large or wide.

Tying the Murder Weapon
On August 31st, 1975, the Visalia Ransacker had entered a home on West Royal Oaks Drive, where he stole a 38-caliber, six-shot, blue steel Miroku revolver with a four and a half inch barrel. Along with the gun, the Ransacker had taken over two hundred 38-caliber wadcutter bullets (a special type of ammunition with a flat front primarily used on paper targets). Naturally, given everything that had been learned during the investigation up to this point (especially with the recovery of the flashlight and the Taurus revolver tied to the Ransacker), along with the previous prowling incidents that appeared to be related to the Ransacker, the police decided to contact the rightful owner of the stolen Miroku. They explained that the burglar who had stolen his gun may have used it to kill someone, and the owner remembered taking the gun out for target practice a couple of weeks before it was stolen. The police told him that if he could identify the place where he had shot the weapon, they could try to recover any rounds that he had fired and possibly compare the ballistic evidence to get a match between the weapons.

The man led officers to an area of the St. John's River – the exact location was at an embankment where Road 204 runs into the river area. Officers scoured the location and were met with success – they collected over seventy bullets believed to have been fired from the gun. They brought them back to the lab for analysis.

Lab work was completed quickly, and the result was positive. The weapons were the same – the gun used to kill Claude Snelling had been stolen by the Visalia Ransacker less than two weeks before the murder. It was official: the police named the Visalia Ransacker as the killer.

Suspect Description

Claude's daughter was interviewed a total of five times by Visalia police – once at the scene, later that day, and three times in October (one of which was a hypnosis session). At each interview, she tried her best to recall physical characteristics of the killer. Unfortunately, she wasn't able to solidly commit to very many descriptors, and the police didn't have a lot to work with when it came to identifying suspects by physical attributes.

She generally described him as a white male with light skin, between 5'8" and 5'11", possibly in his late twenties, medium to stocky build, angry eyes, strong hands, and with a "masculine," low, raspy voice that sounded more like a growl. His mask was a dark ski mask with some kind of white, zigzag stripes (though at one interview she said that they might have been multi-colored). He wore dark clothing and soft shoes that squeaked on the hard floor. They were possibly tennis shoes.

She felt that his hair was a lighter color, either brown or blonde (basing this on the color of the hair on his hands, his eyebrows, and his complexion).

Investigators asked her at each interview if she could commit to a weight estimate, and she insisted that she was unable to guess his weight. Nevertheless, they forced her to provide a number several times, and the numbers she provided ranged from 150 lbs to over 170 lbs.

The ski mask may have had the eyes, nose, and mouth cut out, or perhaps just the eyes and mouth. The white zigzag stripes were near the mouth and may have gone all the way around the mask. The mask seemed to come down to the middle of his neck.

She consistently described his hands as having no odor, no jewelry (rings or watches), and no identifying marks (like a scar). In one interview she stated that they were wet, like he was perspiring.

She noted that his actions seemed deliberate and effortless, like he had planned the kidnapping step-by-step.

At the hypnosis session in Los Angeles on October 23rd, she described his face as very round and his jaw as large. Her description of his clothing at that session was more detailed too: he wore a dark windbreaker that was zipped up all the way to his neck and didn't go past his waist, and the windbreaker had cuffs that were tight around his wrists. He wore dark pants (probably slacks, not jeans) that had no breaks or cuffs.

Context and Analysis

It was through this crime that the Ransacker's true nature was finally revealed. He wasn't an antisocial, childish prankster, and his reason for entering dozens of homes wasn't to play games and steal trinkets. He was seeking to satisfy sexual and sinister desires.

It wasn't common knowledge in the field of criminology at the time, but it's now understood that many rapists, kidnappers, and murderers get their start committing "petty" crimes like peeping and small burglaries. The VR was certainly escalating quickly – entering a house in the middle of the night with five people sleeping in it and attempting a kidnapping was a far cry from any of the behavior he'd exhibited before (or at least, any of the behavior we know about). He'd crossed the threshold of observer to attacker, and it seemed he'd planned the transition carefully. Given the calm and deliberate demeanor with which he committed this crime, it wouldn't be surprising to someday learn that he was responsible for other kidnappings or murders that occurred even before this one.

Not only had he tried to kidnap someone here, but he'd exhibited the most frightening trait of all – he killed another man without any hesitation and without any hint of remorse. He didn't just shoot once, which would've been enough to stop the man from pursuing him as he made his escape, but he shot twice, clearly intending to *kill* him and not merely to stop him. The killing made no logical sense – there was enough time for the VR to escape on foot. By killing Claude Snelling, he didn't really buy himself any extra time, because Snelling's wife was on the phone with police in moments. Perhaps Snelling had a way of identifying him that no one else in the family knew about, or perhaps the Ransacker was so angry at his plan being foiled that he decided to kill in retaliation.

Even to those who have read this book in chronological order, this sudden outburst of violence might have seemed a bit out of the blue. But the subtle hints of this type of outcome were certainly there even in his first canonical crimes with the theft of guns and ammunition. The sexual nature of his ransacking, with the bras and the women's undergarments thrown everywhere, the obvious signs of masturbation with bunched up panties and lotion, the growing body of evidence that he was peeping at victims before or after ransacking their residences, and the prolific, relentless, frenetic manner in which he kept burglarizing the same small area month after month all seemed to paint the picture of an offender who was bound to escalate into something far more dangerous.

It should also be noted that the offender reacted in similar ways during future encounters as well. When he was confronted by a police officer later in 1975, he shot at him. In July 1976, he was interrupted during a burglary and nearly beat a man to death. In February 1977, a teenage boy chased him down and almost caught him. The offender shot him in the abdomen and then shot again – but thankfully the second bullet missed the boy and he ended up surviving. In February 1978, there was an encounter with a couple out for a walk, and the Visalia Ransacker / East Area Rapist shot them dead. During a December 1979 attack in Goleta, one of the victims got free and again, was shot to death. And another man was shot during an attack in Goleta in 1981 when he resisted. With the totality of his known crimes available for analysis, it paints a startling picture of a callous murderer with no regard for human life, willing to kill someone for simply getting in his way.

Kidnapping Theories

It's not known for sure what the VR planned to do with the teenage girl after he led her out of the house. She described his movements, actions, and phrases as pre-planned and deliberate, so it's unlikely that he was just going to pull her out of the residence and then "wing it."

If he was going to put her into his car and drive away with her, where was his car? None of the witnesses along Whitney, Redwood, Gist, or any of the other streets that were canvassed reported hearing any kind of vehicle during the timeframe of the murder, though most of the residents *did* hear the gunshots. Apparently he had brought a bicycle to the scene, but pedaling away with a teenage girl in tow wouldn't have been an easy thing to do. If his vehicle was parked far away, it raised the risk of the kidnapping considerably because his victim could scream or run away at any moment, alerting neighbors all around them in the process and trapping the offender in a troublesome position. That scenario in particular would've almost certainly resulted in him being surrounded by witnesses and maybe even people who could intervene and capture him. Since the kidnapper seemed fairly intelligent and seemed to have a specific plan in mind, that probably wasn't it.

Investigators at the time thought that he intended to drive away with her in one of the vehicles belonging to the Snelling family. They pointed to the fact that he went inside and moved Mrs. Snelling's purse to the back patio before waking up the teenager as potential proof of this theory. They felt that he was searching for car keys.

Detectives and researchers have also pointed to the camper across the street as a place where he may have intended to take the teenage girl. Since the window screen was found all the way over there instead of somewhere nearby, it was clear that the VR had noticed the camper, and that he'd even been over to it. They wondered if the plan was to take the girl out of the house, bring her across the street to the camper, force her inside, sexually assault her, leave her there bound and gagged, retrieve the window screen from the top of the vehicle, replace it to hide his method of entry and delay the finding of the victim, and then make a silent getaway.

It's also possible that he had a residence nearby, or a getaway driver, or that he *did* intend to walk her down several streets. This theory is bolstered somewhat by the fact that there were two suspicious men sighted in a nearby parking lot shortly after the murder, and those two men have never been identified. During the East Area Rapist series of attacks, he led one of his early victims out of the house and quite a distance away to a remote area, where he started the process of assaulting her. For some reason, that attack was abandoned, but it shows that he *did* execute a plan at one point where he took a girl out of the house and led her away on foot.

There's no way of knowing what the exact plans were. Thankfully, that part of the attack was thwarted and the girl was relatively unharmed.

One of the curious events of the evening was the fact that the air conditioner at the Snelling residence quit working around 6:00 PM. It's just a bit coincidental that it went out on the night that the VR struck the house. Nothing was ever found to conclude that the killer had anything to do with the malfunction of the unit, but since the AC didn't work, the family had to open windows. That was a factor that surely could've aided him.

The time and date of the homicide is significant – it was very rare for the VR to strike on a Wednesday/Thursday, and he never struck as late/early as 2:00 AM. His crimes almost always occurred before midnight. The change in day and time was possibly done to avoid any unexpected schedule changes that the family might have had during a weekend, and it might have been done to throw the police off of the true identity of the kidnapper. Another reason that he chose 2:00 AM was probably for the same reason that he often chose it for his East Area Rapist and Golden State Killer attacks – it's the time that most of the city would be sleeping soundly (including his victims) and he'd have a better chance at pulling off his crime.

The "I'll get the rest" message left on the car is significant in several ways. It shows that the killer might've stayed in the general area several hours after the murder, which is almost *crazy* considering he was the most wanted man in Visalia. The sighting of the suspicious person on West Campus Avenue with no shoes on is given a bit more credence given the strong possibility that the killer was still around. The message also seems to show that he knew his victim's first name, and that he even knew where one of her friends parked since the note was placed in a way that she would notice it. As the investigation wore on and more information was revealed, it seemed likely that the VR was keeping tabs on several of her friends and even considering them for alternate or additional crimes. There was an odd sighting three weeks before the murder of a man taking photographs of some of these same young women.

Description Revisited

There were never very many reliable descriptions of the Ransacker, and unfortunately, the short time that the teenage girl spent with the killer didn't provide much more in the way of specifics. It's somewhat notable that she didn't see any hair protruding out of the bottom of his mask, because the prowler her father had spotted several months before had been described as having collar-length hair. In December 1975, a police officer (the same officer who conducted one of her interviews and took her to the hypnosis session, actually) would come face to face with the unmasked Ransacker and would be able to provide a detailed description. His information lined up fairly well with the information that the teenager was able to give.

Crime Scene Map

The daughter was sleeping in the northernmost twin bed in her bedroom on the south side of the residence when the intruder woke her up. He led her through the dining room and then east through the family room. From there, they went out the back door. He took her to the easternmost part of the fence and through the gate, which he had left open. They stopped in the carport, and that's when Claude Snelling emerged. Claude made his way south toward the suspect and toward his daughter, and when he was less than ten feet away from them, the suspect released the teenager and fired over the four-foot chain link fence. He hit Claude in the shoulder, and then Claude went back toward the door a bit. The suspect shot him again, kicked the teenager in the face two or three times, and took off down the driveway, heading west at a jogging pace.

(*map featured on the next page*)

250

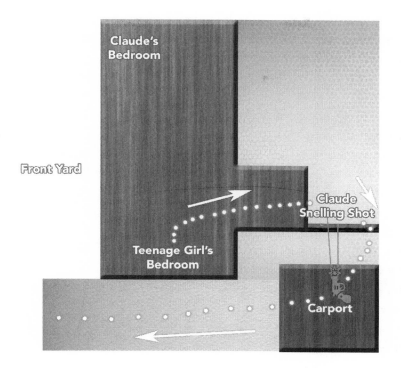

Possible Escape Route

The killer was originally seen heading west from the murder location. Based on the bicycle being abandoned on South Redwood Street, the police are reasonably certain that he'd hidden the bicycle nearby – either on South Whitney Street itself (which would've meant that once he retrieved the bike, he would've had to ride *around* the street to get to Redwood) or perhaps the bike was hidden on Redwood Street, which probably meant that he jumped a fence and traversed a yard to get to it.

After ditching the bicycle on Redwood, it's believed that he stayed in the shadows – keeping near the houses and traveling quickly northward. The flashlight found on the east side of South Redwood Street may have been dropped at this point – it correlated with his northward path. Also found was the displaced ladder, which may have been used by the killer to get to the area near the highway, or may have been used by him to observe the police response from a distance and determine the safest path out of the neighborhood or back to his vehicle.

After traveling north for a bit, it appears he changed direction and headed *back* toward the murder scene, but further north of it. The badminton net might've been downed as he escaped eastward, probably staying as far to the north as he could. The evidence drops off from there. Based on previous patterns, he could've been trying to get back to the College of the Sequoias area, where he might've parked a vehicle, or he may have continued eastward or even turned back to meet with a driver in the parking lot west of the attack area (in the K-Mart parking lot). It's also possible that he lived in the northern part of town and he needed to get across the highway, or that he lived somewhere nearby and he was simply being evasive in his escape path. His escape pattern was very similar to the one he used a few months later when the police were after him following his confrontation with Officer McGowen on December 10th, 1975.

He may not have escaped at all, of course. Based on the note that was found at the school, he may have simply hidden himself and waited for the dragnet to be lifted and the police response to dissipate.

The following is a map of his supposed escape route out of the immediate area, with important evidence drops noted:

(map is located on the next page)

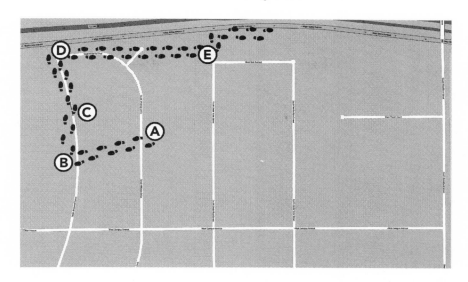

The killer's likely escape route.

A) *Homicide location on S Whitney St*

B) *Bicycle found, front door ajar on S Redwood St*

C) *Flashlight found on S Redwood St*

D) *Ladder moved on S Whitney St*

E) *Badminton net knocked down on Gist Dr*

Evidence Summary

Since this incident was a homicide, the crime was investigated far more thoroughly than any Ransacker crime had been before. Evidence was meticulously collected and analyzed.

The following is a review and summary of the evidence. Much of it has already been discussed in this chapter, but having it compiled in a summary list format will make it easy for readers to reference in the future:

Bicycle

Sometime shortly before or after the homicide, an intruder entered the home of a man living on South Redwood Street. The next morning, he discovered a stolen bicycle in his yard. Two other witnesses saw a man in the area, and shoe impressions matching Visalia Ransacker were found nearby.

The bicycle was stolen sometime after September 9th from a residence on West Tulare Avenue located close to South Giddings Street. The residence was situated to the northeast of Rotary Park and located about a mile and a half or two miles (depending on the route) from the murder scene. It was possibly stolen a day or two before the murder, but it also could've been stolen that night. It's quite a ways to travel, especially if the Ransacker had equipment with him (or the bottle of alcohol that was found). Going by the witness who possibly heard the bike being dumped at 2:30 AM, it does seem likely that the Ransacker rode the bike that night.

When the police were questioning the kidnapping victim, they asked her at two different interviews if the killer could've possibly been a woman. The main reason they asked this was that they actually suspected the nineteen-year-old woman who owned the stolen bicycle to be an accomplice or even the actual killer at one point. The victim insisted that the offender was a man. The rightful owner of the bicycle was completely cleared at the outset of the investigation.

Purse
Mrs. Snelling's purse was located on a brick planter in the backyard of the Snelling residence. The only thing stolen from it was a couple of one-dollar bills. Officers determined that he had taken her purse off of the counter and had looked through it before waking up the victim.

Bottle
A clear bottle of liquid, probably alcohol, was found outside the residence next-door to the Snellings.

Badminton Net
The owners of a home on Gist Drive noticed that the badminton net they'd set up in their backyard had been knocked down overnight. The police felt that it could've been downed accidentally by the killer fleeing the area in the dark.

Window Screen
The window screen that the killer had removed from the back window of the Snelling residence was found across the street on top of a travel-trailer. The offender had apparently removed it, taken it across the street, placed it there, and then made his way back to the target house. The window was quite a large one, measuring over two feet wide and four feet tall – large enough for him to use as an entrance if he would've failed to unlock the back door. The camper that he placed the screen on was a Golden Falcon model, and it was fairly large, measuring about twenty feet in length.

Ladder
A ladder belonging to a resident living on the northernmost portion of Whitney had been taken from their backyard. It was found a short distance away in another backyard closer to State Route 198.

Flashlight

A flashlight was found in the backyard of a residence on South Redwood Street. It was the same flashlight that had been stolen by the Visalia Ransacker on August 30th, 1975, from a residence two doors down.

Screwdriver

A screwdriver was found wrapped in a clear plastic raincoat in a nearby ditch. It's unknown if this drop was related to the Visalia Ransacker, but it should be noted that a screwdriver seemed to be his preferred pry tool throughout his entire crime spree.

The Murder Weapon

Through ballistics analysis, the police were able to determine that the weapon used to kill Claude Snelling was a 38-caliber Miroku four-inch barrel revolver that had been stolen from a VR burglary less than two weeks before the murder.

Note on the Mirror

Sometime between 8:00 AM and 12:37 PM, a note was left in the Mt. Whitney High School parking lot. It stated the female victim's name and then said, "I'll get the rest." The police believed that the killer left the note, and they took it into evidence.

Fingerprints

Scene technicians were able to lift some fingerprints from the rear entryway and from the teenage daughter's room. They were tested against other fingerprint files taken from Visalia Ransacker scenes, but there was no match. They tried to eliminate the prints by testing against family and friends, and all but a few were quickly eliminated. The prints were not believed to belong to the Ransacker, even though there was a portion of the attack where it seemed he wasn't wearing gloves.

After the Murder

It's hard to know if the Visalia Ransacker knew right away that he was suspected of this murder. Whether he did or not, it didn't seem to curb his behavior. Prowling incidents continued immediately, and within eleven days of the murder of Claude Snelling, the Visalia Ransacker burglarized a home.

His threat, "I'll get the rest," seemed to be an ominous warning that he didn't intend to fail again, or that he intended to target the rest of the victim's friends. He certainly seemed to be making good on that threat – the next chapter discusses a young woman who seemed to be targeted relentlessly by the VR.

Prowling Incidents on West Campus Avenue

The Visalia Ransacker had finally revealed himself for what he was – a dangerous, predatory offender. In a flash, he'd gone straight from low-impact burglaries to the most heinous crime of all – the murder of another human being.

The police began scrambling through their files in hopes of latching onto something that could help them identify him before he left the area completely or, even worse, before he tried another one of these crimes. Of course, this brazen offender had *not* left the area, nor did he intend to. His trail was in no danger of going cold.

The Snelling murder was a turning point in the investigation. The police had a better idea of the type of offender they were dealing with, and they began following better leads. Rather than looking for a burglar, they started looking for a sexually motivated stalker.

Claude Snelling's daughter realized quickly that she'd been systematically stalked and targeted. She even told her family that in the week and a half leading up to the kidnapping attempt, she'd felt like someone had been following her on foot and by vehicle. She'd had the feeling that someone was watching her, and the unnerving experience with the prowler outside of her window in late August was essentially confirmation of it.

It turned out that the Snelling girl wasn't the only young lady being stalked in this manner – a few friends and acquaintances of hers were also being targeted and followed.

This chapter discusses events surrounding the young lady who had seemingly been "discovered" by the VR during the commission of *another* burglary – he'd singled out a photo of her on South Redwood Street. That was around the time that her stalking issues began.

Due to a lack of physical evidence and the fact that there are so few full examples of the VR's stalking methods to compare these incidents to, we have to mark the following summary of events as "unconfirmed." But based on everything that we (and investigators) know about the Visalia Ransacker / East Area Rapist, this was almost certainly his handiwork.

VR #116 – *Prowler*
September 1975 | W Campus Ave

-NOT CONFIRMED TO BE RELATED-

A residence on West Campus Avenue had suffered several prowling events, the last one occurring in late September. This was a very busy section of town over the months that the Visalia Ransacker was active, with both this home and the one around the corner suffering nearly a dozen incidents over a yearlong period.

At this particular residence, they experienced everything from a prowler peeping over their fence on different nights, shadows at their windows, "knocking noises," and even harassing phone calls. The phone calls weren't something that had been associated with the Visalia Ransacker yet, but two different victims on West Royal Oaks Drive received calls with violent threats during this general timeframe as well. Both were confirmed burglary victims of the VR, and one of them appeared to be stalked quite a bit by the offender.

Everything seems to line up with the VR, but there are a few details that actually point *away* from the Ransacker in this series of events. In examining the documentation, one of the prowling incidents at this residence seemed a little "off" to us. The report mentions a prowler exposing himself near one of the victims' windows, and in the thousands of pages of files we had examined for this case *and* the East Area Rapist / Golden State Killer case, that didn't really sound like the offender we had been studying. Thankfully, we were given updated information from the witness herself. She clarified that the man did *not* expose himself, and she didn't know how or why that detail had ended up in the police report. She also added that she spotted a prowler on the victims' property at one point and saw him fairly clearly. He had long-curly hair, which is a description that doesn't appear in the reports and doesn't appear in any known Visalia Ransacker description. Additionally, this young woman had a frightening encounter a year before with a young man who was definitely *not* the VR.

While the reports and the witnesses may be at odds with each other on some of the details, one thing is clear – this home was being targeted by *someone*. There are several reasons that investigators feel that the prowling and harassment of this household was committed by the Visalia Ransacker. This first is that these events closely mirror the prowling and harassment incidents that occurred a few weeks later to a family on West Royal Oaks Drive – even down to the content of the phone calls. The family on West Royal Oaks Drive was more clearly a set of Visalia Ransacker victims because their home was ransacked with the VR's M.O. during the time that their stalking occurred. Something else that's notable there is that the stalking of the family on West Royal Oaks Drive began on the exact day that the stalking of *this* family on West Campus Avenue seemed to end – September 22nd.

Another reason is that the teenage girl who lived at this residence had two connections to the Ransacker. Her photo had been removed by the VR at another home on August 30th, 1975 while he was rummaging through their residence, and she sometimes walked in the neighborhood with Claude Snelling's daughter. These walks occurred during the time that Snelling felt that someone was stalking her on foot and by car. Whether the girl at *this* household was first noticed at the August 30th, 1975 ransacking, or whether she was scoped out as part of the reconnaissance that he was doing on the Snelling household is unknown. It's thought that due to all of these stalking events and the other intersections with the VR's activities, this girl was possibly being targeted as a potential kidnapping or assault victim herself.

Another major reason that investigators feel that it was the Ransacker stalking this home is that the home around the corner from this one is the residence that had been targeted by the VR at least three times – the prowler on October 16th, 1974, a ransacking on January 25th, 1975, and an attempted break-in a couple weeks after the stalking at *this* home stopped. Furthermore, a couple days after *that*, a home just a couple doors down on South Verde Vista Street would *also* start to get preyed on relentlessly by a man that the police felt was the Visalia Ransacker.

If this is all a bit confusing, that's understandable. It was a lot to keep track of for the police, too. There are a lot of things happening at this point and many repeat victims in one small area. The takeaway is that this small area of Visalia was a major focus for the VR, just like the little pocket at West Kaweah Avenue, and that alone makes it likely that this young woman (who fit the VR victim profile) was being targeted by him.

In the northwest portion of the Visalia Ransacker's area, this street was considered one of the "big four" – South Redwood Street, South Whitney Street, South Linda Vista Street, and South Verde Vista

Street. They intersected with West Campus Avenue, and this was the area prowled and burglarized the most. These streets were situated to the west of the College of the Sequoias, and many of these homes were quite close to the footpath between West Noble Avenue and State Route 198. It was thought by some that the Ransacker would park near the highway, go across it using one of the streets, and then hug the area between the highway and West Noble Avenue until he arrived at homes that were clear for striking. Then it was thought that he would retreat and cross back to his "safe zone." His shoe prints were found on this path, so we can be fairly certain that he was at least in that vicinity.

A quick note about that footpath: the particular section of it that we've been discussing no longer exists in this part of the city. The landscape has changed, but the trail does still exist in the *eastern* half of the area that the Visalia Ransacker offended in.

The police did what they could to help this family on West Campus Avenue, fully believing that these were Ransacker incidents and that they'd have a chance to nail him while prowling. They even went as far as to station an officer up in a nearby tree to keep watch over the home. The Ransacker wasn't spotted there again. Perhaps he caught wind of it somehow or noticed the officers nearby. There were no further incidents at this address past September 22nd.

September 22nd, 1975 Ransacking

The VR's activities now resembled the East Area Rapist phase far more than they resembled anything that he'd done since beginning his crimes in Visalia. He was peeping and prowling on almost a constant basis, then zeroing in on specific potential victims, burglarizing as he went, and then he'd stalk those potential victims in-person and by phone over a period of weeks. His transformation into the East Area Rapist was more or less complete – he just hadn't successfully invaded a home yet. Everything else about him had settled into the patterns that were utilized in the EAR crime series, and as the rest of the September and October events play out, that will become veery apparent.

With his potential victim on West Campus Avenue in the rear-view mirror for whatever reason (thankfully with no incident of violence), he seemed to be in search of a new target. He apparently found one on West Royal Oaks Drive.

VR #117 – *Ransacking*
September 22nd, 1975 | W Royal Oaks Dr

On Monday, September 22nd, between 7:00 PM and 8:30 PM, the VR entered a single-story home on West Royal Oaks Drive while the victims were away.

He entered by prying open a door and, while inside, he disabled their phone line. This was something that he almost always did during East Area Rapist attacks but hadn't yet done as the Visalia Ransacker. Perhaps it was something he'd thought of after the Snellings were able to call the police so quickly.

This ransacking was extensive, with an intense focus on the teenage daughter's room. He took some of her padded bras, cut them up/disassembled them, and left the remnants in the bedroom. The girl's panties were balled up and placed on her bed. He went to the bathroom, found rolls of toilet paper, and for some reason he stacked them on top of the toilet. He also found a bottle of rubbing alcohol and went back to the teenage girl's bedroom and placed it on her bed.

The VR, who hadn't ransacked a residence since before the Claude Snelling murder, took quite a bit from this scene. He stole a single earring from a pair, two bottles of perfume, six small bottles of makeup/foundation, and a bra. He also stole two wallet-size photos of the teenage girl, both of them featuring her in a beauty pageant. He did *not* steal the piggybank from her room, and may not have even seen it based on its location. Perhaps he'd evolved past piggybanks – while it had been such a staple of his crimes up to this point, he rarely bothered with them in Visalia after the Snelling homicide. Maybe it was an effort to change his distinctive M.O.

He left through the same door he'd used to gain entry.

When the police arrived, they noticed that he'd turned off all of the lights in the residence. The balled-up panties were checked for masturbation emission, but according to the report, nothing was found on the clothing items.

An officer who weighed in with information for this book *does* remember finding telltale evidence that the VR had masturbated to completion at a ransacking around this time period, but he didn't remember which one it was. He wondered if the bottle of rubbing alcohol had been taken to the bedroom at this scene so that the Ransacker could clean up any semen that had ended up on fabric items.

No longer content to simply peep and burglarize, this ransacking was either the beginning of the offender's fascination with this family, or was merely another step in what was beginning to be an escalation pattern related to them. Additional incidents, documented in later chapters, included harassing phone calls and a prowler at the front door in the middle of the day.

The teenage daughter was a fifteen-year-old student at Mt. Whitney High School. How long had the VR been aware of her? Did he learn of her existence during the burglary? Based on his recent activities, almost anything is possible. This young lady had won a beauty pageant and had recently been crowned Visalia's "Ideal Miss," an honor publicly bestowed upon a young lady between ages thirteen and seventeen years old every year. Perhaps the VR had seen her in the paper or had even attended the pageant himself.

The home she lived in was situated less than ten houses west of the home where the Visalia Ransacker had stolen the .38 Miroku revolver that had killed Claude Snelling, so coming across her organically was possible as well. He could've come across the home if he'd peeped his way there and back from South Demaree Street (a possible origin point for the VR) or from a nearby location.

Events related to this family continued for about a month, and despite the Ransacker's initial fascination with the teenage daughter, it seemed that subsequent harassment was directed primarily at her mother.

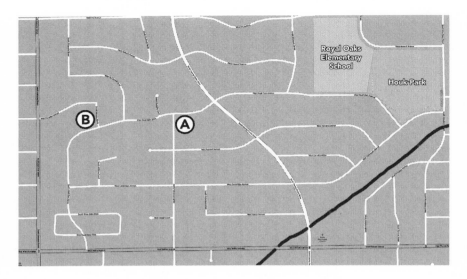

The location of this home, and the home where the gun was stolen that was used to kill Claude Snelling. Both locations are on West Royal Oaks Drive.

A) *Home where the gun used to kill Claude Snelling was stolen from*

B) *This victim's home*

Early October 1975 Prowlers

Even though September had been almost nonstop activity for the Ransacker, he didn't seem to be in need of a rest. Most offenders would probably lay low after killing someone, but the Visalia Ransacker / Golden State Killer was not a typical offender, even in this early phase of his criminal career.

The month of October saw him continue to prowl for new victims, and the second incident we discuss in this chapter is a case where the offender tried to break into one of his victims' homes while they were *still inside*. This incident, which the police didn't think much of at the time, could very easily have been his first home-invasion rape attempt on a couple and an early attempt at the types of crimes he committed as the East Area Rapist. He'd been targeting this particular home for quite a long time, and it appeared that, based on the time of morning that he was attempting to gain entry, that he might've had very sinister plans for them.

Later in the month, a series of Ransacker-esque burglaries occurred in East Sacramento, followed by a home-invasion rape that bears many similarities to the East Area Rapist case. This attack was listed as the first EAR assault for over a year, but later, authorities weren't entirely sure that it was him. As we mentioned in an earlier section, for all intents and purposes, the offender had already adopted most of the tactics he'd use as the EAR, so we'll later explore the possibility that it was indeed the VR/EAR who committed the assault.

VR #118 – *Prowler*
October 3rd, 1975 | S Redwood St

A residence on South Redwood Street had two known prowling incidents. The first one occurred on Friday, October 3rd, 1975.

The adult male living at the house spotted a prowler in his backyard. When the prowler realized that he'd been spotted, he jumped over the fence and disappeared.

Because of the location of this home (situated in an area where the VR had been very active), the police immediately felt that this was the VR. They became convinced later on when the same prowler returned on October 24th – a night where the Ransacker was actively burglarizing homes. At that time, the police found shoe prints on and near the fence at the same location where the prowler had been seen on both October 3rd *and* on October 24th. The shoe prints matched the Visalia Ransacker. Apparently, he was using this man's backyard as one of his entry and exit points to the neighborhood during this phase of his activity.

This residence was on the west side of South Redwood Street, located less than three hundred feet away from where Claude Snelling had been murdered. Behind this residence, where the VR was seen jumping the fence, was an apartment complex that was burglarized by the VR on October 24th, 1975.

VR #119 – *Attempted Break-in*
October 4th, 1975 | S Verde Vista St

-NOT CONFIRMED TO BE RELATED-

On Saturday, October 4th at 4:30 AM, a prowler attempted to enter a single-story home on South Verde Vista.

The residents were inside sleeping at the time. Whether the prowler knew that they were there or not is up for debate, but the timing of this one (4:30 AM) was very different from the typical VR timeframe. At least, different from the typical timeframe utilized when he was merely interested in ransacking. He'd attempted to kidnap the Snelling daughter after 2:00 AM, and most East Area Rapist attacks and murders occurred during the early morning hours (as opposed to the evening hours, which was when most VR burglaries took place).

Luckily, the residents awoke to the sound of the prowler prying at one of their windows, and that seemed to scare him off. The man of the house went to investigate and he couldn't locate the would-be intruder, but he did find multiple fresh pry marks on the window frame.

This household, consisting of a couple in their mid thirties, had long been on the Visalia Ransacker's radar. They'd been prowled on October 16th, 1974, ransacked on January 25th, 1975, and now they'd experienced yet another issue with a break-in attempt.

Their next-door neighbors had recently called the police because they'd spotted a prowler, and incidents two doors down from these victims are described in the chapter "Prowling Incidents on West Campus Avenue." Another house on South Verde Vista Street, discussed later in *this* chapter, also experienced prowling issues, but documentation is lacking on these particular events. All signs pointed to the VR as the culprit in most of these cases, and it seemed he was working multiple targets on the same street. This was a clumsy, noisier version of the exact same pattern that the criminal would employ from 1976 to 1979 during his East Area Rapist phase of attacks – he'd scope out a general geographic area, find a few houses on a street that he was possibly interested in attacking, and then he'd begin prowling, peeping, calling, and doing surveillance on multiple homes on a street at once. After a period of doing this, he'd decide on a morning to attack, and then it seemed he'd begin prowling the street to see which of his "targets" were "available." There would often be a primary target and several backups. He'd then force his way in and assault the chosen victim. Sometimes he would chose a lone women or lone women, and sometimes he would attack couples. Occasionally one of his targets would wake up as he was prying his way inside, and he would flee. It seems that's exactly what happened here. Given the fact that this couple had been on his radar for a long time, the fact that the girl two doors down had experienced a lot of stalking activity and even phone calls, and the fact that this approach had all the hallmarks of the East Area Rapist, this couple was probably quite lucky that they were light sleepers.

We must mention, however, that there's no slam-dunk physical evidence that it was the Visalia Ransacker who tried to enter their home that night. The only other incident like this one up to this point was the Snelling home-invasion, which had taken place a little over three weeks prior. But in light of that event and given the history of this particular residence, the area, the general timing of the event, and our knowledge of the type of offender that the VR *became*, it does seem likely that he was responsible.

The Ransacker was apparently "capitalizing" on all of the stalking intelligence he had gathered over the previous year or so, and he would continue to do this throughout the fall months. He was *clearly* looking to escalate, but he just couldn't seem to pull off an attack. Still, he had a few *more* potential targets that he was working on around town, exactly like when he became the East Area Rapist and he'd stalking multiple targets and areas at once. The activity around a few of these potential victims seemed to continue, but this was the last known issue that *this* particular couple had. By November, the Ransacker had more or less moved out of this area and had begun to again focus his attention on West Kaweah Avenue and a few outlier areas. In the meantime, he continued to stalk the family on West Royal Oaks Drive, he returned to the scenes of several past burglaries, he attempted to break into the home of the ex-wife of one of his past victims, he burglarized homes associated with two family members back-to-back, and more. We'll discuss all of these events as they unfold.

VR #120 – *Prowler*
October 6th, 1975 | S Verde Vista St

-NOT CONFIRMED TO BE RELATED-

It seems another family was being targeted by the VR – another home on South Verde Vista Street experienced a lot of prowling activity in the weeks leading up to October 6th, 1975, which seems to be the last date that anything suspicious occurred at this residence. Paperwork is sadly lacking on these events, and rather than pass along unconfirmed information, we'll simply note that they seemed to be stalked quite heavily, most likely by the Ransacker.

This home was located just three houses away from the residence that had nearly been broken into in the early morning hours of October 4th, and it was right in the heart of the Visalia Ransacker activity of this time period.

October 16th, 1975 Phone Call

The ransacking had taken a backseat to stalking and prowling ever since August had ended. Simply rifling through undergarments and personal items didn't seem to be enough for this offender, whose desire to terrorize and commit sexual offenses had reached a new level.

He'd been relatively quiet since what seemed to have been the failed home-invasion attempt on the morning of October 4th. He lingered on that street for another couple of days, but then that area grew quiet. Rather than being indicative of the offender taking a break, it appeared that two things had potentially occurred: one was that he'd begun focusing his attention back on the West Royal Oaks Drive family, and another was that he may have been gearing up for another attempt at a similar crime – only this time it may have been in Sacramento and it may have been successful. The offender could've been spending a bit of time out of the area in early and mid October stalking and prowling in Sacramento.

We'll discuss other possible activity soon. For now, we need to discuss one of the first *documented* phone calls that the VR made to a victim. We've already discussed two calls that may or may not have been made to victims on West Kaweah Avenue, harassing phone calls made to the targets on West Campus Avenue and South Verde Vista Street, and we've already discussed the phone call made to the man the Ransacker had stolen the Miroku revolver from. It's possible and even likely that he made many more of these to people that he'd burglarized, people that he'd *intended* to burglarize, and people that he'd intended to do much worse to, but it's not documented. One of the problems with the calls is that the police weren't aware of the Ransacker's propensity to engage in this type of behavior until much later in the crime spree. Victims typically didn't report the calls, and the only way that officers learned of them was through neighborhood canvassing, followups with previous victims, and knowing to ask the right questions of the right people. It appears that some of the burglary victims themselves didn't even make the connection between a silent or harassing phone call and the ransacking that had taken place at their home. Documentation of these types of incidents is in poor shape, but more information has started to come out as past victims have looked back on the time period.

Regarding the phone call we discuss in this chapter, it's well documented because the victim contacted the police and gave them a full report. A second phone call that they received a few days later was coupled with a prowling incident, which made for a much more immediate need for the police to be involved.

Phone activity (silent calls and harrassment by telephone) was an integral part of the VR/EAR/GSK's modus operandi from this point all the way through the rest of the 1970s and 1980s. One of the most terrifying aspects of this case is that the calls didn't stop even after the last known murder in 1986 – some East Area Rapist victims received threatening phone calls from the offender even 25 years after their attack, all the way up until 2001 (with other possibilities occurring even in 2004 and 2017).

Note: this incident is classified as "not confirmed to be related" simply because with this being just a phone call, there was no physical evidence or anything *directly* tying the VR to the event. It's merely a technicality – investigators and researchers are virtually certain that the calls are related.

Harassing Phone Call
October 16th, 1975 | W Royal Oaks Dr

-NOT CONFIRMED TO BE RELATED-

Life had almost returned to normal for the family on West Royal Oaks Drive. Their home had been ransacked on the night of September 22nd, 1975. They wondered how long the VR had been keeping tabs on them, especially since the weapon that had been used to kill Claude Snelling had been stolen from another house on their street.

It was 7:50 AM on October 16th, 1975. Thursday morning, and the man of the house had just left for work. His wife was alone in the house. The phone rang, and she picked it up.

"I know you're alone and I'm going to come over and fuck you," a menacing voice said.

She slammed the receiver down.

Authorities felt that the call had been made by the Visalia Ransacker.

The timing of it was precise – occurring mere moments after the husband had left for work. It was *so* precise that a few interesting possibilities are at play. Had the Ransacker watched the house, learned when the husband usually left, and then timed his call for maximum effect? Had he been watching the residence *that morning* to observe the husband leave the home? It's the possibility that might be the most frightening of all, implying that he was stationed nearby and could get to a phone rather quickly. Would that mean he lived close by and could walk, bike, or drive to his residence? Or would he have headed west toward the area where a shopping center was located to use a payphone? It was also possible that the caller was indeed far away from the scene and had dialed remotely with perfect timing because he knew their routine and knew the house would be almost empty.

An interesting note – when the Ransacker had burglarized this family's home, he'd disabled the phone while he was there. An oddity possibly indicating that phone calls were already on his mind.

One thing that represents a shift from what took place during the ransacking is that the target of these phone calls was the mother. At the ransacking, the VR had seemed preoccupied with the teenage daughter. Perhaps either one of them were "acceptable" targets to him, or he'd decided to target the mother with these calls because she would be the only one that he could reliably reach by telephone.

The method that the East Area Rapist used for obtaining the phone numbers of his victims was never really discovered, and police aren't completely sure how he did it. Phone books are an obvious possibility, since he knew their addresses and probably their names. Also, many phone numbers were written down in the residence, often on the phones themselves. Perhaps he had obtained it that way, or had discovered their name and looked it up in the phone book, or he had gone through their mail, or perhaps he had a job where he could easily access information like that.

This wouldn't be the last phone call that the woman received, nor would it be the last time that the Ransacker might've physically been at the residence. The next phone call, coupled with prowling activity, occurred just five days later.

October 20ᵗʰ, 1975 Suspicious Person and Prowler

Ransacker activity was fairly quiet during this portion of the week in October, at least compared with everything that had been happening earlier in the month and during September. Another weekend had passed without any ransackings, and no one else had fallen victim to the VR. After such a busy September and early October, with near-constant stalking, peeping, and prowling reports, it was eerily quiet.

It turns out that this was an incredibly significant week in Golden State Killer history due to some odd activity that occurred in Sacramento *and* Visalia almost simultaneously. Odd prowling incidents occurred in Visalia while burglaries and a home-invasion rape that was thought to be the work of the East Area Rapist occurred in Sacramento. The attack was listed as his first canonical event for about a year, and then it was dropped off the list for reasons we'll explain later. It was very recently put back *on* the list, so we're left with the work of trying to reconcile any activity that occurred in Visalia with any activity that occurred in Sacramento during this time period.

It can be done, but it's dicey. We'll tackle that after working through a few more Visalia events.

VR #121 – *Suspicious Person*
October 20th, 1975 | S Whitney St

-NOT CONFIRMED TO BE RELATED-

At 10:00 AM on Monday, October 20th, 1975, a suspicious person was spotted on South Whitney Street.

The witness who saw the subject was understandably tense and on the lookout – the Ransacker had killed her next-door neighbor, Claude Snelling, five weeks earlier. Her own home had almost been broken into about six weeks before the murder, which added even more purpose to her vigilance.

Lately, she'd been seeing a strange man riding a bike through the neighborhood. The morning of the 20th was the third time that she'd seen this man. He seemed "dirty" and out of place, and given all that had happened, his presence seemed suspicious. When the witness saw him riding past her house on this date, she decided to follow him and get a good description for the police.

Right after saw him ride by, she went outside and got into her car. Even though there hadn't been much time between her spotting the subject and pulling out of her driveway, he was gone by the time she hit the streets. She felt that he might've turned left and headed for College of the Sequoias, so she drove there and looked for him. Unfortunately, she was unable to locate the man or the bike.

She described him as an adult male in his twenties, with shoulder-length brown hair that was wavy, and she emphasized that he didn't seem to belong in the neighborhood. She described the bicycle as very old with large balloon tires.

The subject was never located and as far as police know, he wasn't seen again.

There's very little to suggest a Visalia Ransacker connection, but given everything that had been happening, the neighbor was smart to be vigilant and report the sighting. Not only was the man coming from the general direction that the Ransacker was probably originating from (and escaping to) on several nights that he was active, but criminals like the VR have been known to case homes in the daytime. And of course, they often like to return to the scene of the crime.

The description of long brown hair comes up a few times in the series, and on a couple occasions it was described as curly or wavy. Since the VR was described as having short hair in December, it's possible that the "curly" and "wavy" descriptions existed because, if these subjects were indeed the Ransacker, he could've been wearing a wig.

But it really could've been anyone on the bicycle. This incident seems to be grouped with the other Visalia Ransacker files in every jurisdiction that keeps documentation on the case, so we thought it deserved a mention regardless.

VR #122 – *Prowler*
October 20th, 1975 | S Emerald Ct

-NOT CONFIRMED TO BE RELATED-

On Monday, October 20th at 9:40 PM, a prowler was spotted at a home on South Emerald Court.

A young boy (ten or eleven years old) was dropped off in the cul-de-sac where his home was located. Upon his arrival, he found that the front door to his house was locked and no one else was home. He decided to try the back door, so he went around the left side of the residence and through the side gate. As he rounded the side yard and entered the back, he startled a man who had apparently been standing at one of the back windows. Both the man and the young witness took off running down opposite sides of the house. The boy didn't look back until he reached his next-door neighbor's house, and he explained to them what he'd seen.

The young man only got a fleeting glimpse of the prowler, but he was able to describe him as a white male adult, between 5'10" and 6', about 150 lbs, with light brown hair. The prowler was wearing a blue jacket and jeans.

This description matches other general descriptions of the Ransacker pretty well, but the weight estimate was lower than most of the other sightings. It's unknown whether this was because the boy was young and had a difficult time estimating weight accurately, or if the Ransacker was actually lighter than most witnesses described (with bulk being added by heavier coats or extra items in his pockets). And perhaps the prowler wasn't even the VR.

Some of the official lists of VR crimes used internally by police departments have a "Ransacker Burglary" listed for this address. On some of them, they list an additional prowling incident occurring on October 23rd, 1975 at this address, too. Reports don't seem to exist for either of these additional incidents (which is fairly common for this series, unfortunately), so we're not able to confirm the ransacking or the additional incident on the 23rd. We looked very carefully for additional information, because this part of the crime spree is important due to the timing of the possible East Area Rapist attack in Sacramento that occurred on the morning of the 21st, and that was just a few hours after this prowler was spotted.

The street where this happened backs up to the Houk Park and Royal Oaks Elementary area. The Ransacker targeted this general area many times.

October 21ˢᵗ, 1975 Phone Calls and Prowler

The morning of October 21st, 1975 was when the rape in Sacramento occurred. We'll discuss the details in the next chapter. Roughly seven hours later, the family on West Royal Oaks Drive that had been targeted by the VR before was again being harassed. This time, he didn't seem content to merely make contact by phone – it seemed that he was on the premises as well.

Investigators are almost positive that this incident is a genuine VR event, but since there's no physical evidence or slam-dunk M.O., we've decided to mark this as "not confirmed to be related." Many of our readers require definitive proof or physical evidence before considering an event to be related to the series, and we'd like to err on the side of caution and respect their methods.

VR #123 – *Prowler and Harassing Phone Call*
October 21st, 1975 | W Royal Oaks Dr

-NOT CONFIRMED TO BE RELATED-

The family that lived on West Royal Oaks Drive had been the victims of the ransacking on September 22nd, 1975, and they'd received a threatening phone call on the morning of October 16th, 1975. On the afternoon of Tuesday, October 21st, the trouble continued.

At 1:30 PM, the woman of the house had just returned from running errands. She was home alone. Suddenly, the stillness of the afternoon was broken by noises at her front door. It sounded like someone was trying to open it. Her initial thought was that her son had returned home early from school, but the nature of the noises made her apprehensive enough to look through the peephole before opening the door. The view was completely dark, and she realized that the person on the other side was blocking it with his or her hand.

She stood back for a moment, trying to decide what to do. Hoping to catch sight of the person at the front door, she went to another part of the house and looked out the window. She didn't see anyone on her doorstep. She went back to the door and listened. There were no noises on the other side, so she looked through the peephole. It was unobstructed.

About an hour later (at about 2:40 PM), the phone rang. She picked it up and said "hello," but the person on the other end didn't respond. They didn't hang up, either, and the silence dragged on. She repeated "hello," and asked who was on the other end, but there was no response. The caller hung up.

A few minutes later, the phone rang again. She answered it once more with "hello." This time, the person on the other end spoke.

"How would you like to get fucked?" And then he said her name, and he promptly hung up.

She called the police immediately and told them everything that had happened. One of the questions they asked her was if she felt that the voice from the call received that day was the same voice from the call she'd received on the 16th. She told them that she thought that it was, but added that she couldn't be completely sure.

The police felt that these phone calls were from the Ransacker, and they felt that he was still stalking this woman and her daughter. His frightening behavior toward them was escalating, and it was possible that he was on her premises that afternoon because he was trying to gain entry to her home and assault her. Given what had happened with the Snelling family, and considering the activity related to the families on South Verde Vista Street and nearby West Campus Avenue, investigators began doing whatever they could to prepare for the possibility that this family was next on the VR's hit list.

Given the home-invasion rape that we discuss in the next chapter (and of course, the Snelling incident), it truly is a possibility that he was trying to enter the home to assault her. There were a few instances where he committed back-to-back assaults during the East Area Rapist phase – whether they were committed so close together because he was in a manic state or if he did this because of time-constraints, we still don't know, but committing back-to-back assaults did fit his known profile.

Another thing that fit his known profile were silent, hang-up phone calls. During the East Area Rapist phase of attacks from 1976 through 1979, it was very common for his potential victims to receive phone calls where the caller didn't speak. Sometimes they could hear light breathing and they knew someone was on the other end, but the call would drag on and then end with no words being spoken. It's believed that one of the reasons he did this was to ensure that his victims were home at a certain time so he could plan when to break into their homes and assault them. He also seemed to derive pleasure from hearing them talk to him.

When it came to this family on West Royal Oaks Drive, this was actually the end of the trouble for them. No further reports of Ransacker or prowler activity exist in the files for this address.

Possible 1975 EAR Attack

In 2018, Law Enforcement announced that the Visalia Ransacker and the East Area Rapist are finally confirmed as being the same offender. This has made some aspects of the crime series *easier* to understand, and it's made other aspects of it more *difficult* to understand.

This chapter will explore one of the more difficult areas.

October 1975 was a busy month for the VR, with several incidents attributed to him. There was *also* a handful of crimes in Sacramento that appeared to be his work, and the timeline for some of these events in two different cities is very tight, especially considering that Sacramento and Visalia are two hundred miles away from each other. With so many things going on in two different cities, some of these crimes or sightings *have* to be thrown out in order for one man to be present at all of them... right? Maybe so, and maybe not!

In this chapter, we'll do what we always do and simply present the information, make a few observations and ask a few questions, and then allow the reader to decide what might or might not be possible.

The main thing to note before we get started is that none of these events technically overlap – there *is* enough time for the VR/EAR to make the trip between the two areas and commit all of these offenses – *if* all of them end up being related and he decided not to sleep for a while.

The main incident at play here is a home-invasion rape that took place in Sacramento on October 21st, 1975. Due to a similar M.O. and because the target house was in the exact same area that the EAR would later hit when his crime spree began in earnest in June 1976, investigators at the time felt that this was definitely the first attack by the East Area Rapist. As the months went by and the EAR committed more offenses, they began to question the connection, mainly due to an iffy witness description. Modern investigators have added it back onto their list of canonical EAR attacks based on similarities to the totality of his crime spree and some newly discovered reports detailing EAR-style burglaries that occurred nearby.

To many it appears to be a genuine EAR assault, but there's still room for doubt among some. It seems to be a perpetually open issue that may never be resolved due to a lack of physical evidence.

One of the most notable aspects of this group of incidents is that some of the burglaries that we'll look at in Sacramento have some of the hallmarks of the VR burglaries that were occurring in Visalia. Some of them are so similar that you may wonder if we labeled the city correctly.

It's a complicated series of events, so rather than look at the incidents city-by-city, stepping through the timeline and looking at these events as they happened seems to be the best way to analyze them.

Sacramento: Destruction of Property
Late October 15th / Early October 16th, 1975
10100 block of La Gloria Drive

In Rancho Cordova (an area in Sacramento that the East Area Rapist favored), a driveway lamp was smashed during the late night/early morning hours of October 15th/16th.

Visalia: Phone Call

October 16th, 1975 7:50 AM
3200 block of West Royal Oaks Drive

A harassing phone call was received at a residence on West Royal Oaks Drive. The caller said that he knew the woman was alone and, as a matter of fact, her husband had just left for work. This residence had been ransacked the month before by the VR, so based on that and other harassing phone calls received by other victims that the VR seemed to be targeting, the police have determined that this caller was most likely the Ransacker.

Sacramento: Ransacking

Between October 17th and October 19th, 1975
800 block of Piccadilly Circle

A ransacking occurred at a home on Piccadilly Circle while the residents were on vacation. The burglar gained entry through a sliding glass door in the master bedroom.

Every room in the residence was ransacked. Pictures on the walls were moved, the offender ate in the kitchen, and he left burnt matches on the floors all throughout the home. He stole several size 42 men's suits, a matching top coat, leather jackets, size 9 dress shoes, silverware, a transistor radio, women's jewelry, and coins – including a large number of pennies.

This burglary had hallmarks of *both* the Visalia Ransacker series *and* the East Area Rapist series, making it one of the most interesting crimes that we've come across in our research.

Sacramento: Hot Prowl

October 18th, 1975 between 12:00 AM and 10:00 AM
10600 block of Olson Drive

A "hot prowl" burglary occurred in Rancho Cordova. A man, his wife, and two children were asleep when an unknown intruder entered the home through the back door and took the woman's purse. The family didn't wake up during the event, and the purse was later found in the bushes near the residence. This burglary was fairly close, geographically, to where the October 21st rape would occur.

For those unfamiliar with the term, a "hot prowl" burglary is when the subject enters a home while the residents are still inside.

It should also be pointed out that, interestingly enough, the family of Joseph DeAngelo (the man arrested in 2018 for the Visalia Ransacker / Golden State Killer crimes) lived on this same block – the 10600 block of Olson Drive – for a time in the 1960s.

Sacramento: Ransacking

October 18th, 1975 between 5:30 PM and 9:15 PM
2600 block of Dawes Street

On the evening of the 18th, a ransacking occurred at a home on Dawes Street while the victims were away. This burglary took place even *closer* to the location of the October 21st rape than the burglary we just discussed.

At this scene, the bedrooms in particular were extensively ransacked. Coins were taken from a piggybank, and a .38 caliber handgun (along with ammunition) was taken. Other firearms were left behind, and the family's valuables (such as jewelry, gold coins, and watches) were also left behind. The suspect removed drapery ties from the residence before he left – an eerie foreshadowing of the October 21st rape where the victims would be bound with drapery ties.

Several parallels exist here between this burglary and the typical VR ransacking, such as the coins from the piggybank, the theft of the .38, and the offender leaving behind valuable items.

Sacramento: Ransacking
October 18th, 1975 between 6:30 PM and 9:00 PM
2700 block of Paseo Drive

A couple in their thirties was burglarized while they were away from home. Their house was partially ransacked, and an envelope was torn and left on the coffee table. The burglar stole a clock radio, an M-1 military survival knife, a birthstone ring, and a high school class ring.

The theft of personal jewelry at this scene is consistent with Visalia Ransacker burglaries. The theft of the clock radio is interesting as well, given that as the East Area Rapist, he was prone to stealing those on a semi-regular basis.

Paseo Drive, where this burglary occurred, would be where the East Area Rapist struck on June 18th, 1976 in an attack that's often listed as his first. This burglary is yet another incident that has elements of both the Visalia Ransacker series *and* connections to the East Area Rapist series.

Sacramento: Intruder
October 19th, 1975 after 11:00 PM
10300 block of Malaga Way

A thirty-nine-year-old woman returned home with a male friend sometime after 11:00 PM. They were surprised to find an intruder inside the residence, and he fled when they arrived. The woman found that the chain lock had been engaged on her front door, and that the intruder had left the sliding glass door standing open. Some of the items inside the home had been moved, but nothing was stolen.

The latching of the chain lock was something that the VR did at several of his burglaries, most likely so that the homeowner would be slowed down if he or she were to arrive before he was through ransacking.

Visalia: Suspicious Person
October 20th, 1975 10:00 AM
500 block of South Whitney Street

A suspicious person was seen on a bike traveling on South Whitney Street, which was the epicenter of many of the Visalia Ransacker's crimes.

Visalia: Prowler
October 20th, 1975 9:40 PM
1200 block of South Emerald Court

A prowler was seen in the backyard of a home on South Emerald Court.

Sacramento: Home-Invasion Rape
October 21st, 1975 4:00 AM to 6:30 AM
2600 block of Dawes Street

In the early hours of October 21st, 1975, a man entered the unlocked garage door of a home on Dawes Street. He silently made his way through the entrance that led from the garage to the kitchen and crept through the house until he located the bedroom of an eighteen-year-old girl. She suddenly found herself being threatened with a knife, then promptly tied up with strips of torn towel and drapery cord. The intruder then quickly made his way into the mother's bedroom and woke her in the same manner. He corraled the woman into the same room as the teenager and bound her in a similar fashion. Feeling confident that they couldn't move or escape, he wandered through the rest of the home, located a seven-year-old, tied her up, and left her in her bedroom.

He returned to the teenager and her mother. They begged for him to leave them alone, but their pleas were answered continually with "shut up" whispered harshly. The intruder purposely didn't move his mouth when he spoke, and every word he said was through clenched teeth – perhaps in an effort to disguise his voice. He asked them questions and gave them directions, and if they replied, he'd again whisper at them to "shut up."

He raped the mother and daughter, and he then began ransacking and rummaging through the house. He asked them for money, and he went to the medicine cabinet and rifled through various bottles of medication. He inquired about their contents as he went. The attacker continually called them "ladies," he told them he wasn't "in a hurry," and at times, when it grew quiet, he told them that he was "still here." He cursed at them, saying "motherfucker" several times.

The victims described him as "in control" and "cool, calm, and collected."

The offender took items out of the refridgerator and ate them, and then he sexually assaulted the older two women again. At some point, he moved the seven-year-old girl into the same room as the others. It's unclear, but she may have witnessed one of the sexual assaults – perhaps the reason a newspaper article claimed that he committed what they termed as "sex perversions" on the child.

He finally left the house at 6:30 AM, stealing a ring and some coins on his way out.

The victims didn't get a very good look at the assailant, mostly due to the trauma of the situation and the fact that the room was very dark. One victim felt that he was a black male because of the way he said "motherfucker." The other victim felt that he was a white male. They described him as being in his early twenties, 5'6" or 5'7", 150 lbs, with a thin build. He appeared to wear a homemade mask, military- style camouflage clothing, and he wielded a fairly large buck knife. At a follow-up interview with police, the victim who had initially felt that he was black revealed that it was too dark to determine the race of the assailant, and that he could've been white. The police recreated the lighting conditions, and the victim confirmed that she couldn't determine the race of the assailant based on what she saw during the attack.

The offender was described as having a small penis – a description given in several East Area Rapist assaults. He wore a green army-style t-shirt, a fatigue hat with a small bill and flat top, "Vietnam" boots with leather and fabric, and "bush"-style pants with large pockets. The pants were tucked into the boots and his shirt was buttoned all the way up.

These M.O. factors, some of them quite distinctive, mirror East Area Rapist attacks exactly – even the order in which the activities occur. It seems very likely to many researchers and investigators that this was an EAR attack – especially given the burglary activity in the area before and after the event. It should also be emphasized that this attack was very close, geographically, to EAR Attacks #1, #3, #6, #8, and #15 – not to mention the Maggiore murders.

The victims' estimate of the offender's height was on the low side for Visalia Ransacker / East Area Rapist sightings, but there were plenty of outliers when it came to descriptions of height during both series. In this assault, where the victims couldn't see him very clearly, some of the estimates related to the physical description of the offender might have been a little off.

Visalia: Prowler and Phone Calls
October 21st, 1975 1:30 PM to 2:45 PM
2300 block of West Royal Oaks Drive

A prowler appeared at the doorstep of the same residence on West Royal Oaks Drive that we mentioned earlier in the chapter. On the same afternoon that the prowler appeared, the resident received a hang-up phone call and then a harassing phone call.

Sacramento: Burglary
October 22nd, 1975 Daytime / Evening
10300 block of Malaga Way

Three days later after the thirty-nine-year-old woman scared off the intruder at her residence, her son returned home from work to discover that the house had been burglarized. Only coins were taken.

Visalia: Ransackings

October 24th, 1975 Evening
W Campus Ave, S Redwood St, and S County Center Dr

The Ransacker committed four burglaries and two attempted entries.

This was one of the first extensive strings of ransackings since late August 1975 – a true return to form. It seemed that throughout September and October, he'd been trying to escalate and commit some kind of home-invasion kidnapping or rape offense. It's possible that the attack committed in Sacramento on October 21st was a fulfillment of that and afterwards, he resumed prior offense patterns.

If the attack was indeed him, of course. Now that the basic information has been introduced, the next section attempts to boil down the complicated timeline to a cleaner format so that the logistics can be studied a bit better.

(chart begins on the next page)

The following is a chart of the events broken up by date. The time, city, and type of activity is noted for each entry:

October 16th, 1975
- Early morning/previous night | Sacramento | Smashed streetlight
- 7:50 AM | Visalia | Harassing phone call

Between October 17th and October 19th, 1975
- Time unknown | Sacramento | Burglary

October 18th, 1975
- Between 12:00 AM and 10:00 AM | Sacramento | Hot prowl
- Between 5:30 PM and 9:15 PM | Sacramento | Burglary
- Between 6:30 PM and 9:00 PM | Sacramento | Burglary

October 19th, 1975
- After 11:00 PM | Sacramento | Burglar chased away

October 20th, 1975
- 10:00 AM | Visalia | Suspicious person on bike
- 9:40 PM | Visalia | Prowler on S Emerald Ct

October 21st, 1975
- 4:00 AM to 6:30 AM | Sacramento | Home-invasion rape
- 1:30 PM to 2:45 PM | Visalia | Prowler and phone calls

October 22nd, 1975
- Daytime/Evening | Sacramento | Burglary

October 24th, 1975
- Evening | Visalia | 4 ransackings and 2 attempted burglaries

It's important to note that aside from the events on the October 24th, technically none of the events described can be *confirmed* as being the work of the Visalia Ransacker / East Area Rapist, though the M.O. links are so astounding that most investigators and researchers are quick to include most of them. If the incidents *are* the work of one offender, there's just barely enough wiggle room in the timeline to make it all work.

But the timeline is indeed very tight. Keep in mind that Sacramento is a three and a half hour drive from Visalia under near-perfect conditions, and we have to factor in the need for sleep as well. If the VR/EAR is responsible for most of this, then he did quite a bit of traveling in a small window of time to commit all of these offenses – and on very little sleep.

But as unlikely as some of this might seem at first glance, the East Area Rapist case is filled with examples of him doing just that. Prowling in one area of town, appearing in the next to attack, prowling in another city, making phone calls to other locations, almost all at once. To illustrate this, here are the two examples that show his tightest attack windows:

On October 18th, 1976, the EAR had just committed his seventh canonical assault, which took place in Carmichael (another area in East Sacramento). Less than 24 hours later, he was attempting a rape in Rancho Cordova, which was about nine miles away by car. Not exactly the same type of distance, but it's an example of two attacks within a close timeframe.

In June and early July of 1978, the East Area Rapist alternated attacks between Modesto and Davis, sometimes in short-order and with prowling incidents seeming to occur almost simultaneously. In one instance, he attacked in both cities during roughly a twenty-four-hour period. Modesto and Davis are about a hundred miles away from each other, which is isn't quite the distance between

Sacramento and Visalia, but it demonstrates the same type of proclivity toward attacking and prowling in different cities during the same tight timeframe.

There's more precedent for the offender when it came to traveling great distances for his crimes. During the Golden State Killer murders that this offender committed between 1979 and 1986, the offender sometimes traveled over three hundred miles to commit his crimes. DNA-connected murders occurred in Goleta, Ventura, Dana Point, and Irvine – indications that he wasn't averse to traveling a great distance at all.

Let's take a closer look at the Visalia/Sacramento timeline to see how much travel would really be involved and how many back-and-forth trips would've been needed. We can throw the smashed streetlight incident out as being unrelated if we want to, or we could assume that he spent some days in Sacramento up until the 16th. On the morning of the 16th, he phoned a victim right after her husband left and told her that he knows she's alone. Could the VR/EAR have done this from Sacramento? Absolutely. He could've stalked the victims, determined their schedule, and then rang them up at the appropriate time. If the husband answered, he could've put down the phone. If the wife answered, he knew that she was probably alone, and so he threatened her. It would still make more sense for him to be in Visalia, watch the husband leave, and *then* call, but if we have probable activity from him in Sacramento, it's just as valid to theorize that he could've called her from a distance. Either idea works.

From the 17th until almost midnight on the 19th, incidents are only occurring in Sacramento. The next time we have anything in the VR files is at 10:00 AM on the 20th for the bicyclist sighting. That sighting is one of the least likely ones to be related to the VR series, but it doesn't matter for the purposes of this timeline – we can take it or leave it because there's a prowling incident on the same night in Visalia that *does* seem very likely to be related. Despite a low weight estimate given by the witness, the circumstances and description have a lot in common with the VR/EAR. He'd even hit in that area before.

That puts him as likely being in Visalia at 9:45 PM on the 20th. He could've arrived there anytime during the day, assuming he wasn't the bicyclist.

The home-invasion rape in Sacramento took place about six hours after the late sighting in Visalia. That would give him enough time to drive to Sacramento, prowl, prepare, and commit the crime. Then he seems to be physically present on West Royal Oaks Drive in Visalia about seven hours after the assault. This is a fairly long stretch without sleep, but the EAR phase of the case is full of these. If he had slept at any point during the day on the 20th, then it's not an issue at all, and there seemed to be something in the offender's mental or physical makeup that allowed him to run without sleep while fired up to attack.

There's plenty of time to travel between the two locations. It seems that he made one more trip back to Sac for that final burglary, and then on the 24th, he was definitely back in Visalia committing ransackings. No more activity in Sacramento has been found for the subsequent time period or for any of the months immediately before it.

Obviously, this timeline *does* seem to be more trouble than its worth, but we're certainly not dealing with an offender who was motivated by convenience or logic. The VR/EAR/GSK went through a lot of extra steps to make sure that he couldn't be caught or identified, including traveling great distances and committing crimes at odd times. Committing them back-to-back in different locales even seemed to be part of his strategy – during the earliest East Area Rapist crimes, he would literally alternate between Rancho Cordova and Carmichael almost as if on a schedule, with a Citrus Heights assault thrown into the mix occasionally to keep the pattern from being immediately discovered.

The takeaway is that yes, it *is* possible for him to have committed most or all of the crimes during this time period. Someday it may be discovered that the October 21st rape wasn't him after all, but given the VR/EAR-style burglaries that occurred all around it and how strong the M.O. correlation seems to fit, a link certainly seems possible.

Speaking of the burglaries, let's look one more time at how *similar* some of the burglaries in Sacramento were to the ones that were being committed in Visalia. There are some notable differences of course (burnt matches, stealing outerwear rather than undershirts, etc), but for the most part, they read almost exactly the same. Stealing coins from a piggybank, leaving valuables behind, moving pictures, taking rings that mean something victims... the list goes on. For some, this helps iron out the inevitable problem that arises from including the October 21st rape – if the offender had escalated to home-invasion rapes, why was he content with going back to Visalia to just continue peeping, prowling, and ransacking?

It might be helpful to look at the peeping, prowling, and ransacking through a different lens – with the idea that the burglaries weren't the goal, but rather that the peeping, prowling, and ransackings were just steps in the process of gathering intelligence on potential assault victims and trying to determine the best time/place to strike and invade homes with live victims. It may be that the rape in Sacramento had satisfied that urge for a little while – long enough for him to realize that the stakes were high and that he had to proceed carefully if he didn't want a repeat of the Snelling confrontation. Since he had been so active in Visalia, this type of crime would've increased the heat tremendously. And if he were actually *living* in or near Visalia at the time, the stakes were quite a bit higher to his personal life. It made sense, in a twisted way, to go out of town to another area that was clearly a comfort zone to experiment with this type of crime.

It's difficult, of course, to base too many theories around these events. As we mentioned, many of them are still up in the air. Intelligent readers can decide for themselves which incidents are likely to be authentic VR/EAR events, and whether the M.O. for the rape or the burglaries seems to match what's known about the Visalia Ransacker or East Area Rapist series.

There are still many more points to discuss when it comes to links or potential links between the VR and EAR/GSK series. We dive into those later in the book. For complete details about *all* of the known East Area Rapist / Golden State Killer crimes, our 600+ page book, *Case Files of the East Area Rapist / Golden State Killer* (by Kat Winters and Keith Komos), is available.

October 24th, 1975 Incidents

The crimes that took place on October 24th, mentioned briefly in the previous chapter, were certainly a return to form for the Ransacker. It had been over five weeks since he'd attempted to kidnap the girl at the Snelling residence, and it's quite possible that he'd sexually assaulted a group of women in Sacramento on October 21st (though the event was not connected to the Visalia Ransacker at the time). Now it seemed that he was eager to resume his path of destruction through Visalia.

He returned to the South Redwood Street / West Campus Avenue area for these crimes. Where else? He'd been relentlessly preying on this area since nearly the beginning. It was one street away from South Whitney Street (Snelling murder) and very close to South Verde Vista Street (over a dozen stalking/prowling incidents).

If there was any area that was a comfort zone for him in Visalia, this was it. It was where he'd identified and stalked many potential targets, and after coming down from what might've been an incredibly busy week bouncing between two cities, this was where he could go without having to spend time learning the lay of the land.

VR #124 – *Ransacking*
October 24th, 1975 | W Campus Ave

On Friday, October 24th, sometime between 5:30 PM and 8:15 PM, the VR entered a single-story residence on West Campus Avenue while the victims were away.

He gained entry by prying open the rear sliding glass door. He didn't open any additional doors or windows inside the residence, which was odd for him, though the most likely reason was that the windowsills were covered with decorative items and it would've been noisy and too much trouble to mess with.

Most of the rooms in the house were ransacked heavily. He also opened drawers in the kitchen, but he didn't appear to have rummaged through them.

He stole quite a bit from the scene, making off with coins, cash, a single cufflink from a pair, two single earrings (each from a pair), a new package of men's underwear, a new package of six men's sleeveless t-shirts, and two of the woman's nightgowns. He also stole weapons – a knife from the kitchen and an old policeman's baton/billy club.

His exit was through the same sliding glass door that he had used to enter the residence.

The head of the household was a retired man in his early seventies. He'd worked for the Tulare County government before he retired. His wife lived at the home with him.

Up until the ransackings on this particular evening, the only weaponry that the offender had stolen involved firearms and ammunition. Before this night was over, he stole a knife, a police baton, and a hammer. These are weapons that operate much more quietly than guns – perhaps something that he'd had on his mind since the Snelling incident and perhaps in relation to the rape in Sacramento.

The theft of the police baton deserves special mention here because in early East Area Rapist attacks, the offender appeared to prefer the use of blunt instruments rather than firearms or even knives. In a burglary that preceded Attack #2 in July 1976, the EAR was caught by a resident inside a garage. The EAR, wielding a wooden paddle, beat the resident so badly that he had to go to the emergency room and get stitches put in. At Attack #3, which took place in late August 1976, the EAR beat a woman with an antique police billy club – a club much like the one he'd stole at this very burglary, in fact. In both instances, he had a gun with him, but he preferred the use of the quieter, more "personal" blunt instrument. A few years later, when he began murdering his victims, his preferred method of killing was to bludgeon them to death with a blunt object like a fireplace log, a lamp, or a yard tool.

Even though his major crimes during the VR phase seemed to involve firearms, burglaries like this one hint at events that would transpire later on.

VR #125 – *Ransacking*
October 24th, 1975 | W Campus Ave

On Friday, October 24th, between 10:30 AM and 10:54 PM, the VR entered a single-story residence on West Campus Avenue while the victims were away. This house was situated next-door to the other home on West Campus Avenue that had been ransacked that night.

Just like he had done at the other scene, he entered by prying open the rear sliding glass door. He opened a window to use as an emergency escape route.

It appeared that this ransacking was incomplete, possibly cut short by the homeowners returning to their residence or, more likely, cut short by the police arriving next-door around 8:15 PM. Because he was interrupted at this ransacking and probably fled before doing everything that he wanted to do, the half-ransacked state of the house offered a fascinating insight into his process.

It seemed only the kitchen and the master bedroom had been entered by the VR. In the master bedroom, he opened all of the drawers and removed the woman's undergarments. He tossed some of them into the hallway, and he took the lingerie items and folded them carefully on the bed. He dumped out a jewelry box and placed the monogrammed lid on the bed on top of the lingerie. While in the master bedroom, he also opened a coin bank and took the contents.

Apparently he went for the kitchen next. Four drawers were found to be open, and they were each pulled out about halfway and lined up parallel (each jutting out to the exact same position). It was an odd, intentional display, and it didn't appear that he had rummaged through the drawers.

The responding officers felt that while he was in the kitchen, he saw the lights from the police arriving. He most likely exited the house immediately, and he apparently he forgot his flashlight – it was left behind on the counter.

Since he was known to open windows for the purposes of escape, officers carefully examined the window that he had left open. There were no shoe prints on the other side of it, and none of the dust on the frame had been disturbed. It indicated to them that he had probably fled out the back door near the kitchen (that was one of the reasons that they felt he'd been in the kitchen *after* the bedroom). One investigator wondered if the main reason that he left the windows open was to hear what was going on outside. It's quite possible, though it was also clear that he intended to use the windows for escape since he would frequently remove the window screens.

A man and woman lived at the residence. The woman was about fifty years old and worked as a secretary.

Investigators could clearly tell by the M.O. of these two burglaries that they were Visalia Ransacker crimes. Eager to catch him after the murder of Claude Snelling, they processed the crime scenes as thoroughly as they could.

One of the areas that they spent a considerable amount of time on was the perimeter of the residence. Hoping to find shoe prints that indicated where he had come from or where he'd gone to, what they found instead was a deposit of dirt and leaves on top of a fence. The VR had climbed it. Between that and the fact that the Ransacker had pried the rear sliding glass doors at both homes, the officers surveyed the surrounding geography and generated a few theories as to his comings and goings.

They decided that the VR had probably entered the area from the north, which was made up of a short, hidden road tucked away between West Campus Avenue and West Pecan Court. The road is referred to as Woodland Street. This little alcove of Visalia was pitch black and fairly secluded, making it the perfect cover. The VR had most likely observed the residences and had determined that the coast was clear at both of them. He then probably traversed the backyards, one of which didn't have a fence. When he escaped, he left in a hurry and had apparently scrambled over the closest fenced-in area.

Investigators could clearly see the pry marks in the frame of the sliding glass doors. He had taken a screwdriver with a 7/16" head (not a flat pry tool like he had probably used at some of the other scenes) and had forced it into the track of the doors, easily popping them out and breaking the locks in the process. Future versions of these sliding glass doors would include a deadbolt lock in the part of the track that ran along the floor, making this type of entry a bit more difficult. But at the time, forcing through these doors was a relatively simple process. When he operated as the East Area Rapist, sliding glass doors were his preferred entry point.

The timing of both of these ransackings is probably closer to 8:00 PM, given that officers felt that they had unknowingly scared off the VR when they responded to the first burglary.

Like many of the ransackings before them, these homes are situated immediately to the west of the College of the Sequoias, where Professor Claude Snelling had taught journalism for several years.

VR #126 – *Ransacking*
October 24th, 1975 | S Redwood St

On October 24th, between 10:45 AM and 11:15 PM, the VR entered a single-story home on South Redwood Street while the victim was away from the residence.

He attempted to pry multiple entrances before finally spending what must have been a significant amount of time chopping away at a door and prying it loose.

Once inside, he opened a window. He didn't remove the screen, so was this a possible escape route or had he been spooked by a near-miss with police on West Campus Avenue, which made him decide to listen more closely to the outside? And if interrupted, was he more likely to attack or more likely to flee?

The bedrooms and the kitchen were ransacked. In the bedrooms, he removed women's undergarments from the drawers. The bras were found on the floor in various locations near the rooms they'd been taken from, and the panties were all found stacked neatly on top of the pillows.

He stole a wood-handled claw hammer from the kitchen, and he left a flashlight on a lawn chair outside.

He exited through a sliding glass door.

The head of the household was a female adult, about seventy years old. She was retired.

Tennis shoe prints were found in a northern corner of the backyard. These prints were consistent with other Visalia Ransacker scenes. Technicians determined that the Ransacker had probably entered and exited the property from that location. Another shoe print was found near a door.

Much has been written about the VR's infatuation with high school and college students, but he didn't shy away from toying with the undergarments of women who fell outside of that demographic, either. It's difficult to know if he was aware of the ages of his victims or if he even knew who the occupants *were* at all of the homes that he entered, though. Many homes had photos of the residents on the mantels, nightstands, and walls, and in some cases he could certainly tell by other items in the house who his victims might be. Law Enforcement has theorized that since he intended to embarrass or humiliate women by displaying their undergarments in such a fashion, his infatuation of high school and college students wouldn't have mattered during this activity and that there'd be no age cutoff.

Even though the time window for this ransacking is rather large, it's assumed that it happened after the West Campus Avenue ones because this residence is situated in between those and the ones further west that were ransacked later that night. We *know* that the ones further west occurred after the West Campus Avenue ones based on the time of night that the resident was away from his apartment in one of those, along with some prowling reports from that night, so a pretty solid timeline can be constructed here.

What's odd about the two ransackings that we've just discussed is that the offender left a flashlight behind at *both* of them. How many flashlights did he have on him at any given time? Were either of them taken from the residence and simply moved? The documentation isn't clear. If he had already dropped two flashlights and was still continuing on, does that mean that he had a third flashlight with him? The month before, he had dropped another one on South Redwood Street. Why was he leaving flashlights there and rarely anywhere else?

Since a hammer was stolen at this crime, one quick interesting footnote: the man arrested for the Visalia Ransacker / Golden State Killer crimes, Joseph DeAngelo, was fired from his job as a police officer in 1979 after he was caught shoplifting dog repellant and a hammer.

VR #127 – *Prowler*
October 24th, 1975 | S Redwood St

At 8:30 PM on the night of October 24th, 1975, the resident next-door to the house that was ransacked on South Redwood Street noticed a prowler. A prowler had been spotted near this home just a few weeks before, on October 3rd. On that occasion, the subject had been in a neighbor's backyard and had jumped the fence when spotted.

It seemed he was back, and that he was on the move in the neighborhood. Other neighbors heard noises near their homes during the late evening hours of October 24th, and the noises continued off and on for close to two hours (roughly 8:30 PM to 10:30 PM). One of residents even saw a large figure running in between houses.

After the VR burglarized the home on South Redwood Street, he ransacked an apartment directly behind it on South County Center Drive and then attempted to enter two others. When police began tracking the Ransacker's shoe prints, tracing the route that he took around the apartment complex on South County Center Drive, they determined that the Ransacker had entered the complex from the rear. The apartments backed up to the same backyard on South Redwood Street where a neighbor had spotted the prowler on October 3rd. The spot on the fence that the Ransacker had used was the exact same spot where the resident had seen the prowler a few weeks before. Fresh shoe prints made it clear that he'd again used the same pathway and the same spot, and because of the ransackings that took place on the other side of the fence and the matching shoe prints, the events could be definitively tied to the Visalia Ransacker.

This series of reports gives tremendous insight into the VR's method of operation on the nights he was active. Noises were heard in the vicinity for about two hours, and somewhere in that time window, the home on South Redwood Street was ransacked (maybe even slightly before). It appears that the VR was prowling about, looking for other homes to peep into, ransack, or attack. The next incident occurred sometime after 10:45 PM, which is fifteen minutes after the noises on South Redwood Street stopped. It's a prime example of how much time the VR spent out in the neighborhoods looking for potential victims.

VR #128 – *Ransacking*
October 24th or 25th, 1975 | S County Center Dr

Sometime between 10:45 PM on Friday, October 24th and 1:00 AM on Saturday, October 25th, the VR entered an apartment on South County Center Drive while the victims were away from the residence.

He entered by prying open a sliding glass door. Once inside, he engaged the chain lock on the front door so that he'd be alerted to the resident's return and have enough time to get away.

He ransacked the residence. He didn't come across any women's undergarments because, apparently unbeknownst to the Ransacker, most of the female clothing items were packed into suitcases. These suitcases were located at the residence, but they appeared to be undisturbed. Either he didn't see them, thought they were empty, or there was a psychological reason for him wanting to *only* take things from drawers (perhaps because the items in drawers would definitely belong to the resident and the items in suitcases could belong to anyone, or for some other reason).

He found a container of Vaseline hand lotion in the downstairs bathroom, opened it, and tossed the cap onto the floor. When he was "done" with the lotion, he left the open container in the bathroom. He also went through the bathroom drawers, collected the couple's medications, and dumped all of the pills down the sink.

The offender stole coins, cash, three rings, three single earrings from a pair, and a pin.

The head of the household was a male in his mid/late thirties.

The Ransacker left through the same sliding glass door that he'd used to enter the residence. Outside, his shoe prints were found, and the prints roughly matched shoe impressions found at other ransacking scenes.

The chain lock, sliding glass door entry, interest in medication, and other factors not only mirrored previous VR incidents, but they mirrored the events that had occurred earlier in the week in Sacramento as well. What made this one a little different from previous burglaries was that the VR took quite a risk by prowling and burglarizing an apartment complex. Apartments tend to have decent lighting (which means that there's a better chance of someone spotting a prowler), they're more densely populated (more people to spot something suspicious), and they're usually taller than one story (which means people are on higher ground and can see a burglar from above).

With as much as he'd stolen from the West Campus Avenue ransackings, it's possible that he had to use a vehicle for transportation if he didn't live nearby or have somewhere to stash his spoils. We know that he hit the West Campus Avenue homes first, and it's possible that he parked over there, somewhere near College of the Sequoias. It's also possible that he parked near this apartment complex and traversed over to the college and then back, ransacking along the way. Many of his burglaries around this time period were a bit further west (particularly the West Royal Oaks Drive incidents, which is a street that intersects with South County Center Drive), and a prowler, most likely the Ransacker, was seen escaping to this vicinity. Good cases can be made for him parking on either side of the ransackings that occurred on October 24th.

VR #129 – *Attempted Break-in*
October 24th or 25th, 1975 | S County Center Dr

The VR tried to enter another apartment in the same South County

Center Drive complex sometime late on Friday, October 24th (or possibly early in the morning on Saturday, October 25th) while the residents were away.

He pried at the window but was unable to gain entry.

VR #130 – *Attempted Break-in*
October 24th or 25th, 1975 | S County Center Dr

The VR tried to enter yet *another* apartment in the same South County Center Drive complex sometime late on Friday, October 24th (or possibly early in the morning on Saturday, October 25th) while the residents were away.

He pried at the window but was unsuccessful at gaining entry.

The pry marks found at these cases were studied, and it was determined that all of them matched. Both of these attempts, the *successful* entry at the apartment complex, the ransacking on South Redwood Street, and the two on West Campus Avenue were all pried at with the same tool – most likely a screwdriver with a 7/16" or ½" pry width.

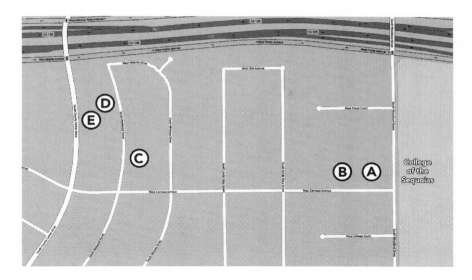

The location of ransackings, the prowlers, and the attempted ransackings that occurred on October 24th, 1975.

A) *VR #124 W Campus Ave ransacking*

B) *VR #125 W Campus Ave ransacking*

C) *VR #126 S Redwood St ransacking*

D) *VR #127 S Redwood St prowling incidents*

E) *VR #128, #129, #130 (a ransacking and two attempts) at the apartments on S County Center Dr*

Late October 1975 Ransacking

The Ransacker had a very particular kind of overconfidence – spending a good portion of September and October skulking about the very same streets where he was wanted for murder. It seemed his compulsion to commit these crimes and his desire to successfully claim a victim outweighed any fear or aversion he had of being caught. There wasn't much physical evidence tying the man himself to any of these crimes, so the smart thing would've been to simply stay out of the neighborhood and go somewhere else.

Since the VR seemed unwilling to do this, and since it seemed his ransacking pattern had resumed, the police began to grow more convinced that he'd stick to the area. Sensing an opportunity to catch him, they began setting traps. One officer would be posted at a dark corner to watch for any suspicious foot traffic. Another would be posted in a tree in the backyard of a family that had been prowled before. Others would patrol by bicycle.

Without any solid leads as to his identity, they felt that their best hope was to catch him in the act.

They also started to gather more information about how he operated. Since the Ransacker was an expert at not leaving any physical traces of himself (like fingerprints) but quite nonchalant about leaving shoe prints, the police installed sophisticated flourescent lights in several backyards to catch any new shoe tracks. This was in hopes of identifying any targets that were in the works and with an eye toward discovering his peeping habits.

These efforts came up frustratingly empty, and it was clear that the Ransacker wasn't in the area to the west of the College of the Sequoias as much as he'd been in the past. Perhaps he became aware of these traps somehow and decided to avoid them. Increased police interest in him after the Snelling murder may have even been what inspired him to make trips to Sacramento, where it seemed he'd been able to burglarize, rape, and terrorize without having to be as careful. And perhaps that was the reason that he began offending in different areas of Visalia once October started winding down.

The first location he chose away from the Whitney/Redwood and Campus area was old stomping grounds for him – a small area of West Kaweah Avenue that only consisted of a handful of homes. It's seems he'd abandoned the potential targets that he was working over on South Verde Vista Street, West Campus Avenue, South Redwood Street, and West Royal Oaks Drive. There were some potential targets on West Kaweah Avenue that he'd had brushes with before, and now it seemed he was turning more of his attention back to them.

The first indication of this was with this ransacking.

VR #131 – *Ransacking*
October 29th to October 31st, 1975 | W Kaweah Ave

Sometime between Wednesday, October 29th at 3:00 PM and Friday, October 31st at 12:45 PM, the VR entered a single-story house on West Kaweah Avenue while the victims were away.

He entered by prying open a door. Once inside, he not only engaged the chain lock to prevent the resident from surprising him, but he put

313

items against the door that would make a loud sound and alert him. The VR also disabled a plug-in light timer (the kind of device that automatically turns lamps on or off based on a schedule that the resident inputs).

He ransacked the bedrooms, taking time to remove women's undergarments and arrange them on and near the bed. He also found a family photo inside the residence and posed it carefully in an odd position at the foot of the bed.

He stole an empty brown leather suitcase, and he also raided the pantry and stole a dozen cans of vegetables and fruit.

At the end of the burglary, he exited through a sliding glass door.

When police responded to the scene, they found a flashlight wrapped in a dishtowel at the front door. They also found a candle in the backyard.

The scene was dusted carefully for fingerprints, but it was obvious to technicians that the Ransacker had worn gloves. Clear shoe tracks were found though, and they were cataloged carefully.

The male victim was the superintendent of a large public park located south of the College of the Sequoias. He lived at the residence with his wife and family.

This ransacking was located in the heart of his West Kaweah Avenue prowling area… a small lane of properties that would eventually end in a shootout with the police (and subsequently, the Ransacker's disappearance). Several incidents occurred in this small area:

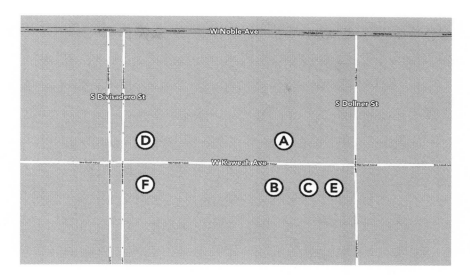

The area of W Kaweah Ave hit hardest by the VR. Some of these marks represent multiple events.

The Ransacker spent a lot of time operating here. Whether it was because he was already stalking the resident on the east side of this short area, or if it was because the homes were near where he originated from (living, parking, etc.), or if there was another reason, we don't really know.

It seemed that in the 1975 ransackings, the offender had dedicated himself to more intricate "displays" of his victims' possessions than he had done in 1974. The burglaries in the second half of 1975 especially saw him doing more with photos, personal items, monogrammed jewelry boxes, and cherished personal possessions. What would be the symbolic purpose of setting a family photo on top of a bed where he had just arranged the woman's undergarments? What was the offender trying to say with that, and what would motivate him to take the time to do it? It's interesting to see how the idea of the family unit and commentary on the sexuality of the woman overlaps in this offender's mind.

The candle in the yard was a good find – in some instances, perhaps he used candles while inside the victims' homes to provide low-level light without attracting too much attention. It would make him less likely to be spotted from the outside than the use of a flashlight or turning on the victims' lights, especially if neighbors knew that the victims were supposed to be out of town. At one of the October burglaries in Sacramento, several spent matches were found in the house. Perhaps he had used a candle at that scene as well. He would've known that this family was away for an extended period because of the light timer that he unplugged, so worrying about neighbors being alerted to his presence is a likely scenario. And he did seem a little extra paranoid or extra careful in this one based on the way that he engaged the chain lock and placed items against the door.

Two other things are worth noting. The first is that the Ransacker was striking on different nights of the week at this point – not just weekends. Perhaps his obsession was reaching a new height, or maybe he was intentionally avoiding the various police stakeouts and patrols that were starting to appear again. While it was theorized by some that he didn't live in the Visalia area based on the burglaries only occurring on weekends for much of the series, at the rate and frequency he was prowling and offending during this time period (and the odd selection of days), it seems likely that he lived in or near the area he was hitting during the last months of 1975.

The second detail worth noting is that he had started routinely abandoning flashlights at the scene. This was the fourth time since September (the first being the one found after the Snelling murder) that he'd done this, and it's a risky thing to leave behind because of potential mistakes regarding fingerprints. The first couple times, the abandonment of a flashlight seemed accidental. Adding more to the mix makes it seem intentional. Not only can fingerprints be found on the flashlights themselves, but some crooks have been caught because their fingerprints were found on the batteries *inside* the flashlights. That wasn't the case here, unfortunately.

November 2^{nd,} 1975 Incidents

Just a few days later, he was back at it again.

The Ransacker obviously didn't want to get caught, but he obviously didn't want to *stop*, either. Police and residents were on high alert, and it must've been getting harder and harder for the offender to steer clear of them. Changing days had helped, but it's possible that the VR still preferred weekends (due to work, family, or some other constraint). When the weekend came, the VR did the logical thing when he didn't change times – he changed areas. Not much, but just enough to stay outside of the dragnet.

It worked in the sense that he wasn't apprehended that night. It probably didn't go as smoothly as planned though, because he was seen by two different residents. Perhaps he wasn't familiar with this part of the city and didn't know where the best shadows were. Or perhaps he knew that he was only passing through and thus was more complacent with his activities. Despite things not going as smoothly as usual, he still got two ransackings in.

In the end, this area seems to have been chosen out of necessity and didn't appear to be part of his long-term plans. No further activity was recorded here.

VR #132 – *Prowler*
November 2nd, 1975 | W Evergreen Ave

A prowler was seen in a garage on West Evergreen Avenue at 7:40 PM on Sunday, November 2nd. He was seen clearly and described as a male adult in his late twenties, "pudgy," with light brown hair. Less than a hundred feet away, two burglaries attributed to the Visalia Ransacker were committed during the same general timeframe, making this an important sighting.

VR #133 – *Ransacking*
November 2nd, 1975 | W Country Ave

On Sunday, November 2nd, sometime between 5:30 PM and 8:00 PM, a single-story residence on West Country Avenue was burglarized by the VR while the residents were away.

He entered the house through an unlocked window. The window had a screen, which he virtually destroyed by forcing his way through it. No pry marks were found, which might indicate that the Ransacker routinely tried multiple doors and windows to see if one was unlocked before choosing one to pry open.

Once he'd made his way in, he opened additional windows and ransacked the home extensively.

No only did he remove women's undergarments from drawers and place them nearby, but he hung some of them on the baby's crib, which was located in a separate room.

He also uncovered a hundred dollars in cash while rummaging through the residence. He left it at the head of the bed in the guest bedroom near the pillows, situated on top of female undergarments.

It was an obvious "look what I found" and "I don't need your money" kind of a gesture, the kind he made all throughout the VR and EAR crimes.

He also left an open jewelry box near the head of the bed. The underclothing, money, and jewelry box were posed/arranged in a deliberate fashion.

He opened the drawers in the kitchen, but it didn't appear that he rifled through them. Other drawers in the house (those not located in bedrooms) were also opened, but those contents didn't seem to be disturbed either. As usual, it was the bedrooms that received most of his attention.

He stole 12-gauge shotgun shells from the residence, an empty purse, and a man's wedding ring. The ring was quite distinctive: it was light gold, had a bright stone on top, and had lines engraved on the side (as well as the number "750" engraved on the inside).

He left the scene through a door.

The head of the household was a man in his mid thirties. He worked as a supervisor at an electric company. Other victims lived in the house as well.

The police went over the scene carefully, and they found latent fingerprints on some of the items that the VR had handled. These prints were carefully preserved and run against prints taken at previous Visalia Ransacker scenes, but no match was found. It was likely that the fingerprints belonged to friends and family.

As we mentioned in the introduction, the crime scenes / incidents on the night of November 2nd, 1975 were geographical outliers, occurring south of any of his usual attack areas.

VR #134 – *Ransacking*
November 2nd, 1975 | W Country Ave

Sometime between 2:00 PM and 8:15 PM on Sunday, November 2nd, the VR entered another residence on West Country Avenue while the victims were away. This home was located next-door to the other West Country Avenue ransacking that took place on the same night.

The VR entered through an unlocked sliding glass door. Like the burglary before it, no pry marks were found, again seeming to indicate that the VR probably checked for unlocked doors and windows before attempting to pry anything open. Of course, it's also possible that he wasn't interested in forcing entry that night and was merely looking for easy hits.

Once inside the home, he opened a window to use as a possible escape route. He removed the screen from the inside and placed it on the bed.

He ransacked the residence. For some reason, this time he threw woman's undergarments onto the *floor* and threw *regular* clothing onto the *bed*.

He found a coin bank, opened it, and stole its contents. Surprisingly, there was a stack of coins in a bedroom that he left alone. Perhaps the VR only cared for coins that were in piggybanks, jars, or purses – he may not have been after the coins themselves, but rather, he might've been interested in what those coins represented.

A window was used for his exit.

The head of the household was a man his mid/late twenties. He worked as an accountant. His family lived there with him.

Shoe impressions were found at the scene. Officers found some of them near the patio, and they followed them through the backyard to a fence. They determined that the VR had climbed over it – his shoe impressions were found on the other side (which was the backyard of a residence on West Evergreen Avenue). The people who lived at the home on West Evergreen Avenue where the VR had climbed the fence had experienced prowling activity that night. Their experience is detailed at the end of the chapter.

The shoe impressions were analyzed. They matched those found at other burglaries committed by the VR.

VR #135 – *Prowler*
November 2nd, 1975 | W Evergreen Ave

At 8:30 PM, a prowler was once again spotted in a garage at a house on West Evergreen Avenue. This was reported by the same resident that had spotted the prowler less than an hour before. The witness felt that it was the same man.

The description attached to this second sighting adds a bit more detail than the first. He was described as a while male, late twenties, with a "pudgy face" and light brown hair. This sighting notes that he had on some kind of mask around his face, but his hair was still visible.

VR #136 – *Prowler*
November 2nd, 1975 | W Evergreen Ave

Prowling activity also occurred at the residence three houses to the east of the garage where the prowler had been spotted.

This resident's dog began barking loudly at the front of the house. It quieted down after a few minutes, but then ran to the back of the house and began barking furiously again. A man was never seen, but noises coming from the yard were reported.

This home sat behind the first one on West Country Avenue that we discussed earlier. It's not known if the prowler was simply passing through this resident's yard, or if he was trying to peep in at the woman who lived there. Nearby shoe prints confirmed that it was indeed the Ransacker who had been on their property, though. It seemed the dog had been an effective deterrent.

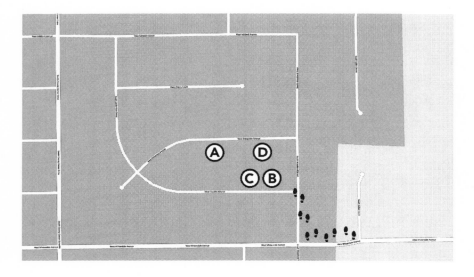

Ransacking and prowling incidents from November 2nd, 1975, along with the location of shoe prints that were found nearby.

   A)   *VR #132 W Evergreen Ave prowler at 7:40 PM and 8:30 PM*

   B)   *VR #133 W Country Ave ransacking*

   C)   *VR #134 W Country Ave ransacking*

   D)   *VR #136 Another prowler on W Evergreen Ave*

Careful tracking of nearby shoe prints showed that the offender had approached the area from the east. They appeared to originate near the intersection of West Whitendale Avenue and South Sallee Court. According to written impressions of the officers, he most likely came from a vacant field. The field is no longer there – now it's a strip mall.

Did the Ransacker park transportation in this dark, secluded area? All of this occurred somewhat early in the evening, but since it was November, the blanket of darkness would've been fairly thick. He would've had more than enough cover.

This tactic, where he parked in a secluded area nearby and then approached on foot, was one that he used quite a bit during the East Area Rapist and Golden State Killer crimes.

November 6th, 1975 Ransackings

The VR might've been avoiding familiar locales on the night of November 2nd, but that certainly wasn't the case on November 6th. Not only did he hit a house for the second time in a little less than a year, but his other two ransackings took place next-door to homes that he'd hit in the past. He was targeting familiar territory, and apparently he worked up an appetite while doing it: he stole quite a bit of canned food from his victims at two of these ransackings.

The theft of food was merely the latest kink in a chain that was getting stranger and more frightening by the day. And speaking of food, he also ate at one of the scenes – a strong parallel to one of the more distinctive behaviors that took place during East Area Rapist attacks throughout the late 1970s.

In *another* parallel to his East Area Rapist series, the offender stole some antique plates at one of these burglaries. He only did that one time in the EAR series that we know of, but it was notable because it was something that seemed so strange. His theft of the plates as the VR was equally odd.

The police had spent considerable time and effort to catch him before, but this was another one of those groups of incidents that made them say "enough is enough" and they committed themselves to spending as much time as they could and as many resources as it took to finally catch him in the act and bring him down.

VR #137 – *Ransacking*
November 6th, 1975 | W Seeger Ave

On Thursday afternoon, November 6th, between 3:00 PM and 4:30 PM, a single-story residence on West Seeger Avenue was ransacked. The victims were away when the burglary occurred.

This house had been hit by the Ransacker before, with the previous burglary occurring on December 16th, 1974 (VR #064).

The point of entry was determined to be an unlocked window. Once inside, he rummaged through the residence and removed female underclothing from the drawers. Rather than arranging them on the bed, as he was apt to do, he left some of the items (mostly pantyhose) on the kitchen table.

A sock filled with silver dollars was found on the floor. It's unclear whether one of the residents had put the coins into the sock or whether the VR bagged them himself. Roughly a month after this ransacking, the police confronted the VR on West Kaweah Avenue and during the skirmish, one of the items that he dropped was a sock that he had stuffed full of coins himself.

He stole cash from the scene and made his exit through a door, rather than a window or a sliding glass door.

A female adult in her mid thirties lived at the residence. She worked as a secretary. Her husband, roughly the same age, worked at a grocery store.

The police examined the scene in the afternoon. They dusted for fingerprints, and they *did* find some latent prints possibly belonging to the burglar. The prints were tested against others, but the result was negative.

Not only is this crime a geographical outlier considering the rest of the series, but the timing was quite odd – it was done in full daylight. When the variables fluctuate this much, it's important to examine everything we know about the burglary to make sure that it's even the same perpetrator. If we can establish that it was, we then need to see if we can find out what made him break his routine.

The modus operandi, plus the fact that the VR struck two more times in Visalia on this date, seemed to indicate that the burglar *was* definitely the VR. This residence was still in his normal attack zone – down in the extreme southwestern portion of it, though. Between the two days that he'd hit the city in November, he'd ventured further south than he'd gone in nearly two years of known/confirmed burglaries.

Since it's not far from where he had just hit a few days before, perhaps it can be chalked up to him simply expanding outward and trying different times of the day/week to throw off the police. It's also possible that he had a personal connection to this part of town – the South Demaree Street ransacking that was believed to be committed by him in June 1973 isn't far away, and if he *did* feel threatened by police but still wanted to continue, it would make sense to stick to a place where he felt most comfortable.

(*map featured on the following page*)

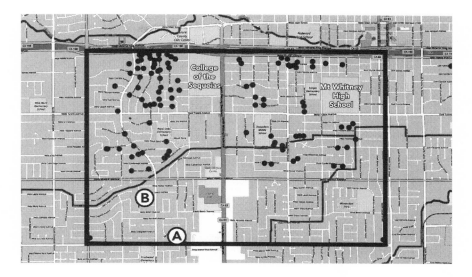

The Visalia Ransacker's normal attack zone makes up the big box, with most incidents marked. Inside are the W Country Ave/W Evergreen Ave ransackings from November 2nd, 1975, and a marker for the home on W Seeger Ave that was ransacked twice.

A) *The area on W Country Ave and W Evergreen Ave that was ransacked on November 2nd, 1975.*

B) *A home on W Seeger Ave that was ransacked on December 16th, 1974 and again on November 6th, 1975.*

We'll note again that this crime was committed in the afternoon and on a Thursday. Throwing the police off is one idea, but it's also possible that his living situation or work situation had changed.

Of course, the biggest oddity is that he'd hit this house before – on December 16th, 1974. What drove him to attack the *same house* in an area that was so atypical for him? What can be learned about his victimology or his stalking method? December 16th, 1974 had also been an atypical day for him to ransack – it was a Monday. What made this location so different?

With what we now know about his stalking activities and his laser-like focus on targeting specific girls and women during this time period, it might make sense to suggest that the woman of the house was a potential victim and that he was considering doing much worse. Entering the home twice over such a long period of time could mean that he had been stalking her for a long time, and now it seemed he was ready to put some of his plans into motion. He might've been assessing the situation one last time before contemplating an attack plan. Thankfully, no documented act of violence occurred at this residence or against this woman.

It's also possible, depending on which way he was traveling home the night of November 2nd, that he'd caught sight of this house again and for whatever reason decided to revisit it the next time he was out prowling. They're in the same general part of town.

VR #138 – *Ransacking*
November 6th, 1975 | W Tulare Ave

On Thursday, November 6th, between 5:45 PM and 9:50 PM, the VR entered a single-story residence on West Tulare Avenue while the victims were away from home. This ransacking was located two miles to the northeast of the house that the VR had ransacked on West Seeger Avenue earlier in the day.

The method of entry was a two-step process – the Ransacker entered a sun room by going through a window that the residents had left open (he had to pry through a window screen to do so, though), and then he pried open a door to get into the rest of the house.

Once inside, he opened curtains in the bedrooms, probably to keep watch for anyone's return or the police, who had no doubt learned of his burglary on West Seeger Avenue. He placed items on and against the door that would make a loud noise if he were to be interrupted. He also wedged a chair under the doorknob at the front door to prevent it from being opened.

The VR began dumping out jewelry boxes and ransacking the drawers in the bedroom. He took the woman's undergarments out and tossed them onto the bed in a seemingly cavalier fashion. On a nightstand or dresser in the bedroom, he spotted the photo of an attractive young female relative and turned it face-down. Nearby were one or more photos of children, and he turned those frames on their side, upside down, or also face-down.

Investigators determined that he ate and drank at the scene. Some of the items he removed from the refrigerator were left out and placed on the floor.

He stole several cans of food from the scene, and he also stole antique plates.

The head of the household was a retired man in his late eighties. His wife lived with him in the house.

The police found several shoe prints at the scene of this crime, mostly on the far side of the backyard. It appeared that the VR had entered the area from West Iris Court, a small street that dead-ended less than a hundred feet behind the residence. Police determined that the size and style of the shoe prints matched the other Visalia Ransacker scenes.

Some analysis was done on the pry marks, and it was determined that the pry tool used was most likely a screwdriver with a 7/16" pry width, which matched several of the other burglaries.

This ransacking was notable in a few ways. For one, breaking into this house was a little more complicated than some of the others because it was a two-step process. Another is that he'd messed with photos before, but it's still one of the more distinctive things that he did.

Two things happened here that echo the East Area Rapist phase of attacks quite loudly. One of them was the eating and drinking at the scene and then leaving the food out when he was done. The EAR would almost always eat and drink at the scene of his attacks (and even during many of his burglaries). Some of these later VR incidents started to show signs of that. Toward the end of the East Area Rapist series and during the Golden State Killer murder series, the offender seemed to drink milk at the scene of his crimes. In this burglary, he left a partially consumed carton of chocolate milk and a bottle of grape juice on the floor near the refrigerator.

Another interesting parallel to one of his later crimes was the theft of antique plates. The VR/EAR stole a lot of interesting things in during his extensive criminal career, and one of the most puzzling thefts was a set of Noritake china that was taken from an East Area Rapist attack in Concord (EAR Attack #37, which took place on October 7th, 1978). It's interesting that he stole antique plates at *this* home as well. By all accounts, it's an odd thing to steal and quite a bulky set of items to transport. In the case of the Concord attack, the VR/EAR used special carriers that came with the set to help him. It's unclear if he had the same luxury at this scene.

Since he stole canned food too, he must've had *some* way of transporting all of these items. And since this ransacking took place so far away from the one earlier in the day, it's possible that he drove to one or both of these locations.

And speaking of the canned food – one does have to wonder if the Visalia Ransacker consumed the canned food that he stole from this scene on the *plates* that he stole from this scene, and what kind of satisfaction that may have given him.

The Ransacker had preyed on this area before. It was located very close to the First Baptist Church of Visalia and close to an area that the Ransacker had targeted in the past. Whether this area was conducive to his activities because the church offered cover, or if he had other reasons, is unknown. But on November 29th, 1974, the house next-door to this residence had been burglarized by the VR and on May 31st, 1975, a residence situated one house away and across the street was burglarized. That's a lot of hits in a tiny area. Like Mt. Whitney High School and College of the Sequoias, the First Baptist Church location appeared to be an anchor point and a hotbed of activity.

VR #139 – Ransacking
November 6th, 1975 | S Oak Park

On the evening of Thursday, November 6th, between 6:30 PM and 10:15 PM, the VR entered a single-story house on South Oak Park while the victim was away from the residence. This home was located roughly half a mile north of the West Tulare Avenue ransacking, making November 6th one of the most geographically spread-out nights in the history of the VR case.

He entered the house by prying open a door. Once inside, he began ransacking.

He stole food and canned goods from the scene, just as he had done on West Tulare Avenue. A large suitcase was also stolen, possibly to transport all of these items.

He exited the scene through a different door than the one he had used to enter.

The woman who lived at the home was retired and about seventy years old. She was a widow.

It's difficult to tell whether this ransacking occurred before the one on West Tulare Avenue. Putting this one first would make sense because of the theft of the suitcase, but even *with* a suitcase, there was a lot stolen on this night.

Stealing food wasn't something that he had done very often, so it's interesting that he did it at two different scenes here. He'd stolen practical items before, but none as bulky or as difficult to carry. Most of the food items were of a variety that couldn't be eaten immediately, but had to be prepared on a stove. Was the VR having money problems? Or was it a new level of thrill to eat food taken from a victim?

This residence was located in the middle of a fairly dense stretch of homes that offered little in the way of cover. A man carrying a suitcase down the street would've looked pretty odd at night, so it's possible that he parked a vehicle nearby. Perhaps he even lived near this residence, had a relative that lived near it, or had some other means of concealing himself.

He wasn't a complete stranger to this area. In fact, on October 23rd, 1974, he'd ransacked the house next-door. Just like on West Seeger Avenue and West Tulare Avenue, he was returning to very familiar ground.

It *is* it odd that on this night he hit two houses next-door to locations that he'd previously ransacked, and that the other ransacking of the night was of a residence that he'd already burglarized. Seeing how far apart these were from each other makes it even stranger:

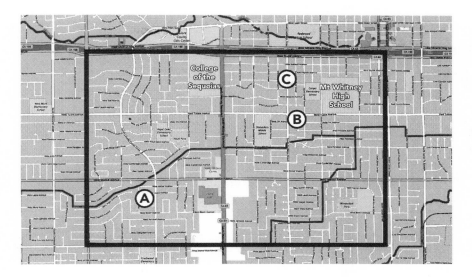

The ransackings that occurred on November 6th, 1975. The box indicates the zone that all of the VR's burglaries took place in.

A) *VR #137 on W Seeger Ave. This house had been ransacked before (on December 16th, 1974).*

B) *VR #138 on W Tulare Ave. Two houses nearby had been ransacked in the past, one on November 29th, 1974 and the other on May 31st, 1975.*

C) *VR #139 on S Oak Park Street. The house next-door had been ransacked the year before (on October 23rd, 1974).*

Was he making or finalizing plans for another live victim? It wasn't outside the realm of possibility that he'd attempt another violent crime. Regardless of his true intentions, he covered a lot of ground and stole a staggering amount of items on this night. Even though it was all spread out, he managed hit areas that he'd been to before and he hit them with precision. It means *something*, and whatever it meant, it probably wasn't good. The police formulated a response and decided to launch more focused patrols and stakeouts.

November 9ᵗʰ, 1975 Prowler

Police Stakeouts
November 7th through November 9th, 1975

The escalations and changing patterns of the Visalia Ransacker were concerning police, who wanted badly to bring him to justice for the murder of Claude Snelling. The stalking incidents that they were uncovering and the Ransacker's return to so many areas that he'd hit before seemed to indicate the possibility of another tragedy in the works.

As the police had done at the end of 1974, they organized a special patrol to stake out key places that the Ransacker typically struck. Without any fingerprints to identify him, their best hope was to catch him in the act, and they were determined to do so.

Starting right away on Friday, November 7th, 1975, half a dozen officers went out on patrol. They paired up and staked out three different key locations. Some were stationary, and some moved around their areas.

Unfortunately, nothing out of the ordinary occurred on Friday. They went back out on Saturday. Still nothing.

Stakeouts are a tricky thing, and much of police work is a waiting game. Undeterred, the officers went back out on Sunday.

That was when the call came in.

VR #140 – *Prowler*
November 9th, 1975 | W College Ct

-NOT CONFIRMED TO BE RELATED-

At 7:25 PM on Sunday, November 9th, a prowler was spotted on West College Court. The initial description was that of a medium-to-heavyset white male.

Officers got the call, and it sounded promising. West College Court is located immediately to the west of the College of the Sequoias – a hotspot for the VR. The vague, general description seemed to match. Excited, they raced over as quickly as they could.

Response time was almost immediate, but by the time they got there, the prowler seemed to be gone. The police fanned out, but they were unable to locate him in the darkness.

The witness who'd called in the incident provided more details. The prowler had been seen hiding in the shadows nearby. He was standing still, as if he was waiting for something, and he was smoking a cigarette. The witness didn't feel that the subject knew he was being watched.

The subject then suddenly sprung to life and moved along the perimeter of the home. Then he attempted to *break into* the home. Suddenly he stopped – it seemed that something had scared him off. (According to one report, the subject actually gained entry to the house successfully, but then left immediately).

The witness got a decent look at him, but it was too dark to make out any distinct features. The description given was that of a white male, mid twenties, 5'10", and roughly 175 lbs.

By the time the police arrived, it seemed that the man had left the area (or had hidden himself well), because officers couldn't locate him. There's no notation in any of the documentation about any shoe prints being found at the scene that night, but the officers did return to the scene the next morning. Unfortunately, they were unable to locate any additional clues. Investigators do believe that this was likely a Ransacker sighting, but with no physical evidence and no M.O. traits, we're forced to leave it designated as only a *possible* incident.

While it was disappointing that the extra manpower assigned to the case hadn't netted the Ransacker, it's possible that this alert witness and a quick police response had at least prevented a burglary.

This home was just southeast of the intersection at South Verde Vista Street and West Campus Avenue. If this was the Ransacker, it was an area that he knew well and had visited many times before.

One final note – during the East Area Rapist phase, he seemed to smoke quite a bit while prowling during 1976 and most of 1977. Cigarette butts were commonly found in places where he'd positioned himself to watch a home or on trails that he'd used to enter and escape a neighborhood. He even stole cigarettes from a few of the first two dozen victims.

Police Stakeouts

Undeterred by what felt like a near miss on November 9th, the Visalia Police Department took a few days to regroup and re-strategize. Then they increased their efforts.

On Thursday, November 13th, they sent out more patrols. Instead of six officers, this time they sent out nine, and they covered four different areas instead of three. They worked in pairs (two officers to a quadrant), with one of them patrolling the area in a squad car. Like before, some of them hid in the shadows and kept watch on nearby residences, and some of them covered their beat on foot or on bicycles.

On Thursday all was quiet, but on Friday the 14th, it seemed that they might be catching another break.

A suspicious person was sighted at 9:20 PM at the intersection of West Myrtle Avenue and South Dollner Street. A witness reported the sighting, and officers responded as quickly as they could. It seemed that they were too late – the subject had already left the area. Nothing further could be developed, though they did canvass the vicinity and speak with every neighbor. None of them had been outside their residence at the time of the sighting, so the identity of the mystery person remains unknown. Since the person didn't appear to be doing anything terribly out of the ordinary, the officers moved on.

The police tried their patrols again with the same tenacity on Saturday night (the 15th) and Sunday night (the 16th), but the Ransacker failed to appear.

It's unknown whether the VR had planned to offend. Could he have somehow observed the officers looking for him, heard them discuss it on a police radio, or somehow learned of their plans? Or was he simply busy with other things and couldn't find an opportunity to prowl or ransack?

The lack of success was undoubtedly frustrating for the police. If the prowler on November 9th was him *and* the suspicious person on the 15th was him, then he'd already been given two tastes of the cops on his heels. It would stay that way for the rest of the month, with various prowling incidents occurring and the cops being at the scene within minutes. But somehow he continued to elude police and avoid capture.

November 20ᵗʰ, 1975 Prowler

The extra Visalia Ransacker patrols, which were expensive for the force and required a lot of personnel, had yet to net anything substantial. After the 16th, they were paused, and the Visalia Police Department pondered its next move. It had been a couple weeks since a ransacking had occurred, but several calls about prowlers had been coming in and their prompt attention to them might've been preventing more crimes.

One of these calls came in on November 20th. Full details don't seem to be available to us (or perhaps anyone), but at the time, there was something compelling enough about the event to convince police that they needed to step up their patrols again.

VR #141 – *Prowler*
November 20th, 1975 | S Wellsley Ct

-NOT CONFIRMED TO BE RELATED-

At 5:00 PM on Thursday, November 20th, a man was seen prowling on South Wellsley Court. The homes on the street were under construction at the time, and the prowler was seen entering a half-built residence.

This home was located in the southwest corner of the VR's typical attack zone. It was one of the houses situated on the cul-de-sac.

A detailed description of the incident and the prowler isn't available, but investigators at the time believed that the prowler was the Visalia Ransacker. This certainly seemed to be an area that he was expanding to, having hit in the general area on November 2nd and November 6th.

November 23rd, 1975 Prowler

Police Stakeouts

Irked at another near-miss and feeling that the Ransacker would be back over the weekend, the Visalia Police Department decided that it was time to go all-out. Nearly twenty-five police officers were gathered together on the evening of Friday, November 21st for a special patrol. They were split up into teams and deployed all across Visalia for the evening. Based on past patterns, they felt almost certain that the Ransacker would show up that night and be caught in the act. The memory of the busy Thanksgiving weekend of 1974 was still fresh in a lot of their minds.

Nearly every major VR hot zone across the city was covered. Some of the teams were hidden in trees, garages, or bushes. Some patrolled on foot, some on bicycle, and some by vehicle.

Unfortunately, the Ransacker was a no-show. There were no prowlers or burglars spotted, and no related calls came in. In hindsight, one of the mistakes made that night could've been an overreliance on using police radio to broadcast plans and positions. It didn't dawn on them at the time that he might be listening in – radios that could listen to police band were somewhat common back then (now those frequencies are typically encrypted). A week or two after these patrols, they silenced their radios.

The lack of success on their stakeouts was just part of the job. They tried again full-force on Saturday, November 22nd. The same officers took their same positions. Unfortunately, not a peep from the offender.

Sunday, November 23rd, was the same story – almost. The officers took their positions and waited until about 10:00 PM before disbanding. Some stayed an hour later. Disappointed by their results but happy that they took a proactive approach, the patrols had all been called home sometime after 11:00 PM. About forty-five minutes after the last team called it quits, a possible Ransacker incident occurred.

Unfortunately, the police wouldn't find out about it until much later, or else they could've modified their plans. The following entry is a description of this event.

VR #142 – *Prowler*
November 23rd, 1975 | W Royal Oaks Dr

-NOT CONFIRMED TO BE RELATED-

On Sunday, November 23rd, right before midnight, a resident on West Royal Oaks Drive spotted a prowler near his home. The prowler seemed to be attempting to gain entry, but he was chased away.

There isn't any detailed documentation for this event, and it wasn't reported at the time that it happened. Police found out about it later.

Interestingly, this residence was located directly across the street from the home where a significant VR burglary had happened on August 31st, 1975 – the burglary where the murder weapon used in the Claude Snelling homicide had been stolen.

The timing was interesting. Did the VR observe the officers patrolling different areas for him, and is that why he waited until they packed up for the night before attempting to enter a home? Midnight was quite late for him if burglary was the only thing on his mind. He may have had more sinister intentions.

It's also possible that the prowler wasn't the Visalia Ransacker at all. Nothing ties him to this directly, though he had spent quite a bit of time working this street in recent weeks.

The home on West Royal Oaks Drive that the Ransacker had been stalking extensively was located to the east:

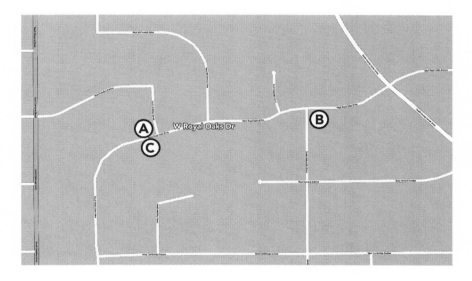

The VR-related events that took place on West Royal Oaks Drive.

A) *Prowler incident on November 23rd, 1975*

B) *A residence that had been ransacked and stalked by the VR in September and October 1975*

C) *The residence where the gun that killed Claude Snelling was stolen by the VR on August 31st, 1975*

December 1st, 1975 Incidents

It seemed that the police and the public had been successful at chasing off prowlers and keeping the Visalia Ransacker at bay for a few weeks. Patrols didn't stop, but they *did* start to slow down. The Ransacker hadn't burglarized a home in almost a month.

But he wasn't through. He seemed determined to continue ransacking, and on the night of December 1st, 1975, he apparently deemed it safe enough to venture out. Since it was a Monday, he probably felt that the patrols would be at their lowest level. And he was right.

VR #143 – *Ransacking*
November 30th to December 3rd, 1975 | W College Ave

Sometime between Sunday, November 30th at 9:00 AM and Wednesday, December 3rd at 3:00 PM, the VR entered a single-story residence on West College Avenue while the victims were away.

He entered by prying open their door. Inside, he created a familiar scenario – bedrooms ransacked and women's underwear taken out of drawers and arranged carefully in different locations. For some reason, he also decided to turn all of the panties inside out.

He stole holiday postage stamps (both Easter and Christmas), an attaché case, binoculars, and a shaving kit from this residence.

Shoe prints were found – the same size and style of tennis shoe prints found at the other ransackings.

Apparently at this ransacking, postage stamps were acceptable in lieu of Blue Chip stamps. The attaché case was possibly taken to help him transport some of his stolen items, though he'd taken suitcases and other items like that before, so it's possible that these types of items simply appealed to him. It's not known if it was monogrammed or not – if it seemed like it had personal significance, he was more likely to steal it.

The theft of the binoculars has interesting implications, given that this offender possibly staked out homes and observed them prior to making an approach. He clearly looked for homes that were vacant, but he also liked to peep. Both of those were activities that could've been assisted by binoculars. He could've also used the item to help him scout an area for police patrol units. He'd stolen a pair of binoculars before, at VR #066 on December 21st, 1974.

He'd taken a shaving kit before, too, and given his likely age it shouldn't be an odd thing to steal if he was in the market for practical items. Some of the descriptions given by witnesses who got a good look at the VR mentioned that he had the body of a man in his late twenties but had a very, very youthful face. Witnesses almost unanimously said that it was round, pudgy, and that the Ransacker had teenager's skin texture. One even questioned whether he was able to grow facial hair or not. Perhaps he was just a fan of the close shave, or perhaps there was even a medical condition involved.

The timing of this ransacking can't be pinned down due to the residents being away from their home for an extended period of time, but given its general proximity to other events on Monday, December 1st, it's likely that this burglary happened on the same night as those. It's not known which order it would be placed in. It was off to the east of the others, so if they occurred on the same night, it's possible that it was either the first or the last one of the evening. The theft of the attaché case could've been in anticipation of a night's haul, or it could've been taken out of necessity because he was weighed down by full pockets.

The fact that this burglary was off by itself a bit may not have anything to do with when it occurred – it may have more to do with the couple whose name was attached to this house. After this weekend, the next time that the Ransacker hit the streets was on December 8th, and it was just for a one-off hit in a part of town that he never really went to. The victim in *that* burglary was the *mother* of the man whose name was associated with *this* burglary. Because of the odd geography and the fact that these happened back-to-back, that's a little more than coincidental! It's another solid thread that's been put together in the process of cracking the offender's selection methods.

VR #144 – *Ransacking*
December 1st, 1975 | W Beverly Dr

On Monday, December 1st, sometime between 5:40 PM and 9:50 PM, the Visalia Ransacker entered a single-story home on West Beverly Drive while the victims were away.

The point of entry was a pried window.

The Ransacker didn't get very far in this one. Before he could begin tearing through drawers, it appears that something changed his mind and he decided to leave. That something was most likely the family dog – the dog was inside the house at the time and typically didn't care for strangers.

Before leaving, he did take some coins and some paper money from the residence.

The head of the household was a man, about fifty years old, who worked as an attorney. He lived there with his family.

Fingerprints and partial shoe prints were found at the scene. The technicians were particularly interested in the fingerprints, because they were hoping that the Ransacker's possible run-in with the dog might've caused him to slip up and touch something. After being carefully lifted, catalogued, and compared with previous ransackings, it was determined that unfortunately, there was no match.

The shoe prints, however, were the same as at other scenes. Based on the method of entry, the shoe prints, and the proximity to other incidents that occurred Monday night, this entry was definitely believed to be the work of the Visalia Ransacker.

The residence was a corner house positioned immediately to the east of the College of the Sequoias. It was two or three blocks directly south of the next two incidents we'll discuss.

VR #145 – *Ransacking*
December 1st, 1975 | S Central St

On Monday, December 1st, sometime between 8:30 PM and 10:45 PM, the Visalia Ransacker entered a residence on South Central Street while the victims were away. Like the previous one, the home was situated on a corner.

He entered by prying open a door. Once inside, he opened a window and ransacked the residence, stealing a man's ring in the process.

Shoe prints were found nearby. They matched the VR's tracks from other scenes.

The head of the household was a retired man in his early seventies. His wife lived at there with him, and she worked as an office manager.

The house adjacent to this one was pried at on the same night, but apparently the Ransacker couldn't get in. Details are covered next.

VR #146 – *Attempted Break-in*
December 1st, 1975 | W Kaweah Ave

On Monday, December 1st, the Visalia Ransacker attempted to enter a house on West Kaweah Avenue at 9:50 PM. This home was adjacent to the South Central Street ransacking that occurred on the same night. Based on the shoe impressions found at both scenes, it appeared that the South Central Street burglary was committed before the Ransacker attempted entry here.

The victim, a woman, was *in the home* while he attempted to enter it. She was in bed, asleep.

The woman woke up to the sound of someone prying at her back door. At that point she started turning on lights inside the house. She went to different doors and windows to look outside, but she wasn't able to see anything.

The woman checked her back door and saw several gashes and pry marks near the lock. Luckily, the Ransacker hadn't been able to gain entry and he'd left when the woman was alerted to his presence.

The pry marks were examined, and they matched the marks left at other recent incidents related to the Ransacker. Shoe prints at the scene also matched.

It's unknown if the VR even knew someone was in the home – it's possible that he made a mistake. It should be noted, however, that this victim had a connection to one of his previous victims... she was the ex-wife of a man who was burglarized by the VR on November 2nd, 1974 (VR #046). Whether this is a significant connection or merely coincidence has yet to be determined.

The woman worked as a nurse at Kaweah Delta Hospital. One of the other significant connections in this case was *also* tied to this facility – a previous victim was a physician there. It was the man whose home was ransacked, and then the next day, his *assistant's* home was ransacked. It should also be noted that during the East Area Rapist / Golden State Killer phases, many of his rape and murder victims had connections to medical facilities. None of this necessarily means anything significant, but they're important details to point out.

Did the VR plan on assaulting her that night? If he had gone out to assault someone that night, would he have also ransacked the other residences? And wouldn't he have waited until later on in the night like he'd done in the Snelling case, the attempted entry in early October, and possibly the rape in Sacramento?

The answer to those questions actually might show some sophistication on the part of the offender. This woman worked nights, and she would've been leaving for work in about an hour. Could the Ransacker have known that, and did he deem this his best chance at attacking her under the cover of darkness? He'd apparently prowled this area of town very thoroughly.

And burglarizing earlier in the night doesn't preclude him from assaulting someone. On the night of December 29th, 1979, he committed several burglaries before he gained entry to Dr. Robert

Offerman's home, where he committed a *double homicide.* And during the EAR series, it wasn't uncommon for there to be burglaries in the area when he was ready to attack. If anything, the burglaries seemed to work him up even more.

It's impossible to know for sure what his intentions were regarding this entry, or what his intentions might've *turned into* had he gained entry and realized that she was inside. Luckily, we never found out.

As with some of the other events from this night, this home was located directly to the east of the College of the Sequoias (the college is located just to the west of the following map). The home was adjacent to the property line of the South Central Street burglary discussed earlier in the chapter.

(map featured on the next page)

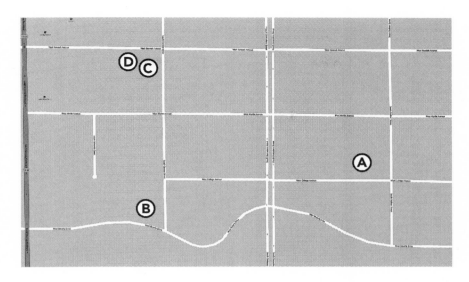

VR incidents from December 1st, 1975.

A) *VR #143 ransacking that took place between November 30th and December 3rd on W College Ave*

B) *VR #144 ransacking on W Beverly Dr*

C) *VR #145 ransacking on S Central St*

D) *VR #146 attempted entry on W Kaweah Ave*

About ten days after this incident, West Kaweah Avenue would be the scene of the Visalia Ransacker's final confirmed activity – a confrontation with the police.

December 8ᵗʰ, 1975 Ransacking

All throughout late November and early December, officers continued to patrol the town on a fairly regular basis, sending out about six deputies per night. On Monday, December 8th, they had three teams of officers (two officers per team) looking for the Ransacker. About an hour into their shifts, the call came in that another burglary had occurred.

VR #147 – *Ransacking*
December 8th, 1875 | W Sue Ave

On Monday, December 8th, a single-story house was entered by the VR while the victim was away. The burglary occurred sometime between 6:30 PM and 7:10 PM.

He entered by prying open a sliding-glass door. Once inside, it appeared that he went straight to the master bedroom and began ransacking.

He removed the woman's undergarments from drawers and began tossing them onto the floor and the bed. Jewelry boxes were dumped out, and a few items from them were stolen.

The VR didn't open any additional windows, and he didn't ransack any other rooms. He left through the same door he'd used to enter the residence.

The victim was a woman in her mid fifties. She worked as a sales clerk.

The police were called in. They dusted for fingerprints, and they found several that they were eager to test. Unfortunately, none of them matched previous findings.

They also found shoe prints in the victim's backyard and in the yard to the side of the house. These prints were a match for other Visalia Ransacker scenes.

The police felt, given the narrow time window and the seemingly incomplete ransacking, that the homeowner had surprised the VR while he was still inside the residence. He possibly escaped without her knowing that he was even there. If so, this is significant because it shows him fleeing rather than acting with violence.

One thing that's a little odd about the scene is that he didn't open any additional windows. Perhaps he didn't feel the need to because of the layout of the house, or perhaps he didn't always open them right away and we're mistaken when we assume that it was one of the first things that he did inside a residence. He might've ransacked a bedroom or two first, then opened the "escape hatches." It's also possible that he closed the window behind him when he made his escape. It should be noted that in East Area Rapist series of burglaries, very rarely was a window or door left open. Perhaps he'd already evolved beyond the need to do that.

This burglary was located fairly far to the west of the Ransacker's typical strike zones. While it can't be known for certain how he ended up there, an interesting connection can be found when studying this location – a connection we discussed in the previous chapter but need to touch on again.

The connection involves the people tied to recent burglary addresses. A researcher named Mason Tierney assisted us in working through some of the names attached to this and other addresses, and it was found that the victim in *this* ransacking was the *mother* of the man tied to the West College Avenue address (VR #143) from the last time the VR was out.

Is it coincidence that the VR ransacked the home with a certain man's name tied to it, and then on his next outing he went outside of his usual comfort zones and ransacked his *mother's* home?

This is a very interesting pattern, especially in light of the attempted entry on December 1st at West Kaweah Avenue where a previous victim's ex-wife was targeted. Two family connections – one on December 1st and then another on his next outing, December 8th. That would be even *more* of a coincidence.

Very rarely do these types of things come up throughout the Golden State Killer's sweeping list of crimes. At first glance, very few of his victims have had any connection at all. But digging deeper, patterns do start to emerge. Three East Area Rapist victims in a row ate at the same pizza place. Several of them had ties to the same military base. Some of them had gone to the same hospital for surgery. But those aren't nearly as interesting as what we have here.

These mother/son, husband/ex-wife, and doctor/assistant connections in the Visalia Ransacker series are some of the clearest relations that can be found among any of his victims. And it's probably not coincidence that these are found during the early phase of his criminal career – in the future, he probably still selected victims who were related in some way (at least on occasion), but he was clearly a bit more careful about letting time or distance pass before acting on anything. It's also possible that he went on to selected people with relationships that were a bit more removed, or with relationships that were harder to determine in retrospect.

Shoe Prints on W Kaweah Ave

Shoe Prints Found
November 1975 | W Kaweah Ave

In November, the residents of a home on West Kaweah noticed vague shoe impressions in their yard. The prints appeared to be congregated near their nineteen-year-old daughters bedroom and bathroom windows. They contacted the police.

These residents were understandably on-edge – the apartment over the garage had been ransacked in July, and as the ski-masked perpetrator made his escape, he'd come face-to-face with the nineteen-year-old daughter. Shortly afterward, it seemed that someone had started peeping in at her during the night.

The police surveyed the yard, but they weren't able to notice much due to the autumn leaves that had since covered the ground. Realizing that the offender might return (and keeping in mind all of the Ransacker activity on this street), officers suggested that they keep the ground near the windows free of leaves and debris. They recommended that the area be checked every few days for fresh prints, and if they found any, the police were to be notified at once.

More Shoe Prints Found
December 9th, 1975 | W Kaweah Ave

The family had been faithfully raking under the yard and checking for shoe impressions. Nothing had been found in the weeks since they'd spoken to the police.

On December 9th, however, they were startled to find new prints under the windows. The peeper had returned.

The police were called immediately, and they sent someone over. The officer inspected the shoe prints and noted that they were consistent in size and pattern with the Visalia Ransacker. He also noticed circular marks in the dirt, and discovered that the Ransacker had gone next door, brought over a flowerpot, and had stood on it to get a better vantage point into the windows.

Knowing that another "VR Patrol" was scheduled for the next night, the officer came up with an idea – he and his partner would stake out the residence in hopes of catching the Ransacker peeping in at the teenage girl.

This officer, a brilliant and dedicated man named William McGowen, would soon become the only person who ever came close to arresting the Golden State Killer during his entire crime spree.

December 10th, 1975 Ransacking

All across Visalia, teams of officers working in pairs had been patrolling and staking out key areas known to be frequented by the Visalia Ransacker.

Their efforts had yet to find success, but a few suspicious persons had been found wandering the streets at night and they'd been taken in for questioning. One of them even had the exact same style of shoes that the Ransacker did, which caused a little bit of excitement at first, but the suspect was cleared.

While all of this searching was going on, the VR was still prowling the night, and he was apparently doing it right under their noses. The shoe prints found on West Kaweah Avenue was proof of that. And on the night of December 10th, the police were out in force and stakeouts were again in place. And once more, the Ransacker was on the move.

Officers were as careful as they could be, and radio chatter was kept to a minimum. Like every night, they hoped that *this* would be "the night."

And it finally was!

But first, the night started with a burglary. Based on the way that events played out, the Ransacker apparently liked to burglarize homes before going on his regular peeping routes. On December 10th, he decided to hit West Laurel Avenue.

VR #148 – *Ransacking*
December 10th, 1975 | W Laurel Ave

Sometime between 6:30 PM and 8:15 PM on Wednesday, December 10th, a single-story residence on West Laurel Avenue was burglarized by the Visalia Ransacker while the victims were away for the evening.

Once he entered the home, he opened a bedroom window to use as a quick escape route.

He spent a lot of time in the master bedroom, ransacking the drawers and removing the woman's underwear, lingerie, and other garments. A sweater was also removed from a drawer.

He stole cash, some rings, three books of Blue Chip stamps, and three loose stamps. He stole a copious amount of coins: several rare silver dollars, loose change, some collectible coins, and some foreign coins.

One of the rings that he stole was a George Washington University class ring, dated 1948. It had a large red stone on it, along with the owner's initials. Another engraved ring was stolen as well.

Inside the son's bedroom, he found a bottle containing over 1,500 pennies. He took *all* of the pennies, but he left the bottle – moving it to the *daughter's* room and placing it on her bed.

The VR apparently exited through a sliding glass door, leaving it open as he made his way out of the home.

The burglary was discovered later in the night, after the events of the next chapter had unfolded. Officers found shoe prints at the scene, and they matched the Visalia Ransacker's.

Due to the significant events that took place later that evening, the Visalia Police Department brought in a team of crime scene experts from Fresno. They spent the night pouring over the trace evidence left at this burglary. Their work was so extensive that the residents had to spend the night with friends.

An article was published in the Visalia Times-Delta that explored this ransacking in-depth from the victims' point of view. It explained how they returned home at 10:30 PM and noticed that a drawer in their kitchen was open – their first indication that something was wrong. More drawers in the house were found open, and a Crème de Menthe decanter had been broken on the floor, staining the carpet. Once they arrived at the bedroom, they saw that it had been ransacked.

The article also mentions that the resident, a doctor, had a medical bag on the premises and that hadn't been touched. The Christmas presents in the home had been left alone as well. The wife's jewelry box was found on the other side of the house, and the family's elderly dog, "Popcorn," had not succeeded in scaring off the intruder.

This ransacking on West Laurel Drive was the last *confirmed* burglary committed by the Visalia Ransacker in the area. When all was said and done, he'd ransacked over *one hundred homes*. There were two more events in 1976 that were possibly tied to him, but other than that, he disappeared into the night.

After the events that we describe next, of course.

The McGowen Shooting

<u>VR #149</u> – *Attempted Homicide*
December 10th, 1975 | W Kaweah Ave

Background

Police officer William McGowen had been one of the most tenacious investigators on the Ransacker case – dedicated through and through to bringing the criminal to justice. A College of the Sequoias graduate, a Navy veteran who served his country, and a career police officer who served his community, McGowen was known across the town for his professionalism and work ethic.

It was in this competent opponent that the Visalia Ransacker finally met his match.

Pre-Attack Timeline

Note: Several of the relevant timeline events have been discussed in other chapters. The basics of these events are included in this chapter in order to provide a complete view of all information pertaining to this incident.

February 16th, 1975: Ransacking of Neighbor's Residence

A family living on West Kaweah Avenue suffered a ransack-burglary while they were out for the evening. Coins and cash were stolen from their home, and women's panties/bras were taken out of drawers and arranged on the bed. The burglar picked up a wedding photo of the daughter (she was a College of the Sequoias student) and a photo the middle-school-aged son and threw both pictures to the floor. It was determined that the crime was committed by the Visalia Ransacker.

This family lived next-door to the nineteen-year-old woman who would later become a target of the VR, and it's at this house that the police would later position themselves during a stakeout to catch him. Her face-to-face encounter with the VR is described in the next entry.

July 24th, 1975: Ransacking of Victim's Residence

The nineteen-year-old woman was startled by a man emerging from the apartment over the garage. As he came bounding down the stairs, he noticed her and seemed to panic, pushing her down roughly and fleeing the residence. The encounter happened so quickly that she was unable to provide a good description, but she could see that he was wearing a ski mask and that he had "strong arms."

November 1975: Shoe Prints at Victim's Residence

The mother of this same woman noticed vague shoe prints in the yard. The prints were located under the nineteen-year-old's bedroom and bathroom windows, indicating that someone had been peeping in at her. The police told them to keep the area clear of leaves and other debris so that they could get a clear shoe impression, and they also instructed them to call immediately if any more shoe prints materialized. The mother began checking the yard every couple of days.

December 6th, 1975: No Shoe Prints

On this date, the mother checked the yard for shoe prints. She didn't find any.

December 9th, 1975: More Shoe Prints

The mother checked the yard again, and this time she *did* find prints. She called the police. Officers at the scene noted that the impressions matched the Visalia Ransacker's shoes in both size and style, and they were even able to note something at the house next-door (the home that had been ransacked on February 16th): the Ransacker had used the neighbor's planter to stand on while peeping.

December 10th, 1975 6:00 PM: Ransacker Patrol is Deployed

In an effort to catch the Visalia Ransacker in the act, seven officers were deployed across different target areas that the VR was known to frequent. Two officers were positioned the vicinity of the home on West Kaweah Avenue where the shoe prints were found. Officer McGowen was hidden in an open garage located next-door to the target residence (he was hidden at the same home that had been ransacked on February 16th – he hoped the VR would use their planter again), and another officer was positioned across the street. One was in a squad car patrolling the general area, and four were on foot nearby (the closest backup officer being about three blocks to the west).

These patrols had been mobilized on more than two dozen other occasions throughout the Ransacker's crime spree, but the officers had yet to encounter the VR. They were hoping that the night of December 10th would be different.

December 10th, 1975 Sometime after 6:30 PM: Ransacking

On the 1500 block of West Laurel Avenue, the Visalia Ransacker broke into a home while the residents were away for the evening. He ransacked the residence, removed women's undergarments from drawers, and rearranged them on and near the bed.

He stole three books of Blue Chip stamps (as well as some loose stamps), cash, loose change, several collectible coins, several foreign coins, a class ring (engraved with initials), a gold ring (engraved with initials), and other miscellaneous rings. He also stole a thimble and over fifteen dollars in pennies. It was a fairly big haul for him – the coins alone weighed about ten pounds.

This location was about half a mile to the south of the home on West Kaweah Avenue where McGowen and his partner were waiting for the VR.

The McGowen Shooting

December 10th, 1975 8:30 PM: Attempted Homicide

On West Kaweah Avenue, McGowen's partner was positioned across the street from the potential target house. He'd only been there about two and a half hours before something caught his eye. Straining to see through the darkness, the officer noticed the outline of a man traveling through the shadows. The subject, moving against the shrubbery in a crouched position, made his way to the opening of the garage where Officer McGowen was hiding. The subject stood, peeked inside, and then, apparently not seeing McGowen, started moving away from the opening and toward the side of the garage. As the subject made his way to the back gate, McGowen rose up silently and began following him.

The officer followed the man all the way to the back gate and observed him for a moment as he tampered with the lock. Then, capitalizing on the element of surprise, he clicked his flashlight on and trained it at the prowler's head.

"Oh my God!" the subject shrieked, spinning around and facing the officer. He squinted at the bright light of the flashlight beam. "Oh no! Oh my God, no!" His voice was high-pitched and frantic.

"Police officer! Hold it right there!"

The suspect, who was wearing something like a stocking cap or ski mask rolled up on his head, reached up and removed it with his right hand. He tucked it into his right pocket in a distracting manner and took off running. Going only a few steps, he used momentum to propel himself over the gate. The subject made a hard landing in the backyard belonging to the house where McGowen had been hiding.

"Hold it! Put your hands up!" the officer ordered, also jumping over the fence. The suspect began running around in the yard almost in a zigzag or circular pattern. "Oh my God! Please don't hurt me! Oh my God, no!" he continued to scream in a high-pitched, feminine voice.

McGowen fired his service weapon into the ground several feet away from the subject. This acted as a warning shot and also alerted his partner across the street to the confrontation. The partner had already observed the situation, however, and was on his way.

Shortly after the weapon discharged, the prowler ran straight for the fence bordering the next property. He easily scrambled over it, landing in the same yard where his shoe prints had been observed the day before.

"Police officer! I told you to put your hands up! Stop or I'll shoot!"

McGowen continued to track the subject with his flashlight through the wide spaces between the fence slats. He held the flashlight up and away from his body just like he'd been trained to do at the Los Angeles Police Academy several years before.

"Don't hurt me! Oh my God! Please don't hurt me!" the man continued to shriek. He stopped running, and then positioned himself only five feet away from the officer. He turned to his side, carefully ensuring that only the right half of his body was facing

McGowen.

"Look! My hands are up!" he squealed. He raised his right hand, but as he did this, he began surreptitiously digging around in the folds of his jacket with his left hand.

Before McGowen could react, the subject pulled a gun out from his jacket, spun to face him, and fired a shot. The policeman fell backward.

The other officer had just arrived to assist, and he saw McGowen lying motionless on the ground. He got on his radio and called for help as he watched the shooter run through the gate on the other side of the fence.

As this was happening, the homeowner, his wife, and two visitors inside the target house heard the gunshot. Then they also thought that they heard another one.

The homeowner looked out his window just in time to see a man run through his back gate. He charged out after him and quickly caught sight of the man, who by this time was walking (not running) next to the fence on the other side of the house. The shooter turned, looked at the homeowner, seemed to pause a moment, then took a running start and jumped over hedges that ran along the side of the yard.

Back on the other side of the house, McGowen had pulled himself to his feet. Dazed, he asked if he'd been shot. Amazingly, it was discovered that the bullet had hit his flashlight directly on the lens. Other than some cuts near his right eye (from flying glass) and some powder marks on his face, the policeman was relatively unharmed. He was transported to the hospital, where he was later treated and released. The bullet meant for McGowen's head was eventually found embedded in his flashlight batteries.

December 10th, 1975 8:45 PM: The Scene

On his way out of the yard, the shooter had emptied his pockets of some of the loot that he'd stolen at the West Laurel Avenue ransacking that night. The money and coins were found tied up in a sock on the ground near the West Kaweah Avenue house. A few books of Blue Chip stamps, also stolen at the ransacking that night, were found as well. The police found out about the burglary a couple hours after this shooting occurred, which confirmed for them that the Visalia Ransacker was indeed the man they were after.

December 10th, 1975 8:45 PM: The Chase

Every on-duty unit from the Visalia Police Department was called in, all off-duty personnel were called in, the California Highway Patrol was summoned, and the Tulare County Sheriff's Office also came in to assist the chase. Nearly seventy officers descended on the area.

Police congregated at the hedges where the shooter was last seen. Officers unfamiliar with the situation were brought up to speed, and everyone got to look at the subject's shoe prints. There were plenty of examples – impressions were found in the dirt and the flowerbeds, tracks were found on the patio, and others were found near the street. They were later matched to shoe prints left at other Visalia Ransacker scenes, helping prove that the shooter was indeed the VR.

Officers followed his trail six houses to the west of the shooting location, and then they noticed that the impressions appeared to hook north and travel up South Divisadero Street. There was a small break in the trail, and then it picked up again at the site of a house under construction on West Noble Avenue. There he seemed to have vanished for a bit, but an officer noticed more tracks two or three houses to the east of the corner of South Divisadero Street and West Noble Avenue. It appeared that the shooter had traveled west from the scene of the shooting, then one block north, and was then headed back east *right past* the general location of the shooting that he'd just fled from.

The tracks were a bit more visible at that point, and it appeared the Ransacker had run east, parallel to State Route 198. Due to a copious amount of crushed branches, leaves and shoe prints pointing various directions at one certain location, it appeared that he'd hidden himself near a palm tree across from the corner of West Noble Avenue and South Dollner Street. In fact, if you visit Visalia today, that palm tree is still there – perhaps the only living eyewitness to the killer's identity during the Visalia series.

Another officer found more shoe prints heading east behind houses near West Noble Avenue and South Giddings Street. A few more were found on the east side of Giddings (where the Pentecostal Lighthouse Church is located today). The police realized too late that this area was outside of the perimeter that they had set up. The Ransacker had foiled them by retreating in the opposite direction that he had taken off in initially.

The police wondered if the Ransacker had crossed the highway into the north section of town at Giddings Street, thus getting even *further* outside of the perimeter. A tracking dog was brought to the scene, and the dog's trail ended virtually at the same area where the officers had lost him. It was assumed that he had parked transportation near the church, and that he eluded the dogs and police officers by fleeing the scene by vehicle or bike.

Unfortunately, the search for the shooter that night ended without an apprehension. Once again, the Visalia Ransacker had dodged the police and had melted into the night.

December 10th, 1975 10:30 PM
The residents on West Laurel Avenue returned home to find that their house had been ransacked. They contacted police, who quickly made their way to the residence. As the homeowners took inventory of what had been taken, the police were able to cross-check it with items that the Ransacker had dropped at the confrontation on West

Kaweah Avenue. The distinctive coins, the amount of loose Blue Chip stamps, and some of the other items were a match. Based on the M.O. displayed at scene of the West Laurel Avenue ransacking, it was clear that the VR was responsible.

Specially trained scene technicians were called in from Fresno to go over the burglary with a fine-toothed comb. They hoped to discover trace evidence that could lead to the Ransacker's identity. The homeowners had to spend the night with friends while the technicians worked.

December 11th, 1975 Morning
The ransacking victims on West Laurel Avenue were allowed to return home.

October 24th, 1976: Burglary
Nearly a year after the McGowen shooting took place, the nineteen-year-old woman (now twenty) who had originally been targeted on West Kaweah Avenue had another strange occurrence: her house was burglarized. She was still living at the same residence, and many investigators felt/feel that the burglary was the work of the Visalia Ransacker. It seems possible that he'd returned to the home to take care of unfinished business. No one was harmed in this incident, but it's one more potential example of the VR's long memory.

Suspect Description
William McGowen saw the Ransacker clearly – perhaps the best sighting of any witness – and as a trained Law Enforcement professional, his description was given quite a bit of credence.

He described the shooter as a white male, 25 to 35 years of age, 5'10", and 180 pounds or more. He had a round face, a cleft in his chin, a wide jaw, and his nose had a distinctive shape when his profile was seen (like a slope). He had a "thick neck."

His hair was short and light blonde, with no sideburns. It was longer on the top and parted on the left side. The officer described it as a "military haircut" – it was shorter than most boys and men were wearing at the time. An interesting note – because his hair was so short, the police went to several barbershops to see if anyone was familiar with the suspect's description.

McGowen also described the shooter as having light skin with no sign of whiskers or stubble. Under hypnosis, the officer described him as "baby-faced."

He described the Ransacker's shoulders as large and round, and said that the suspect had a large lower half with big legs, large hips/thighs, and a large behind (or "rump," as the report puts it). His feet were described as "stubby."

The VR was wearing tight pants that looked like blue jeans, a brown and green camouflage jacket with elastic cuffs, converse tennis shoes that were a low-top style and dark in color, and brown cotton gloves. The cap he was wearing was very thick, and it gave the impression of a ski mask rolled up.

McGowen described him as running slowly and running in a "funny manner, like his knees were together." This may be because of eleven pounds of coins that he had in his pockets, or it could be another example of the strange gait that was sometimes described by witnesses.

He drew his gun and shot with his left hand.

The neighbor who observed the subject described him as 5'10", about 180 lbs, and said that he was "large" and had a "large frame."

A month and a half later, after the VR case had gone quiet, another officer created a sheet that summarized and collated a bunch of

Visalia Ransacker facts. In this description, the officer gave the age range of "20-25." The modified age range was an amalgamation of several Ransacker sightings.

A composite drawing was made of the suspect shortly after the encounter:

(drawing featured on the following page)

The Visalia Ransacker as described by Officer McGowen. This was the first sketch created based on the incident.

McGowen didn't feel that it was an exact likeness, so about a month later two more drawings were done – one of the perpetrator's face and one of his profile:

Another sketch made of the Visalia Ransacker based on input from Officer McGowen.

A composite sketch made of the Visalia Ransacker's profile as he appeared on the night that McGowen was shot at.

Unfortunately, William McGowen passed away a number of years ago, and he was never able to identify the Ransacker through photographs or lineups.

Context and Analysis

Some of our research in the VR case involved looking for similarities and overlaps among VR victims in hopes of finding commonalities to help explain why the Ransacker focused on certain individuals over others. Since this was the second of the two big events typically associated with the Visalia Ransacker case (the other being, of course, the Snelling homicide), it seemed especially important to examine the different variables related to the young woman who was being targeted by the Ransacker at this location. Both this home and the Snelling household experienced multiple visits from the VR over a period of months. In fact, the known visits to this residence on West Kaweah Avenue add up to quite a few:

- July 24th, 1975: Burglary
- November 1975: Peeping (and perhaps many instances before that)
- Early December 1975: Peeping
- December 10th, 1975: Peeping and Confrontation
- October 24th, 1976: Burglary (suspected of being the VR)

What's interesting is that this nineteen-year-old woman and the young lady at the Snelling household had very little in common when it came to personality, interests, and activities. Perhaps it was the First Baptist Church that was the commonality – both young ladies were associated with the church (one of them volunteered heavily and the other one worked there). Aside from that, there doesn't seem to be any distinctive physical or behavioral trait that they shared in common.

Regardless of how these victims were originally selected, this confrontation was a long time coming for the VR. Because of how frequent and thorough the police had been in their stakeouts and their special patrols, it was really only a matter of time. Was the VR prepared for this eventuality? He had a mask on top of his head and a firearm handy, which indicates that he *was* prepared to protect his identity and he was ready to react violently, but did he specifically plan out what he would do and how would he react? Or was he improvising?

It seems that everyone familiar with this shooting has a slightly different take on what was going through the VR's mind when he began squealing and running haphazardly. An expertly preplanned response of cascading distractions? A burst of activity while he decided whether to shoot or flee? Genuine panic? Would anyone who knew him in his normal life recognize this type of behavior, or was this something completely out of the ordinary for him?

Did he shoot the officer intending to kill him? It's believed that he aimed squarely at the only part of the officer that he could see, which was the flashlight. Some see this as proof that the VR must've been a terrific shot, able to shoot through fence slats *and* able to hit his target on the bull's-eye. Some believe he was simply lucky. Others fall somewhere in between, noting the comparable shooting distance in the Claude Snelling case.

We *can* be reasonably sure that he intended to kill the officer – probably because McGowen saw him without his mask on and could possibly identify him at some point. It seems that he was simply creating distractions and buying time so that he could find an opportunity to kill him. Regardless of what his actual plan was, this event is always listed as an "attempted homicide."

There's some question as to whether there were two shots or one. Witnesses nearby felt they heard two. Some of the documentation only refers to one, though it can't be assumed that there wasn't a second shot based on how things are worded. An officer who wasn't at the scene tells us that there was only one. It may not seem like it matters, but it does – two shots are far more deadly than one, though it would've only taken one shot to end the officer's life.

The escape route that he chose was clever. When the homeowner saw him leave, it appeared that he was heading east over the shrubs. However, shoe tracks indicated that he actually took off in a westerly direction. He went that way for a while, and from there he went north. Then he ran back east *past the general area where the crime had occurred*. And he apparently kept going. If he had access to transportation parked east of the crime scene, it took some quick thinking (or preplanning) to initially start heading west and north *away* from the safety of his vehicle or bike. It's a similar pattern to the escape act that he'd performed after the Snelling homicide. In that instance it seems he also went west, north, and then east past the crime scene. The escape out of West Kaweah Avenue can be charted more accurately than the escape from the Snelling murder, thanks to the many shoe impressions that he left, as well as the tracking dog and the larger police force that was combing the area.

(*map featured on the following page*)

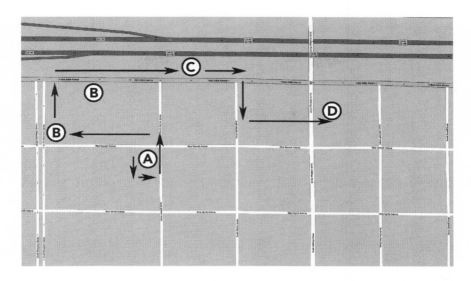

Based on the evidence, this is the VR's likely escape path.

A) The location of the shooting on W Kaweah Ave

B) Areas where clear shoe impressions were found on W Kaweah Ave and W Noble Ave

C) The area where tracks and broken branches on the ground indicate that the VR hid for a period of time

D) The church parking lot area where the trail ended

While it's believed that he took transportation from that general area, it's also possible that he found another way of escaping, such as crossing the highway into the north section of town.

The description that Officer McGowen gave of the shooter bears little resemblance to the description given of the East Area Rapist in June 1976, which was one of the factors that kept the VR and EAR cases from being easily connected for over forty years. One of the more interesting parts of McGowen's description is the heavier lower half of the subject. Some investigators believe that when his pockets were stuffed with coins and stamps, it made the VR's lower half look larger than it really was.

The fact that the Ransacker was wanted for homicide in the Snelling case certainly wasn't enough to scare him away from Visalia – he kept right on stalking and offending without missing a beat. This time, his reaction was very different, though. Perhaps because his face had been seen, perhaps because he'd had such a close call and was almost caught, or perhaps for some other reason, the Visalia Ransacker seemingly vanished after this confrontation with McGowen, completely gone from his typical patterns and attack area.

There was one more incident in mid January, but most of the subsequent prowling, peeping, and burglary offenses (such as those committed by the so-called Dollner Street Prowler) appear to have nothing to do with the Visalia Ransacker. The one exception, of course, is the burglary that occurred at this victim's home in October 1976. We'll review that in a later chapter.

After the Shooting

Even though this was basically the last time the VR was known to be on the radar in Visalia, McGowen and his colleagues continued to work the case for the next several years, even into retirement. McGowen kept case files, notes on various suspects and strategies, and continued to work leads. It's that amalgamation of data, and the work of other retired officers such as John Vaughan, that allow people like *us* to pick up the case so easily and continue to build on it.

William McGowen passed away on October 26th, 2005 at the age of 66. His legacy lives on because of the difference he made in his community, the difference he made in this case, and because of everything he did for his fellow officers. One of those fellow officers is his son – a man who grew up to follow in his father's footsteps and join one of the local police departments.

An area where the Visalia Ransacker hid while escaping the scene of the McGowen shooting. Photo by Bill Harticon.

January 18ᵗʰ, 1976 Prowler

Over a month had passed since the shooting on West Kaweah Avenue. Suspects were being developed, leads were being chased down, and the hunt for the Visalia Ransacker was still in full swing.

Meanwhile, just a few blocks east of the VR strike zone, two young teens had what might've been the town's last experience with the Ransacker before he moved out of the area and began more permanent operations in Sacramento.

VR #150 – *Prowler*
January 18th, 1976 | S Burke St

-NOT CONFIRMED TO BE RELATED-

It was 11:00 PM on Sunday, January 18th, 1976. A fourteen-year-old girl and her sister were in the living room.

Out of the corner of her eye, the fourteen-year-old noticed a figure at the window. She turned to get a better look and was startled to see a man peeping in at them.

The girl screamed. Realizing that he'd been spotted, the prowler simply turned and walked away at a leisurely pace. Both girls went to the window to watch him as he made his way out of their backyard and walked in the direction of East Kaweah Avenue. They never saw him at their window again.

The girls described the subject as a white adult male, early twenties, 5'11", 190 lbs, with a round face and light-colored short hair. His complexion was light, and he was wearing a dark camouflage jacket. Their description matched other descriptions of the Visalia Ransacker.

When pressed for details on the jacket, officers found that it was identical to the one that the Ransacker had worn on the night of December 10th when he'd shot at Officer McGowen.

The location of this incident was very atypical – it was quite a bit east of the Visalia Ransacker's attack zone. A map is below:

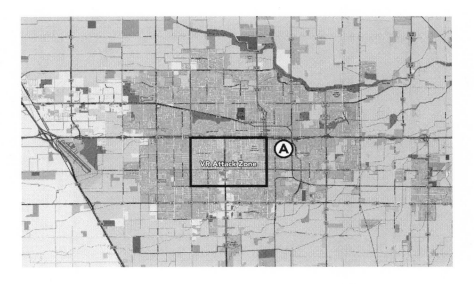

The box indicates the area where all of the previously known VR incidents occurred. The marker shows where the January 18th, 1976 peeping incident took place.

Toward the end of his known crimes in 1975, it was clear that the VR was targeting some different areas and starting to branch out a bit geographically, so appearing outside of the known strike zone isn't a deal-breaker when considering whether this incident fits the known crimes. If this incident *was* him, as most investigators believe, then it helps give us an idea of what his mindset was at the time. It appeared that he was still peeping, expanding his geography, and for some reason, he even still wore the same jacket that he'd had on the night of his brush with the police.

The offender's reaction in this sighting has some of the earmarks of the calm, collected, brazen, sexually motivated criminal that the VR had proven himself to be. Sightings of the same offender in Sacramento during his East Area Rapist years often played out the same way, with a suspicious man appearing at a window or fence who simply walked away at a calm, leisurely pace when spotted.

The First EAR Attack

It was May 1976. A twenty-three-year-old woman living in Rancho Cordova started to get the feeling that she was being watched. An older, dark-green car appeared to haunt her as she went about her daily life on Paseo Drive, a street not far from where the October 21st, 1975 home-invasion rape had taken place. The car, whose driver would turn his face completely away from her when she looked at him, finally stopped appearing in early June.

That was around the time her neighbor started hearing noises at his fence every night. Someone was climbing it, and they were passing through so often that some of the slats were broken. A side gate was also being used and the homeowner got so tired of the night-time intrusions that he nailed the gate shut.

The woman on Paseo Drive felt uneasy. She lived in the house with her father, but her father was on a trip and she was alone for several weeks. Adding to her stress was the telephone – it would ring, she'd answer it, but there'd be nothing but silence on the other end. The silence would drag on… the caller neither spoke nor hung up.

On the night of June 17th, 1976, she went to bed – tired from working and uncomfortable from dealing with cramps. Midnight passed, and she was sound asleep. She slept so soundly that sometime after 3:00 AM, she didn't hear the neighbor's dog barking. She didn't hear the commotion in her backyard as a man tried to cut her telephone wire, or the sound of him furiously chipping away at her doorjamb and freeing her deadbolt. She didn't even hear the man wandering through her house, finding Johnson's Baby Oil in a cabinet and lubricating himself with it. It was the sound of someone tapping on the frame of her bedroom door that finally jarred her awake.

The bedroom light was flipped on. Squinting in the brightness, she saw a masked man. He had no pants on and his penis was erect. Instinctively, she drew the covers over her head. At once he was on top of her, ripping them off and digging a knife into her temple.

Snarling hoarsely through clenched teeth, he issued a warning: "If you make one move or sound, I'll stick this knife in you." He'd already, in fact, dug it in so deeply that part of her pillow was soaked with blood.

Then, he announced the reason for his intrusion.

"I want to fuck you."

He stood beside her now, flashing his knife and tersely ordering her to remove her nightgown. As she did, he wandered through the room with an air of apparent anxiousness until finally stopping in front of her.

"Roll over," he snarled. She did. He pulled her arms behind her back and tied her hands very tightly with ligatures he'd brought with him – some kind of cord, rope, or twine. Again he was moving about the room, rummaging and collecting items that he could use to reinforce her bindings. He supplemented the ligatures on her wrists with a cloth belt from her closet.

Again he ordered her to roll over, and then he raped her. During the sexual assault, he touched her breasts only briefly. When he pulled out, he wiped his penis with the bed sheet and tossed the bedding onto the floor. She couldn't tell if he'd climaxed or not, but would find out much later from a crime lab report that he had.

When the horrendous assault was over, he asked her if there was money in the house. She began to answer, but he interrupted her, ordering her through clenched teeth to "shut up."

Again he wandered the bedroom, collecting more items to tie her up with. He gagged her with a slip that he found nearby.

With his victim even more secure, he began moving through the room once more, rummaging and ransacking as he went. He returned to her side, held the knife close, and warned her that if she made any movements he'd kill her.

And then he was gone... but just from the room, not from the house. She heard him tearing the residence apart, pulling at drawers loudly, and opening and closing a paper bag as he explored.

At one point she heard whispered voices, as if two people were talking. A louder whisper said "I told you to shut up!" The whispering continued as drawers and cabinets were opened and shut in various rooms. Despite the apparent conversation, the victim felt that the assailant was by himself, and that he was talking to an imaginary accomplice.

After a few moments, there was silence. No more paper bags opening, no more drawers being slammed, and no more hushed conversation.

The house was a mess – drawers open, papers and items strewn about. The victim's purse was found on the patio, its contents dumped out onto the lawn. Ten dollars were stolen from the scene, some silver dollars were taken, and packs of Winston cigarettes were missing.

The attacker was described as a white male, early twenties, 5'9", 160 lbs. He was broad-shouldered, with a fairly muscular build. His legs were muscular with dark hair, and his arms had a lot of dark hair as well. He was described as "not well-endowed." He whispered hoarsely through clenched teeth, and his jaw didn't seem to move when he talked.

The assailant wore a dirty white or gray tight-fitting mask made of a coarse-knitted material, which was constructed with a seam down the middle. It had eye holes, but no holes for the nose or mouth.

His clothing consisted of a dark navy blue or black t-shirt with short sleeves and a pocket on the left breast. He wasn't wearing any pants. His gloves were a coarse material similar to the mask, with elastic bands near the wrist (similar to garden gloves). He wore tennis shoes.

There was no way of knowing it at the time, but this was the Visalia Ransacker. He'd changed methods, he'd changed locations, and it seems he'd even changed appearance. The VR had clearly thought about his failings at the Snelling incident, utilized the skills he'd honed on West Campus Avenue, South Verde Vista Street, South Redwood Street, and West Kaweah Avenue, and he'd become something even more monstrous than before.

Tragically, the attacks didn't end with this assault in Rancho Cordova. A month later, he invaded the home of two sisters in Carmichael who were staying by themselves. He tied both of them up and repeatedly raped the younger one. He tried this type of attack again in August, just a couple of houses away from the woman he'd assaulted in June on Paseo Drive. In a scene very reminiscent of the October 21st, 1975 assault, this home was occupied by a mother, teenager, and a young daughter. The tables turned on him this time, however – the mother fought him off before he could sexually assault any of them and he was forced to retreat.

Undeterred, he continued to commit home-invasion rapes in the East Sacramento area throughout 1976 and beyond. All the while, Visalia was chasing leads and wondering where their offender had gone to – worried that he'd graduated to bigger and bolder offenses somewhere else.

Indeed he had... but before moving on completely, it's possible that he paid Visalia one final visit in October 1976.

October 24th, 1976 Burglary

By October 24th, 1976, the Visalia Ransacker / East Area Rapist was two hundred miles away in Sacramento, and he'd already committed eight sexual assaults. The offender had upped the ante quite a bit from his Visalia days – entering homes in the middle of the night, sadistically binding his victims, assaulting them, ransacking their homes, and leaving without a trace.

An incident that occurred on a night in October 1976 gave investigators a reason to believe that he'd returned to Visalia for some reason. Perhaps he felt he had a score to settle, or maybe he was merely in the area for family or work purposes. Whatever the reason for his possible return, he may have actually gone back to the scene of his confrontation with McGowen.

VR #151 – *Burglary*
October 24th, 1976 | W Kaweah Ave

-NOT CONFIRMED TO BE RELATED-

On the night of October 24th, 1976, a home on West Kaweah Avenue was burglarized.

This was the residence belonging to the nineteen-year-old woman (now twenty) who had been peeped at by the Ransacker in November and December 1975. He'd burglarized the upstairs apartment at this residence in July of that year, and on December 10th, he'd shot at Officer William McGowen while trying to escape.

There wasn't anything in particular that tied this burglary to the Visalia Ransacker series other than a suspicion by officers that the VR had returned to take care of unfinished business. There was also a sighting of a prowler near this street around the same timeframe, but it didn't offer anything special in the way of details. The Visalia Ransacker crimes had not yet been tied to the East Area Rapist crimes, and the police department had no idea that the VR had already committed eight rape/attempted rape crimes in East Sacramento, so that didn't factor into their investigation at all.

The next East Area Rapist assault to take place after this burglary was on November 10th, 1976 in Sacramento, and the previous one had been on October 18th, 1976. There was a wide window of time where the offender could've made it to Visalia and back.

Again, this incident has been proposed as being related simply because the burglary was suspicious and the victim had been targeted before by the Ransacker. It may or may not be related. Knowing the full extent of how the offender operated from the early 1970s all the way through to the mid 1980s (and beyond, counting harassing phone calls), it probably wouldn't surprise anyone if this *was* the VR committing one final crime in the area – the town where he got his most prolific start.

Profiles

In an effort to understand the man that they were hunting, the police made two attempts at profiling the Visalia Ransacker. Their hope was that an overview of his behaviors and the likelihoods of various attributes that the killer might possess could serve to narrow the suspect pool and help generate leads.

The first profile was made in-house, and it was generated about a month after the Claude Snelling murder. The second one was made with outside assistance after the crime spree had ended. Even today, both profiles provide interesting insights into this series of crimes.

October 1975: First Profile

In early October 1975, an officer at the Visalia Police Department attempted to gather all of the information known about the Visalia Ransacker in hopes of discovering a pattern that could help lead to identification.

The profile began with the observation that the Ransacker was primarily active on weekends (Friday, Saturday, and Sunday) and that he tossed around women's underclothing in a more "exaggerated manner" than other clothing at the crime scenes. The tossing about of women's clothing was certainly one of the most distinctive M.O. traits found at VR scenes.

The officer also noted that the Ransacker frequently took money and Blue Chip stamps, and that he sometimes also took cosmetics and female underclothing. When it came to jewelry and other valuable items, he noted that the Ransacker didn't tend to take items of value, but that he would rather take personal jewelry or a single earring from a pair.

The profile included about a dozen different instances of the Ransacker leaving items against the inside of doors, constituting what the officer termed as a "warning system." The tendency of the VR to open multiple windows and/or doors as a means of quick escape was also in his report.

He emphasized that the Ransacker took pistols and ammunition, but that would leave other types of firearms behind.

There was some commentary on his breaking and entering skills – the officer noted that there were over a dozen instances where the Ransacker pried at a particular entrance or lock but couldn't find a way to force it open. His conclusion was that the offender was "not proficient in forcing entry."

He noted that the Ransacker sometimes removed, destroyed, and/or stole photos of girls or children.

The report also states that the Ransacker vastly preferred operating on east-to-west streets as opposed to streets that ran north and south. At the time the report was compiled, the Ransacker had hit east/west streets *twice* as much as he'd hit north/south ones.

It's interesting to note that at this point in the investigation (two months before the McGowen shooting), the officer who compiled this report felt that the Ransacker was on the younger end of what ended up being the proposed age spectrum. He described him as likely being a white male, early twenties, 5'8" to 5'11", between 150 and 180 lbs, with collar-length brown hair. Many of these descriptors clearly came from the Snelling incident, which was the main focus of the investigation at the time. The idea that he was younger was probably based on the general feeling that the burglaries seemed immature and childish to many of the officers.

The profiler felt that the VR had a connection to Mt. Whitney High School (either at the time that the crimes were being committed or in some years past).

He speculated about the Ransacker's home life, feeling that the killer might've lived at home with his parents and because of that, he had to be home at a certain time. It was a logical explanation for why the VR ransacked so early in the evenings. He also felt that the VR couldn't be seen carrying larger items into the house without arousing suspicion. It was assumed that he walked or rode a bike to the ransacking locations.

The officer believed that the Ransacker most likely had an unhappy life and had been unhappy while he was in school.

His explanation for the theft of the single earrings was that the VR probably collected them or frequently wore a single earring himself.

The officer even spent time speculating about where the VR could've lived. He felt that he most likely *did* live in the strike zone (which he defined as South Demaree Street on the west, State Route 198 on the north, South Court Street on the east, and West Walnut Avenue on the south).

No further information had been developed at that time. Looking back on these ideas and having the full dataset of the crimes at our disposal (plus forty years of advances in criminology), clearly the thinking on some of these theories has changed over time – but there's a lot that this officer got right and a lot of good police work involved in this profile.

Once a couple months had passed and the Visalia Ransacker was spotted clearly at the McGowen incident, some of these ideas were adjusted. They felt that the VR was between twenty-five and thirty-five, and that due to McGowen not recognizing him and no one turning in any solid tips based on the composite sketches, the idea was proposed that he *didn't* live in the attack zone. Officers felt that he could've been living in the north side of town, or perhaps somewhere like Woodlake or Exeter. It was even possible that he was living as far as Bakersfield, a location south of town – and officers eventually learned that he ended up referencing Bakersfield twice as the East Area Rapist. Bakersfield was ruled out because it was too far, but forty more years of history have shown us that it's not unheard of for sexually motivated offenders commute significant distances to commit their crimes. Generally, though, Woodlake or Exeter seemed to be the most likely origin point.

The time constraint that the officer noticed (the burglaries occurring early in the evening) could've indeed been imposed by family (parents or a wife), or perhaps by his occupation. Since he passed up several items of value, many officers felt that he had a source of income apart from burglaries, especially once they bumped the age estimate up to a higher number.

A possible connection to Mt. Whitney High School was a classic "chicken or egg" problem. Did he choose his ransacking areas because of a connection with that particular school, or did a connection to that particular school show up because of where he had chosen to offend? Teenagers on the south side of town went to Mt. Whitney High School, and teenagers north of the highway went to Redwood High School. Since all of his crimes occurred south of the highway, only teenagers who went to Mt. Whitney were his victims. There were three instances of Redwood connections throughout the crime spree, however – three staff members of Redwood High School (some of them retired) were ransacking victims.

One area of the profile that modern theory has additional insight on is the motivation behind the theft of single earrings. It's easy to see why they initially thought that the VR was simply collecting these – most of what he stole constituted a "collection" of sorts (coins in piggybanks, coin collections, and collections of Blue Chip stamps). One of the theories that resonates with us is that he took these small, personal items to cause a specific kind of feeling of loss in his victims. It's also thought by some that he took those "collections" because the victim had spent so much time accumulating those things, and that there was a psychological thrill in undoing their efforts. That might explain why a jar of pennies might be taken, but cash might be found and then displayed on the bed. There's a statement of sorts there, and if researchers and investigators are reading it correctly, the statement is "I took your pennies that you spent so long collecting, and look, I found your hidden cash and left it behind because I'm not doing this for the money, I'm doing this just to mess with you." The idea behind the theft of a single earring may be the same – "When you go to put your earrings on later you'll realize that I've been here and I took it. I'm not doing this for the money or I'd take both. I just like the little jolt of fear and violation you feel when you realize I took it. I have control."

Officers working the case at the time were fairly advanced in their thinking, and they realized that they weren't dealing with a "normal" run-of-the-mill burglar. Since there were probably deeper psychological reasons for why the Ransacker did what he did, they brought in a psychologist to help them make another, more advanced profile of the Visalia Ransacker.

February 1976: Second Profile

The new profile created in February 1976 produced several angles that the police had not considered before. The ideas and insights generated during these sessions were part of some very forward-thinking police work for the time period.

The profiler came up with the following theories and observations:

The underlying motive for the crimes was sexual in nature. Burglary was secondary to the offender – he was primarily a prowler/peeper.

The offender was voyeuristic and received gratification from seeing his victims' intimate possessions.

It's possible that he went home and masturbated to the burglaries, sometimes with the items that he stole. He may not have always masturbated during the commission of the crime.

He probably kept the items that he took, according to the profiler. Some of the current investigators aren't so sure – some feel that he was too evidence conscious and that he dumped most the items as soon as he completed the burglaries.

He most likely spent a lot of time peeking into windows, and had probably looked into hundreds of homes. Most of this activity was not noticed and not reported to the police. Weeks or months later, he probably returned to some of those same residences to burglarize them.

The offender did not necessarily live in Visalia. After going over the behaviors and evidence, the profiler felt that he could've been coming to Visalia for the sole purpose of "entertainment and gratification." The feeling at this point was that if he didn't live in the area of the crimes, then he had to live fairly close. They specifically mentioned

Woodlake or Exeter as possible origin points – they were eyeing areas that were far enough away but not very populous. They felt that if he were living in a bigger city, then he would be offending *there* instead of Visalia. Exeter in particular was on the radar at various points, given that one of the guns that the Ransacker had stolen was found near there.

He probably lived alone or with an elderly relative. It was impossible to know for sure though, and he could've been married. Regardless, he was a "loner." This was a little different than what the thinking had been earlier in the series, which was that the Ransacker had to hide his activities from his parents.

Neighbors, peers, and fellow workers probably considered him "weird" in his daily life.

The offender most likely did not have a common mental illness. He was not mentally retarded, and he could probably function effectively during the daytime.

The profiler felt that the VR enjoyed the high risk and the danger associated with the types of crimes he was committing

The general consensus was that the offender was gone from the area, but that he would continue his pattern of peeping, prowling, and burglarizing in another location.

To sum up the analysis, the profiler said that the offender could be leading a very ordinary existence. He wouldn't call attention to himself, and he'd be fairly isolated and reclusive. He'd probably have very few social relations or friendships, and he could live in his home or his neighborhood for a long time without neighbors knowing very much about him.

The Investigation

The investigation into the VR case was sweeping and thorough. Police identified close to forty viable suspects early on, and they began systematically clearing them one by one.

Since Claude Snelling's daughter had been a primary target, a main focus of the investigation started there. Her life was examined thoroughly, but nothing significant could really be found. She was very involved in the church, and connections she had there were turned inside out to no avail. She worked part-time, so her co-workers were looked at. Nothing there, either. She couldn't recall anything specific that stood out in the time leading up to the murder... she did have a general feeling that she was being watched or followed by car, no one in her personal life had behaved in a creepy or inappropriate way toward her. There hadn't been any situation where someone had asked her out and she'd had to turn them down.

She didn't feel like she was stalked by anyone she knew, and she told the police that she didn't think she'd ever met her attacker before.

Since the Visalia Ransacker had a history of targeting Mt. Whitney High School students, the school population (past and present) was examined for possible suspects. Witnesses felt that the attacker was definitely older than a high school student, but the investigation was all-encompassing and over twenty persons of interest were generated from the high school or from an association with it. A few of them were cleared easily, and close to a dozen more of them had almost nothing to possibly tie them to the series other than a passing physical resemblence or a few hours of their lives on September 10th, 1975 where they didn't have a solid alibi.

The police worked a different angle, wondering if Claude Snelling himself had been the actual target all along. Investigating Claude's life for suspects was just as difficult as it was for the investigators who examined his daughter's life – Claude had no enemies and was universally liked. No one from the church, the college, or from anywhere else in his life could be found who might have had a motive for his murder. Still, the police pressed on, even looking at some of his students as potential suspects. Claude's daughter was asked if she'd ever accompanied her father to work or if she'd ever spent time at the college. She had not.

Other persons of interest were generated in the case, many of them developed independently of the Snelling investigation. Local sex offenders, known peepers, and locals who had been charged with kidnapping in the past were looked at as possible suspects. Even the girl whose bicycle had been stolen by the VR was a possible suspect at one point – proof that investigators were leaving no stone unturned.

Depsite hundreds of hours being spent on these persons of interest, the Visalia Ransacker could not be identified.

Granted, the police didn't have a lot to go on. In over thirty ransackings where they'd collected fingerprints, not a single one could be matched. They had descriptions of his shoes and matching impressions, and from that they were able to determine that he'd been wearing a pair of size nine low-top Converse All Stars, probably black in color based on eyewitness reports. But the shoe wasn't distinctive enough to make an identification, and the Ransacker could change shoes whenever he wanted to.

One person of interest *was* developed from the shoe angle, though. One night during the VR crime spree, an officer noticed a man walking in the darkness. The officer approached the subject and noticed that his shoes matched the Visalia Ransacker's, so he quickly asked the man to come with him to the police station. The subject was cooperative, and after questioning, it was determined that the individual was not the Visalia Ransacker.

At the beginning of 1976, the suspect list had grown to contain nearly a hundred persons of interest. One of them looked promising – a young man who had attempted to kidnap a teacher from Mt. Whitney High School. But over time he too was cleared, along with many other promising suspects.

Early in 1976, a computer specialist from Sacramento was brought in to help the officers sort through some of the information that they'd compiled. He also helped them look for other possible crimes in other areas that could be tied to the Visalia Ransacker. The process was very involved, but the specialist came up mostly empty-handed. Little did he know, the Visalia Ransacker was in the process of moving to his own city.

For a time in early March 1976, it seemed the Visalia Ransacker was back. An area of South Dollner Street located in the southern portion of the VR's attack zone experienced a lot of prowler activity. Witnesses caught him in the act several times, and they provided a description that vaguely resembled the Ransacker. The police began working the area immediately, using every forensic tool at their disposal in hopes of finally catching the VR. The press ran with the story that the Ransacker appeared to be back.

It turned out that the prowler had clearly left some fingerprints. Hoping that this would be their big break, they conducted stakeouts and followed a few of the leads that they'd generated. They even learned of a stolen bicycle, which reminded them of the Snelling murder.

The case proved to be a fairly simple one – the prowler was caught by police within a couple of weeks. They ran the fingerprints, researched his history, and examined him for any possible Visalia Ransacker ties. Unfortunately, examination of his record showed that he was in prison during several of the ransackings. This "Dollner Street Prowler" was not the VR.

As spring came to a close and summer started, the VR investigation started to slow down and run out of avenues to pursue. In June, the East Area Rapist began hitting in Sacramento. As that crime spree wore on, investigators in Visalia started to notice some similarities between that offender and their own Visalia Ransacker.

In February 1977, over a year after the McGowen incident, the Visalia Police Department made contact with the Sacramento Sheriff's office and they exchanged some basic information. On May 17th, 1977, the Sacramento police released a composite sketch of the East Area Rapist. Visalia officers were struck by the resemblance to their own sketches of the VR. The two officers that had been part of the December 10th, 1975 stakeout on West Kaweah Avenue got in the car and immediately made their way to Sacramento. They were followed by to two more Visalia Police Department officers.

They met with officials in Sacramento. The conversation was not a good one – something went wrong politically during that meeting and both parties came away with negative views of each other. They took their fued to the newspapers, and words were said that seemed to dig an insurmountable rift between the two departments. The years that followed can be charitably characterized as "lacking in cooperation."

Things cooled decades later, but both cases still remained unsolved for many years.

The East Area Rapist

Introducton to the EAR

The offender known as the "East Area Rapist" was a prolific, sexually motivated home-invasion criminal who began operating in Northern California in the mid 1970s. It's generally accepted that his first attack was in June 1976, though the October 1975 attack that we presented earlier in the book has gained quite a bit more traction among investigators as a possible first attack.

He continued attacking victims in their home until 1979, when he moved his operations down to Southern California and began a murder spree that lasted until 1986. DNA evidence connects three of his rape crimes to most of the Southern California murders.

He targeted middle and upper-middle-class people in their own homes in the late night or the early morning hours. A typical attack involved the victim(s) being awakened from a sound sleep by a flashlight beaming into their eyes. They'd barely catch a fleeting glimpse of a masked intruder (one who wore a different mask to every single crime) before their hands were bound tightly – so tightly that circulation was restricted and their hands would turn purple. The East Area Rapist, speaking through a harsh whisper and clenched teeth, would often claim that he was just looking for "food and money." With his victims securely bound, he'd then begin ransacking the residence. If a couple (rather than a lone woman) was being attacked, he would lead the female out of the bedroom and leave the male behind. Dishes from the kitchen were then stacked on the man's back so that the assailant would hear him if he moved or tried to escape.

The assailant would sexually assault the woman, usually multiple times, amidst a constant barrage of verbal and physical threats. He'd often use a gun or a sharp object (like a knife) as a control weapon to gain compliance. After lording over the house for up to three or more hours, the offender would silently make his escape, taking with him a few personal items belonging to his victims and most of whatever cash was lying around.

Time and time again, month after month and year after year, the East Area Rapist eluded police. Not a single blatant clue to his identity could be found. As he moved into Southern California in 1979, he began killing non-compliant victims with gunshots and compliant victims by bludgeoning. Decades later, this phase of the crime spree earned him the name "Golden State Killer." Even with the higher stakes, nothing substantial related to the offender's identity could be uncovered.

Before all was said and done, the East Area Rapist had committed home-invasion rape attacks in several jurisdictions, including areas east of Sacramento like Rancho Cordova, Carmichael, Citrus Heights, Orangevale, and Foothill Farms. Other places he offended in included Stockton, Davis, Modesto, Concord, San Ramon, Danville, San Jose, Fremont, and Walnut Creek. He murdered victims in Southern California locations like Goleta, Ventura, Dana Point, and Irvine.

Two of the murders occurred in Sacramento on February 2nd, 1978.

Despite so many attacks and so many potential clues left behind, the cases remained unsolved for over forty years. Investigators had no idea where this killer had came from or where he had disappeared to after the series concluded.

Of course, as early as 1977, some were noticing key behavioral similarities between the East Area Rapist and the Visalia Ransacker. The prolific number of offenses, the sexually motivated nature of the rummaging and ransacking, the amount of time that both offenders spent inside the residences, the theft of personal items rather than items of value, timelines that interlocked well, and various other crosspoints raised many interesting questions over the years. There were certainly attributes that *didn't* match as well, which made investigation quite difficult.

Connections between the VR and the EAR

If you've read our book *Case Files of the East Area Rapist / Golden State Killer,* you've been through an intense study of the EAR/GSK crimes. Now that some light has been shed on the Visalia Ransacker offenses, some interesting analysis can take place.

Dozens of attributes and connections have been proposed and studied between the EAR series and the VR series, but since have finally announced that the two men are the same, we only need to tackle some of the main ones. We'll start with some of the general characteristics that both of the phases shared in common – attributes that set them apart from other crimes and other criminals of the era. Then, we'll discuss some of the more specific behavioral connections. We'll even look at some behaviors that *weren't* the same, because examining how this offender evolved over time can also be quite illuminating.

Some of the connections include:

Committing a high volume of offenses in a short period of time
The number of crimes committed in both the VR phase and the EAR phase are staggering – over one hundred burglaries committed in Visalia from 1973 to 1975 and over one hundred burglaries committed in Sacramento and beyond from 1976 to 1979. Not only were these crimes committed in high numbers and in small areas, but the offender committed them without ever getting caught. Even before the VR and EAR were tied together, this pointed to a similar type of criminal who spent a significant amount of time planning and organizing his crimes. Serial offenders who are able to commit that many offenses are not the norm.

Preferring personal items over valuable ones
This is more or less consistent between both phases, though in the East Area Rapist phase he did steal more items of higher value during many of his attacks. Throughout all of the crimes, he gravitated toward monogrammed or engraved items such as class rings. As the EAR, he frequently stole the wedding rings from his victims, and as the Visalia Ransacker, he once stole a man's wedding ring that had been left on a dresser. He often focused on lower-end jewelry, unique pieces, items of a more sentimental nature, and costume jewelry. As the East Area Rapist, however, he was known to sometimes steal high-end items and valuable jewelry that didn't have a personal connection to his victims.

Spending a long time inside residences
It's extremely rare for either a burglar or a rapist to spend a lengthy period of time inside a victim's home. However, both the VR and the EAR series were notable for this behavior. The EAR would spend up to four hours in a victim's home, and judging by the mess he made

and the intricate displays of women's underwear he arranged as the VR, he was also spending a significant amount of time in *those* homes, too. Usually burglars and rapists commit their crimes and then get away as quickly as possible in order to minimize risk, but this offender was never in a hurry to leave. It seemed that spending time in a victim's home added to the satisfaction he received from his crimes.

Shooting during confrontation

The Visalia Ransacker had two instances where he shot at a pursuer, intending to kill them, and the East Area Rapist had two instances as well. As the Golden State Killer, two *more* instances can be added where the offender shot people who resisted him.

The VR shot Claude Snelling twice as Snelling approached him during the September 11th kidnapping attempt. Shooting someone twice is clearly an intention to kill them – and he *did* kill him. He also shot at Officer McGowen, directly hitting his flashlight (which would've been the only visible target in the darkness), earning himself an Attempted Homicide charge.

The EAR is believed to be responsible for shooting a teenage boy who was pursuing him on the night of February 16th, 1977. He shot the boy square in the stomach at close range, and then he shot at him again but missed – again, clearly intending to kill him. The EAR is also believed to be responsible for the double homicide of Brian and Katie Maggiore on February 2nd, 1978 in Sacramento. It's believed that they confronted him while he was prowling. He chased the young couple and shot them to death.

In the Golden State Killer series, he shot and killed a man named Robert Offerman during an attack. It appeared that Offerman had worked his bindings loose and had confronted him. After killing Offerman, the GSK then executed the man's date, Alexandria

Manning. A year and a half later, a man named Gregory Sanchez was also shot by this offender under similar circumstances during an attack in the Goleta/Santa Barbara area.

Oddly enough, there were several times when the offender was confronted, challenged, or even about to be captured and he *didn't* shoot his pursuer. It's possible that in those instances, the offender didn't have a gun on him, was out of ammunition, couldn't get a clear shot, or something else stopped him. Perhaps the issue isn't as cut-and-dry as it seems, but the commonality does exist at least in some form.

Ransacking

He seemed to derive sexual pleasure from rummaging through the belongings of his victims. The only difference between the VR and EAR series was that the rummaging occurred at different points. The East Area Rapist committed over one hundred burglaries between 1976 and 1979, and he typically did not rummage and ransack during these burglaries. In fact, the vast majority of them were so discreet that the victims didn't even know that someone had been in their home until hours or days later. In stark contrast to the East Area Rapist burglaries, the rummaging and ransacking was apparent to the victims *immediately* in the Visalia Ransacker series. Homeowners would enter their residence to find every drawer in the house opened, contents strewn about, minor damage to their possessions, underwear and clothing everywhere, and various windows / doors left open in the residence.

The rummaging and ransacking during the East Area Rapist phase occurred during his home-invasion rapes, not his burglaries. He typically entered the home while his victims were sleeping and, once his victims were securely bound, he began tearing through their drawers and closets. He would engage in this behavior in between sexually assaulting the victim as well. This, along with eating the victim's food, seemed to sexually excite him. Perhaps the idea of invading the victim's privacy and handling items important to them while they were there to see him do it gave him a feeling of power, importance, dominance, or the thrill of seeing things that he wasn't supposed to see.

It should be noted that since the EAR's pre-attack and post-attack burglaries weren't terribly messy and they didn't share much in common with the Visalia Ransacker, it's easier to see how investigators could not immediately connect the two.

While rummaging, the offender gravitated toward stealing personal items from his victims. As the VR, he tended to steal items such as keepsake piggybanks and personalized jewelry. He also made a point of stealing anything that the owners spent their time collecting, such as Blue Chip stamps, coin collections, collectible stamps, and change jars. After taking these items, the VR would often show very little regard for them – balling up stamps, storing collectible coins in a sock (where they'd clang against each other and lose their value), and sometimes he'd discard the items altogether at a nearby location. This type of behavior can be read as the offender wanting to rob someone of their time and effort. It seemed to be a paradigm designed to insult or annoy his victims.

As the East Area Rapist he *also* stole personal items. It can be argued that some of the items taken during the EAR phase seemed to be more in the nature of "trophy" items or things that were taken to relive his crimes later. He still took keepsakes and coins, but he also took driver's licenses and school identification cards. This could have been an extension of the same type of behavior seen in the VR series though – as the VR, he typically wouldn't have access to items like identification cards because his victims weren't at home while he was there.

The EAR *also* discarded several of the stolen items near the scene of the burglary, or sometimes he even deposited them in other homes that he burglarized or attacked. It seemed to be a "game" designed to show his victims that their personal items meant very little to him and to show them that he was here, there, and everywhere.

One of the unanswered questions about this case is whether the offender kept these items, and how long he might've retained them. The thefts seemed to be designed around causing pain and inconvenience for his victims, but he certainly may have kept some of the items for himself as "souvenirs" for a period of time.

Leaving Cash Behind

Cash would sometimes be left behind at Visalia Ransacker and East Area Rapist scenes. He did this far more as the VR than as the EAR, but the manner in which the cash was left out, almost as if on display, was similar.

The Visalia Ransacker would often rifle through every nook and cranny of a house, and as he did, he sometimes came across cash that the residents had hidden. When he found cash in this manner, he would often display it prominently on a bed or a kitchen counter rather than steal it. In a similar vein, sometimes when he came across piggybanks, he would empty them out and leave them upside down or on their side, making it obvious to the owner that he had fleeced them. When rifling through a jewelry box, he would either dump it out and leave the contents strewn about, or he would leave the lid of the jewelry box on the bed or the counter to show the owner that he had been through it.

As the East Area Rapist, his actions were more of a mix. He stole most of the cash he came across, which amounted to thousands upon thousands of dollars over the years. If he came across hidden cash, he typically stole it. As one victim put it, he took "anything of value that wasn't nailed down." From one scene, he stole $4,000 worth of jewelry. There *were* instances, however, where the EAR left cash behind. When he did, it was left in a prominent place on the counter or dresser, just like in the VR series. In one instance, he found a victim's hidden store of cash, and he took exactly half of it and left the other half behind. That's not typical behavior for a robber or home-invasion rapist, so it's something that sets these crimes apart from others.

Victims receiving hang-up and threatening phone calls

One of the more distinctive components of the EAR's M.O. was that he would make hang-up and threatening phone calls to victims and potential victims both before and after he attacked them. There are hundreds of such calls described in the East Area Rapist series. He'd even continue to call victims for years after their attacks – in one case, he called a victim *twenty-five years* after he attacked her. Another victim felt that she was receiving hang-up phone calls from him up until 2017 – over *forty years* after her attack.

As the Visalia Ransacker, he didn't make nearly as many phone calls, but he did make quite a few. This part of his M.O. was unfortunately underreported, misunderstood, and sometimes completely written off. It's only in recent years that the information has been compiled, and the parallel between this behavior as the VR seemed to match up well with his behavior as the EAR.

Perhaps it's not surprising that this didn't jump out to anyone as an important possible link, though. These crimes took place in an era where crank calls and harassing phone calls were quite common. It probably didn't always seem terribly odd to victims who were receiving these obscene or strange phone messages, particularly victims who were burglarized and hadn't encountered the offender in their home.

It does seem to speak volumes about the VR/EAR that he chose to engage his victims in this way. Simple burglary or rape was clearly not the only objective for him – there was much more going on psychologically. The phone calls went beyond reconnaissance – they were short bursts of connection, terror, and low-risk ways of violating his victims. He, the anonymous harasser, could attempt to create the illusion of mystery and power over them even through the phone. In former victims, it was a way to randomly intervene in their life and create a cascading uneasiness that could last for months or years after a singular phone call.

Stealing bicycles

On the night of the Snelling murder, police believe that the Visalia Ransacker stole a bicycle from one residence, used it to transport himself to the attack scene, and then ditched it shortly afterward at a *different* residence. This is the only known incidence of the VR stealing a bike.

There were a handful of incidents where the East Area Rapist *also* stole a bicycle from one home, committed a crime at another home, and then ditched the bike at yet another home. In a chilling parallel to the Snelling crime, one of these was a double homicide (Offerman/Manning).

This certainly isn't the most unique connection between the two phases – an offender stealing a bicycle to commit a crime elsewhere and then ditching it as he or she makes a getaway is a somewhat common offense. But it's unique enough, given the totality of the connections, to be addressed and included here.

Using lotion at the scene

Starting with some of the Ransacker's earliest crimes, it seemed clear to police that he was using hand lotion to masturbate while he was in some of the homes. As the East Area Rapist, he would often use hand lotion or baby oil to lubricate himself before assaulting his victims.

This choice of lubricant seemed to be made out of convenience to the offender rather than preference, at least in the early crimes. It was also something that he'd have a logical explanation for if he were ever caught with it.

Home-Invasion Rape

If someone were to do a very basic side-by-side comparison of the criminals without nuance, without context, and without depth, then they would look quite dissimilar. After all, the East Area Rapist was a home-invasion rapist and the Visalia Ransacker was not. In the two years that the Ransacker offended, the Snelling incident was the only crime that seemed to come close.

The other side to this coin is that the Snelling incident *does* seem EAR-like in many ways. It's important to keep in mind that home-invasion rapes against strangers are quite rare, as are home-invasion kidnappings of strangers. One could argue that even though the actions themselves were different, the spirit behind them was the same – to be brazen enough to enter a home full of people in the middle of the night and attempt to commit a sex crime is something somewhat rare that both of these series shared.

Many crimes of this type against strangers are based around opportunity. Most offenders would *not* see a small home with five people in it as an ideal kidnapping opportunity. It's not – and that's one of the reasons it failed. A parallel can be found in the East Area Rapist series. For his third attack in 1976, the EAR entered a home occupied by three people – a mother and her two daughters. The mother overpowered him and the women escaped. Again, most offenders would not have seen this as an ideal home-invasion rape opportunity.

Furthermore, while the Ransacker never committed a home-invasion rape, it could be argued that his attempts at entering occupied homes toward the end of his crime spree may have been. Fortunately, the offender didn't get far enough for us to find out.

Panties

The Visalia Ransacker had a preoccupation with women's undergarments. Not only did he remove them from drawers and closets, but he carefully arranged them in deliberate displays. In the East Area Rapist series, this behavior appears to be absent, for the most part. This was an area where there *wasn't* much similarity between the offenders.

This difference is explained by some as the EAR now attacking live women and not having any need to offend by proxy with panties or lingerie. It's still quite peculiar that the East Area Rapist committed roughly 125 burglaries between 1976 and 1979 (burglaries where he didn't attack anyone, that is) and he didn't engage in the same type of behavior with women's undergarments. Since this type of behavior is certainly one of the more common ones that sexually motivated burglars display (even though the Ransacker had a decidedly different take on it), it's not surprising that investigators were perplexed by the lack of similarity here. As the Ransacker, he made such a mess when he burglarized a home, and as the East Area Rapist, there was often scant trace that he'd even been there (only during a burglary, not during one of his attacks). An empty container of applesauce in the trash can, a few pieces of jewelry that belonged to someone else, a missing package of cigarettes, a window left unlocked, a piece of rope under the couch, some envelopes moved from one side of the drawer to another – one or two of these were often the only indications that the East Area Rapist had even burglarized a home.

Of course, if the goal was to do reconnassaince for a possible attack, then why tip off the homeowners that he'd been there? Why put them on high-alert? The difference between the two phases could be explained as easily as that. When he was the East Area Rapist, the rummaging and ransacking took place *during* the attacks. That was when he was getting his sexual gratification, and the ransacking seemed to be an integral part of that.

To be fair though, there were a few instances that we're aware of where the EAR displayed VR-like behavior when it came to women's undergarments. In both Stockton attacks, the East Area Rapist removed a pair of pantyhose, tied them in a knot, and poked a hole in the crotch with his finger. In a pre-attack burglary in Walnut Creek, the EAR stole a woman's nightgown. During Attack #22, he brought several items of clothing out from drawers and laid them out in a peculiar display in the living room while the assault was ongoing.

Single earrings

One of the most peculiar things that the VR did on a fairly regular basis was the theft of a single earring from a pair, sometimes from multiple sets of earrings at one scene. He'd take one and leave the matching one behind, breaking up the set. We theorized elsewhere in the book that this puzzling, quirky behavior was a smug attempt to instill fear in his victims at a later date – as they went to put on their jewelry, they'd notice that an earring was missing and know that he'd been there. He also rendered the set of earrings useless, because most of the victims would only want to wear the set, not a single earring. He also could have done this to show them that he wasn't stealing the earrings for the value (or else he'd take both), and he wasn't stealing them because he was going to use them for anything (they were only useful to someone as a set), so he was probably doing it simply to show his disregard for them.

As the EAR, he didn't really engage in this behavior. In fact, only one instance is documented – Victim #6. This particular victim may have been "special" to him in some way, because her house had been burglarized in an EAR-style burglary in spring of 1973, about three and a half years before the home-invasion rape took place. This burglary occurred before the Visalia Ransacker series was even underway, so it may or may not be related.

Assaulting a victim outside

One of the leftover mysteries in the Visalia Ransacker case is the logistics of what he planned to do with Claude Snelling's daughter after he brought her outside of the home. Investigators unanimously believe that he planned to sexually assault her, but they're unsure of what the VR's exact plans *were*. Did he plan to steal the Snellings' vehicle and kidnap her, and was that why he went through the wife's purse before waking the daughter? Did he plan on assaulting her in the camper across the street where he had placed the window screen? Did he have transportation nearby? Or did he plan on assaulting her outside?

Attacks that occurred during the East Area Rapist phase may give us some clue. There were several early assaults where he led victims outside:

- In Attack #6 on October 9th, 1976, he extracted his victim from her home and assaulted her in the backyard. She was home alone, but it's not known whether he knew that or not – he tied the inside doors together with rope so that they couldn't be opened, which seemed to indicate that he thought there might've been someone else inside the house.

- In Attack #8 on October 18th, 1976, he attacked a young woman as she was getting out of her car. He led her into someone else's backyard, which had been "prepared" with strips of towel laid out to use as bindings. He bound the victim and then left without assaulting her.

- In Attack #9 on November 10th, 1976, the East Area Rapist took a teenage girl out of her home while she was alone. He led her down a canal and a long distance away from her residence. When they ended up at a remote outdoor location, he undressed her but didn't sexually assault her.

- In Attack #10 on December 18th, 1976, the EAR again took a teenage girl out of her home while she was there alone. After assaulting her briefly in the backyard, he took her back inside where he assaulted her again.

These outdoor elements are interesting in light of what happened at the Snelling home. In the Visalia Ransacker series, there's not enough data to know if the VR was simply transporting the teenager somewhere else, or if there was actually going to be an outdoor element to this attack like there was in some of the EAR assaults that occurred in 1976.

Antique police billy club
At the East Area Rapist's third canonical attack, which took place on August 29th, 1976, the offender used what looked like an antique police billy club. The description of it vaguely matched the club stolen at a Visalia Ransacker burglary on October 24th, 1975. In July, the EAR had beaten a man with a blunt object that's sometimes described as a billy club, but closer examination of the case reveals that the weapon in that instance was more like a wooden paddle.

Stealing piggy banks
One of the Visalia Ransacker's most distinctive trademark behaviors was virtually absent in the East Area Rapist phase. In over a hundred burglaries and over fifty attacks, there are only a handful of instances where the East Area Rapist actually stole a coin bank or piggy bank.

One of them was in a pre-attack burglary on his fifth victim. Ironically, this was also the first EAR-phase attack where he made a threatening phone call (not just hang-up phone calls), and it was where began stealing personal jewelry from nearby neighbors. Perhaps the offender made a concious effort to change certain aspects of his M.O. for his first few attacks, and then when he felt that he wouldn't be connected to Visalia (or perhaps when his urges got too strong), he began reverting back to some of his VR-like behavior.

Since he had upped the ante considerably in his EAR attacks, perhaps he no longer felt the need to take the piggy banks. He was hurting his victims in other ways. He still, however, seemed to have a fascination with coins – he would often steal coins from residences during his attacks. One of the attacks where he did this was Attack #35 (June 24th, 1978 in Davis), where he stole seventeen rolls of pennies.

Left-Handed
It wasn't known for sure if the East Area Rapist was left-handed or right, but several victims felt that he *was* left-handed, especially during the earlier crimes in the series. A victim who was shot by the EAR on February 16th, 1977 and ended up surviving the encounter noted that the offender had fired the gun with his left hand. Witnesses to the two shootings committed by the Visalia Ransacker *also* felt that he fired with his left hand.

Shoe Size
Both the VR and the EAR left shoe prints that ranged from about 8.5 to 9.5.

Characteristics like the VR/EAR's possible race, height, and hair weren't specific enough or distinctive enough to draw comparison – they were traits shared by a large portion of the population.

Investigation into the Connections

Other connections exist – the offender relying on creek beds to move throughout the cities that he attacked, the fact that he never left fingerprints, the put-on voice that he used, and more. One of the most interesting ties wasn't a behavioral of physical characteristic at all, though – it was timing. One prolific sexually motivated offender stopping and then another one starting up six months later (two hundred miles away) certainly raised some eyebrows among investigators who began working these cases.

Viewing the information as we've presented it, it might seem almost obvious that there was something to the Visalia Ransacker / East Area Rapist connection idea. Keep in mind that this is a list compiled after countless people have spent their entire careers working on the cases, studying the nuances, and over forty years later, finally discovering that the Visalia Ransacker and the East Area Rapist / Golden State Killer were indeed the same offender. It's a cherry-picked list created with the benefit of much hindsight. For decades, the two cases were plagued with witness descriptions that didn't match up, timeline issues during October 1975, the lack of any matching fingerprints or physical evidence, and jurisdictional issues.

Speaking of the jurisdictional issues, in the previous chapter we discussed how the spirit of cooperation between Visalia and Sacramento had fizzled out in the 1970s. Thankfully, in the late 1990s and early 2000s, there was renewed interest in working together. An investigator from Orange County named Larry Pool spearheaded several projects to try to determine whether a link between VR/EAR could be proven or not. While he wasn't able to put the issue to rest one way or the other, he added a vast amount of information to the body of knowledge surrounding the VR case. Our research has benefitted greatly from the facts and resources that he was able to put together.

While it was unknown for many years whether the VR went on to become the East Area Rapist, it was more or less accepted by everyone involved that, unless injured, killed, or apprehended, the Visalia Ransacker would continue to escalate and would go on to become some kind of serial offender *somewhere*. Earlier in this chapter, we described the general East Area Rapist M.O. and the rape crimes that he went on to commit. Now we'll explore an even darker series of crimes that he's responsible for – the Golden State Killer murders.

The Golden State Killer

Before all was said and done, the East Area Rapist had committed roughly fifty home-invasion rapes. He'd begun in Sacramento, hit Stockton twice, and then he'd started moving around the state. Modesto, Davis, Concord, San Ramon, San Jose, Danville, Fremont and Walnut Creek were terrorized by him from 1975 or 1976 all the way through the summer of 1979.

Following a close call in Danville and then another one in San Ramon, the EAR made a large geographic move – very similar to when he'd left Visalia for Sacramento. In the fall of 1979, he resurfaced in the Goleta/Santa Barbara area – 325 miles away from the Northern California region he'd been hitting so hard for over three years.

Strange phone calls, prowlers, and shadows at windows became the norm for days or weeks in September. Then, in the early morning hours of October 1st, 1979, he finally made his presence fully known.

A young Goleta couple had been in bed for hours. Their house was set back from the road – barely visible. It was situated next to a dry creek bed, similar in many ways to Evan's Ditch in Visalia. Nights were usually dark and quiet.

But on this night, all was not quiet. The Goleta couple woke suddenly to the sensation of someone violently kicking their bed. All of their senses burned at once.

"Wake up! Wake up!"

Like the hiss of a snake, the intruder gave them orders in an angry rasp. The bright beam of a flashlight darted back and forth between their eyes.

"Don't move motherfucker, or I'll kill you." He ordered them onto their stomachs. Claiming that he just wanted money, he threw ligatures onto the bed and forced the woman to tie the man up. "Tie it tight or I'll kill you."

She complied.

This was how almost every East Area Rapist attack started. Caught off-guard and paralyzed by fear, his victims would obey his commands and hope against hope that they would survive the ordeal. His threats had qualifiers. "Do this *or* I'll kill you. Give me money *or* I'll kill you." While they all felt that he would kill them without hesitation, as long as that essential "or" was present, there was always hope for survival.

That's how it had been for years.

This time, however, as the attack progressed, that crucial "or" went away. With a move to a new location, it seemed a new boldness had come over this offender – the man who had at first appeared so harmless in Visalia as he stole piggybanks and lined up bras now had something new in mind.

"I'll kill 'em. I'll kill 'em," he chanted in the kitchen. The woman, whom he had led out of the bedroom shortly after the man was tied up, heard him say this phrase over and over. "I'll kill 'em. I'll kill 'em."

There was no "or."

She was blindfolded. He loomed over her, and his flashlight beam crawled over her naked body. He masturbated while he did this.

"Now I'm going to kill you," he said. "Cut your throat."

This was a *statement*, not a threat.

When she heard him go back into the kitchen, she knew that she could either stay and die a horrific death, or she could at least *try* to escape. Her hands bound, her feet bound, and her eyes blindfolded, she rolled into a standing position and started hopping as quickly as she could toward what she thought might be the direction of the door.

She hit the wall, but somehow was able to keep her balance. As she slid along the perimeter of the room, the bindings around her ankles came loose. She moved faster, and she quickly found the doorknob. After struggling with it for what seemed like an eternity, it opened.

"Help me!" she screamed, running blindly down the driveway. As she filled her lungs and prepared to scream again, her body slammed into the side of her neighbor's house. Dazed, she stumbled back.

Strong hands pushed her to the ground, and she felt gloved fingers in her mouth. "I told you to be quiet!" the offender hissed. She felt a knife at her throat as he pulled her back into the house.

Meanwhile, the male victim had heard the commotion and, thinking that the intruder had just killed his girlfriend, he rolled off the bed and hopped into the backyard. His cries for help went unanswered by neighbors, so he curled into a ball and hid behind a tree.

After the offender had forced the woman back into the house, he went to check on the man. Realizing he was gone, he stepped into the backyard to look for him. The male victim watched the assailant from his hiding place. He held his breath and prayed that he wouldn't be found.

The woman took this opportunity to get up and run away again. She was able to free her feet and remove her blindfold just enough to head straight out the door and down the driveway. Screaming for help, she ran into the middle of the street. A car had to stop to avoid hitting her.

By this time, the next-door neighbor, an FBI agent, had heard the cries for help and he'd summoned the authorities. Grabbing his service weapon, he went outside to assist the couple. As he approached their home, an unmasked man in jeans and a gray/blue plaid shirt whizzed past on a bicycle.

The FBI agent pursued the subject by car. A few streets away, the bicyclist realized that he was about to be caught, so he jumped the curb, hopped off of the bike, dropped his knife, climbed over a fence, and disappeared into the darkness.

Officers descended on the area, but the subject couldn't be located. In a scenario that echoes the Snelling murder, it was determined that prior to gaining entry to the victims' home, he'd stolen the bicycle from a residence located a few streets away.

The local police viewed this as an isolated incident, but it was learned years later that this was the work of the East Area Rapist. He'd not had a chance to place dishes on the back of his male victim, and some of his other behaviors hadn't had a chance to reveal themselves in the attack, but as the years wore on and the offender returned to the area, he eventually left DNA in the city that made the link conclusive.

The Visalia Ransacker had grown even meaner and *more* vicious in the four years since the Snelling murder. By now his home-invasion rapes numbered in the fifties, and he was beginning a new chapter in his crime series – home-invasion *homicides*. Just like he had shifted several elements of his M.O. when he made the change from Visalia to Sacramento, he was making shifts to his M.O. as he made the change from Northern California to Southern California.

The next time he entered an occupied home in the Goleta/Santa Barbara area, it was in the early morning hours of December 30th, 1979. His victims on that morning were not nearly as fortunate as the ones from October 1st. Robert Offerman and Alexandria Manning were found shot to death.

Apparently, Offerman had broken free of his bonds and had confronted the offender. Just as Claude Snelling had been shot for daring to challenge him, just as William McGowen had been shot at, then the Sacramento teen, and then Brian and Katie Maggiore, so too was Robert Offerman. Police were able to determine that even after Offerman had been wounded, he'd bravely continued to go after the intruder. This resulted in him being shot three more times. The bound Alexandria Manning was then shot to death execution-style.

Before leaving the house, the killer callously helped himself to their leftover Thanksgiving turkey.

Several burglaries had been reported on the night Offerman and Manning were killed, some of them reminiscent of the same old Visalia Ransacker patterns. Personalized jewelry, a flashlight, and some coins were some of the only things stolen during the five burglaries committed that night.

His next attack occurred in Ventura in March 1980. Sadly, those victims didn't survive the night, either. Unlike the December 1979 scene, where it appeared that he'd killed Offerman and Manning because Offerman had resisted, Lyman and Charlene Smith of

Ventura were unquestionably the targets of an intentional, premeditated murderer. Their bodies were found a few days after the attack. Charlene had been raped, and both of them had been bludgeoned to death with a log from their own woodpile.

The scene repeated itself with a couple in Dana Point late in August 1980. Keith and Patrice Harrington were found bludgeoned to death in their bed. Patrice had been raped.

These crimes, occurring so far apart geographically, weren't immediately tied together. No one knew that the Visalia Ransacker had moved two hundred miles to become the East Area Rapist, and no one knew that the East Area Rapist had traveled over three hundred miles to begin a series of murders. By moving around and changing jurisdictions, he was keeping the police in the dark and preventing connections from being made. In Southern California, he took crucial evidence (like the murder weapons and the ligatures) away from the scene. Very little could be found that could help identify the man responsible for these crimes.

In February 1981, he struck in Irvine. A lone woman, Manuela Witthuhn, was raped and bludgeoned to death in her home.

July 1981 saw him back in Goleta, where he committed the murders of Cheri Domingo and Gregory Sanchez. The killer apparently encountered resistance from Greg Sanchez – he shot Sanchez in the face before bludgeoning both of them to death.

Nearly five years went by without any known crimes. A few victims during this time period received hang-up phone calls and whispered threats on their phone line, but there were no known victims of violence. That changed on the night of May 4th, 1986.

In a scene somewhat reminiscent to the Witthuhn murder several years before it, a woman staying home alone in Irvine named Janelle

Cruz became the Golden State Killer's last known murder victim. She was found in her bed the next day, bludgeoned to death. And like most of the others, she'd been raped.

Again, most of these crimes weren't tied together initially. There was no physical evidence, there was little in the way of obvious M.O. elements that could be analyzed, and there were no solid leads to go on.

The offender was careful – he'd always been careful. He planned, he stalked, he anticipated, and he was as evidence-conscious as any other offender the state had dealt with. He'd accounted for everything – almost. One thing that he *hadn't* taken into account was the future. Shortly after his crime spree ended in 1986, forensic DNA technology came onto the scene.

DNA was able to close gaps in this case that traditional investigative techniques couldn't. It was through DNA processing conducted in 1996 that investigators were finally able to determine that the Smiths, Harringtons, Manuela Witthuhn, and Janelle Cruz had all been killed by the same man.

As more and more labs came "online" and DNA technology advanced, two jurisdictions where the East Area Rapist had struck in Contra Costa County found three rape kits related to the EAR case that hadn't yet been tossed out due to the statue of limitations. They were tested against each other, and it was determined that they were matches. The same offender had committed those three crimes. In 2000 and 2001, they were tested against the murders that had occurred in Southern California. They were a match.

The East Area Rapist had indeed become a serial murderer, the man later dubbed the "Golden State Killer."

In 2011, DNA samples were discovered on a bedspread taken from the Domingo/Sanchez murder scene, and that DNA was *also* a match for the Golden State Killer. While no DNA has ever been discovered among the evidence taken from the Offerman/Manning case, that too is thought to be related due to overwhelming M.O. links and even some physical evidence – namely, that the twine and shoe prints were the same between the Offerman/Manning case and the October 1st, 1979 attack.

So DNA technology had proven that several of the murders in Southern California were perpetrated by the same person. It had proven that the rapes in Northern California were perpetrated by the same person. And it had proven that the Domingo/Sanchez murders had been perpetrated by the same person. It was creating breakthrough after breakthrough in the EAR/GSK case.

What else could it do?

The Arrest

The Visalia Ransacker case (and it's bigger cousin, the East Area Rapist / Golden State Killer case) remained unsolved for over forty years. Lead after lead was chased down, and each one branched off into dead ends. Rather than help resolve the mystery, each lead and each clue only seemed to deepen it. Thousands of tips were worked by very tenacious detectives and researchers over the years, but that one elusive tip that could break the case wide open had yet to materialize.

There was no doubt about it – after so many years had passed, there was very little hope of the Visalia Ransacker case being solved on its own. With no fingerprints, no usable DNA, and no breaks in the case since 1975, the opportunity for solving it through police work, witness recollection or some other traditional method seemed to be behind us. The biggest hope for solving the VR case seemed to be through the identification of the East Area Rapist / Golden State Killer (a case where DNA *was* workable) and a hope that solving that case would solve this one.

DNA technology had advanced exponentially over the past several years, and it was clear to anyone who followed the industry that eventually, no one (dead or alive) would be able to escape its reach. Someday, the EAR/GSK would be identified. But how long would it take for technology to advance far enough to do it?

Some argued that since the case hadn't been solved in forty years, waiting another ten or twenty more years for DNA technology to catch up was inconsequential. But actually, *time was of the essence*. The crimes had occurred decades ago – family and survivors of his assaults had already started to die off. The killer himself, believed in 2016 to be somewhere between sixty and seventy-five years old, wouldn't be long for this earth either, if he was even still alive. The goal was always to catch him while he was still living so that he could face what he'd done.

Realizing that traditional investigative methods had failed, the jurisdictions working the EAR/GSK case (which in 2016, grew to include the FBI) began pouring resources and efforts into utilizing the most cutting-edge technology available to them *now*. There was no time to wait for something else to come down the pipeline.

DNA had always been what had moved the needle in this investigation. As explained in the previous chapter, there were seven canonical murder scenes — five of which had DNA. Three of the rape cases also had samples that had been preserved. But at the time these crimes were committed (1975 through 1986), forensic DNA technology didn't exist, and the offender was so shrewd that several of his crimes remained unconnected until the mid 1990s and early 2000s (and in the Visalia Ransacker case, even beyond). Evolving DNA technology had always led the way when the investigation hit roadblocks.

It was called on again in 2017, when three cutting-edge technologies were utilized to finally identify and arrest a suspect in this case.

The technologies were open-access ancestry-focused DNA databases, deep familial matching, and "touch DNA."

The suspect identified with them was a man named Joseph James DeAngelo.

428

The process was simple in theory, but it took decades of technological innovation to allow these techniques to intersect. And still took hundreds of hours of human input, skill, and intelligence.

The idea for the past several years had been to gain access to large private databases such as 23andMe or Ancestry.com and run the offender's DNA sample through it in hopes of a direct match or a match to a close family member. Those hopes were dashed time and time again when the private database companies denied the requests, citing terms of service and privacy issues. No legal or ethical workaround could be found, and the idea was shelved with the hope that someday, the environment would change to the point where investigators could try again.

Meanwhile, open/public databases were on the rise. Websites like ysearch.com, geni.com, dna.land, and gedmatch.com began offering some of the same types of services and data access that 23andMe and Ancestry.com did. They consisted of profiles that were voluntarily donated and made open to everyone. On many of the websites, the data could be used for almost any purpose. Every time investigators looked at these websites, tens of thousands of new profiles had been added. It seemed to be a reasonable alternative to the private DNA database companies.

A Match is Made

Paul Holes was a member of law enforcement in Contra Costa County. He'd worked the EAR/GSK case for over twenty years and had played a key role in tying the EAR rapes to the GSK murders in 2001. He was also part of the team that felt the time was right to search public databases for answers.

Investigators obtained an untouched sample of the offender's DNA from Ventura County – the jurisdiction where the Golden State

Killer had murdered Lyman and Charlene Smith in March 1980. Paul Holes requested that a police lab convert the sample into a format that could be used in these ever-growing open-access DNA databases. He submitted the data into one of them, gedmatch.com, and hoped for a hit. This website was one of the repositories that used autosomal DNA technology, which lends itself well to deeper familial matching.

Up until very recently, familial testing technology could only find a DNA relationship match against a father, mother, brother/sister, or son/daughter. Recent advances allowed for much stronger comparisons and very distant relationships to be matched – several levels of grandparents, nieces/nephews, and all the way to great-great-great uncles/aunts and fourth cousins.

Humans have 46 chromosomes. These chromosomes are structures inside the cells of your body containing DNA blueprints that dictate how your body will look, work, and can even account for a predisposition to certain illnesses. This DNA profile is unique, and the odds are beyond astronomical for these DNA blueprints to match another random person anywhere, dead or alive. The chromosome structures are paired off into 22 pairs called autosomes (and one pair called the sex chromosomes, which influence characteristics related to gender). Generally, each autosome is made up of one chromosome from your mother and one from your father. The portion of each chromosome that you get isn't usually a perfect split – you're likely to get more material from either your father or your mother and thus end up resembling one of them more in some way. Your parents, of course, are made up of the same kind of autosome split derived from *their* parents, and so on. Thanks to autosomal DNA analysis, which is quite sensitive to identifying and matching unique characteristics in these autosomes, common DNA profiles can trace these different chromosome characteristics back several generations.

So Paul Holes and his team didn't *need* the offender or his immediate family to be in the database. He just needed *some* kind of match from some kind of ancestor or relative to give him a starting point. The investigators felt that surely, someone in these open-access databases would be a distant relative of the EAR/GSK. With the latest familial matching technology, they could match all the way up to a ninth-degree relative, so their chances looked good.

The results came back. There was no direct match, which was probably too much for anyone to hope for anyway. Serial killers who have left DNA at their crime scenes probably weren't the biggest users of these types of websites. But the team still met with success – their fishing expedition netted about a dozen profiles that were distantly related to the EAR/GSK's sample.

Utilizing tools on Ancestry.com that facilitate the formation of complex family trees (not *data* from Ancestry.com, just *tools*), they set to work. Holes and a team that included a civilian genealogist were able to create two dozen family trees. Because the samples that they'd matched were fairly distant (relatives like third cousins, people who shared a great-great-great grandfather with the Golden State Killer), the trees ended up branching out to roughly 10,000 different suspects. This was still a sizable pool to sort through, but it was much smaller than the retirement-age male population of California and beyond, which was what they *had* been working with.

After doing a lot of traditional investigative work and researching the most viable individuals on these family trees, only a few profiles bubbled to the surface. By April 2018, most of these had been worked through, and the most promising suspect was eliminated through the DNA test of a close relative. Officers looked at the next one.

Joseph James DeAngelo, a seventy-two-year-old man living in Citrus Heights near Sacramento, California, was shopping at Hobby Lobby on April 20th, 2018 when officers approached his empty vehicle in the parking lot. Unbeknownst to DeAngelo, they carefully swabbed the door handle and left.

The swabs were carefully transported to a crime lab and explored for "touch DNA." This technology, still fairly new and cutting-edge, is so sensitive that it can generate DNA profiles based on tiny particles and skin cells. Analysis was completed, and the profile was compared to the Golden State Killer's.

The samples shared several common markers and appeared to be a 47% match – a fairly significant match for this type of technology. Not an absolute lock by all standards, so detectives wanted more proof.

On April 23rd, 2018, they surreptitiously took samples from Joseph DeAngelo's trashcan, which he'd placed at the curb. A piece of tissue came back as a match with a likelihood ratio of "47.5 Septillion" (that's twenty-four zeroes) indicating that they'd finally found a match for their GSK DNA samples.

An Arrest is Made

The Sacramento County Sheriff's Department immediately began planning an arrest.

"We were able to surveil him," Sheriff Scott Jones explained. "We got a feel for some of his activities, or lack thereof. Got some information regarding his routines, we got some information relative to what he might do if confronted or apprehended. Based on the information we were able to glean from that surveillance, we developed a plan to wait for him to come out of his residence rather than approach him in the residence or when he's out and about in a vehicle."

On Tuesday, April 24th, 2018, at about 5:30 PM local time, Joseph James DeAngelo was arrested at his home on Canyon Oak Drive by armored police working for the Sacramento Sheriff's Department.

"When he came out of his residence we had a team in place that was able to take him into custody," Sheriff Jones told reporters at a press conference held the next day. "He was very surprised by that. It looked as though he might have been searching his mind to execute a particular plan he may have had in mind, obviously speculation on my part, but he was not given the opportunity. It happened almost instantaneously, and he was taken into custody without incident at all."

Joseph DeAngelo was held on a warrant from Ventura County Sheriff's Department. After seven hours, the suspect was booked. It was 2:29 AM on April 25th, 2018.

Listed as 5'11" and 205 lbs, DeAngelo was charged by Sacramento County for the February 1978 murders of Brian and Katie Maggiore. He was also charged by Ventura County for the murder of Lyman and Charlene Smith – two counts of first degree murder with three special circumstances (murder during commission of rape, murder during commission of burglary, and multiple murders).

A press conference was held at noon on Wednesday. Several district attorneys appeared, along with Sheriff Scott Jones, FBI Special Agent Sean Reagan, and Bruce Harrington – the brother of murder victim Keith Harrington.

Sacramento County District Attorney Anne Marie Schubert remarked that it was fitting that the press conference was held on April 25th, which happened to be "National DNA Day."

Filings and Court Appearances

The day after the arrest, Orange County District Attorney Tony Rackauckas charged Joseph DeAngelo with four counts of murder: the Keith and Patrice Harrington case from August 1980, the Manuela Witthuhn case from February 6th, 1981, and the Janelle Cruz case from May 5th, 1986. The charges included the special circumstances of multiple murders, robbery, burglary, rape, sodomy, and lying in wait. Santa Barbara followed them on May 10th, 2018 with four murder charges – the Robert Offerman and Debra/Alexandria Manning case and the Cheri Domingo/Gregory Sanchez case.

On April 27th, 2018, Joseph DeAngelo appeared in a Sacramento County courtroom before Judge Michael Sweet for an arraignment hearing. Handcuffed to a wheelchair and appearing to be weak or sedated, DeAngelo's answers to the judge's questions were barely audible. His head often drifted to the side as if he were having a hard time holding it up, and he offered little in the way of body language. Attendees noted that he was breathing very deeply.

DeAngelo spoke little. When the judge asked him if "Joseph James DeAngelo" was his true and correct name, he whispered "yes." The judge made him repeat his answer with more volume. He was asked about the status of his representation. He hesitated before answering, and his answer was barely audible.

Judge Sweet asked DeAngelo if he understood his questions, and the defendant repeated, "I have a lawyer." Public Defender Diane Howard accepted the appointment to represent DeAngelo.

On May 2nd and 3rd, DeAngelo's lawyers fought unsuccessfully to prevent the prosecution from obtaining more DNA samples from the defendant and from taking photos of his genitalia. Over the next month, they also fought to keep the search and arrest warrants from

434

being completely unsealed. The warrants were unsealed and released on June 1st, 2018 with several redactions, most of them aimed at protecting victim and witness privacy.

One of the most interesting aspects of these warrants is the fact that they address the Visalia Ransacker link.

The Visalia Ransacker Case

"Joseph James DeAngelo has been called a lot of things by Law Enforcement," said Tony Rackauckas, District Attorney in Orange County on April 25th. "He's been called the East Side Rapist, the Visalia Ransacker, the Original Night Stalker, and the Golden State Killer. Today, it's our pleasure to call him defendant."

This remark, given at an April 25th, 2018 press conference held to announce DeAngelo's arrest, was the first public indication that Law Enforcement had uncovered information that finally tied the Visalia series to the EAR/GSK crimes.

Unfortunately, investigators have declined to publicly reveal the exact nature of the information that links the Visalia Ransacker to the East Area Rapist / Golden State Killer cases, and much of the arrest/search warrant is redacted in that regard.

Obviously, until a verdict is reached in a court of law, it's unknown and unproven whether Joseph DeAngelo is guilty of any of the crimes he's been charged with. The arrest/search warrants themselves offer a little insight into the arrestee's history in the area, however. The warrants note that in 1973, DeAngelo took a police officer job in Exeter, California, which is located near Visalia. Further research has concluded that the exact month was May 1973, which is also the first month that the first burglary by the VR was thought to have been committed. The warrants also state that around 1974, DeAngelo attended Kings County Public Safety Academy, a police academy affiliated with the College of the Sequoias in Visalia. Claude Snelling worked at the College, and many other victims had affiliations with the school as well. A few months after the McGowen incident, he transferred to Auburn, which is northeast of Sacramento.

Again, living near Visalia or Sacramento is not a crime. Upcoming legal proceedings will settle the issue once and for all – is Joseph DeAngelo the Visalia Ransacker?

Innocent Until Proven Guilty

As of this writing:

- Joseph DeAngelo has yet to be charged with any crimes related to the Visalia Ransacker series.

- He has yet to be arraigned by any other county other than Sacramento County.

- He has yet to appear in court for any other crimes other than the murders of Brian and Katie Maggiore.

- He has yet to enter a plea or stand trial.

We must be clear – until proven in a court of law, Joseph James DeAngelo is innocent until proven guilty. He's merely been arrested and charged with these crimes.

This is a large case and, assuming that the defendant will plead "not guilty" and will live long enough to see trial, it could move very slowly.

Tulare County, the jurisdiction where the Visalia Ransacker crimes were committed, has yet to file any charges against DeAngelo for the murder of Claude Snelling. It's unknown if this will occur.

Pending the results of the trial or any other major outcome, more information will undoubtedly be added to this book. In the meantime, updates can be found at our websites:

www.goldenstatekillertrial.com
www.visaliaransacker.com
www.coldcasewriter.com
www.goldenstatekiller.com

Other Possible Connections

While the Visalia Ransacker series represents the Golden State Killer's first canonical crimes, they're not necessarily his first forays into burglary or violent offenses. The evolutionary process for offenders like him isn't always sequential. He may have explored several tangents or he may have experimented with different modus operandi during his development. It's thought that there could be dozens of crimes that have yet to be connected to his overall crime spree – before, during, *and* after.

In particular, officers and investigators have combed through over 35,000 police files in search of offenses that might've been committed by the Golden State Killer in the years *prior* to his known crimes.

By going through these files, Law Enforcement was able to identify and reconstruct the criminal careers of several unknown serial offenders from the general timeframe of the early 1970s. More information is still being developed on these offenders in case the crimes can be tied to the Golden State Killer series. For now, they remain question marks. It's an ongoing process.

The crimes/offenders discovered that seem to have a decent chance of being related to this case include following unidentified serial offenders and isolated crimes:

- Exeter Burglaries
- 1972-1973 Cat Burglar
- The East Sacramento Flasher
- Cordova Meadows Burglar
- The Sarda Way Assault
- The Jennifer Armour Murder

Exeter Burglaries

The recent investigative linkage of the Visalia Ransacker to the East Area Rapist / Golden State Killer series has set several jurisdictions into high-gear when it comes to examining the areas where the Ransacker may have operated. Investigators are taking a closer look at the Tulare County area in particular to examine locations where the Visalia Ransacker crimes occurred, and to scout any areas where the man accused of the Golden State Killer crimes, Joseph DeAngelo, had lived and worked. Due to several personal and professional ties uncovered in the suspect's past, the police are taking a particular interest in the Exeter area.

Exeter, California is a city in the San Joaquin Valley at the foothills of the Sierra Nevada Mountains. It's located about ten miles to the east of Visalia and, like Visalia, it's located in Tulare County. Today, Exeter's population is roughly 10,000 people. In the late 1960s, it was less than half of that.

In the late 1960s, there seemed to be a few more burglaries on the books than usual. The early 1970s saw crime begin to increase in a slightly more dramatic way, and some of the crimes even featured an offender who would enter homes while the residents were still inside.

Investigators who have offered information about this series point out that some of the crimes in Exeter seem to have parallels with a crime series that started in *Sacramento* in the early 1970s – a hot-prowl burglar that seemed to operate in the Rancho Cordova, Carmichael, and Citrus Heights areas. We'll discuss those crimes shortly.

By themselves, a slight uptick in burglaries doesn't mean much for Exeter. But given the scale of the Visalia Ransacker series that occurred less than a dozen miles away and the various connections that the man arrested for the GSK murders shares with the area, it's certainly something that's being researched further. The police are currently in the process of obtaining existing reports and unpacking any crimes that might be related. Due to the impending prosecution of DeAngelo and an uncertainty regarding how Tulare County may or may not proceed regarding charges related to the Snelling murder, it will be interesting to see how this plays out. It's been learned so far that several of these burglaries took place while Joseph DeAngelo was in the Navy and out of the area, so it's hard to say at this point what that might mean when it comes to determining who might or might not be considered responsible.

The Visalia Ransacker's estimated age at the time of the McGowen shootings was 25-35, which would have possibly made the VR 19-29 at the time these crimes seemed to begin.

1972-1973 Cat Burglar

Between 1972 and 1973, a prolific "cat burglar" (or rather, an offender committing "hot prowl" burglaries) haunted the eastern portion of Sacramento County. Just like the East Area Rapist, he seemed to prefer Carmichael, Rancho Cordova, and Citrus Heights.

His M.O. was fairly consistent across incidents, which helped detectives tie the crimes together. Often striking several times in one outing, the burglar would enter an *occupied* home late at night, open an additional door to use as a potential escape route, and begin quietly rummaging through the house. He collected purses, wallets, and valuable coins as he went. There were a few occasions where he stole food and/or alcohol as well.

The burglar was considered dangerous, having been seen armed with a gun on at least one occasion.

What was odd about this burglar was that he seemed to be motivated by more than simple theft. It wasn't unusual for police to find the spoils of the night abandoned somewhere nearby, though even when he did drop a wallet or a purse, he would almost always keep the driver's license.

The damage to the homes was negligible and the financial loss was minimal, but the attacks were incredibly eerie. The burglar spent time in the bedroom with victims while they were asleep, targeting both couples and lone women alike. Usually the victims wouldn't wake up, but they'd know he had been in there based on items having been moved or taken.

Sexual motivation or curiosity was apparent in some instances – such as the time a woman living by herself woke up to the burglar fondling her breast. She shouted at him and ordered him out of the house and interestingly enough, he obeyed and left peacefully.

The geographical ties between this series and the East Area Rapist series shows an interesting relation. The "cat burglar" began by targeting homes in the immediate area of where the October 21st, 1975 rape would occur and victims #1, #3, #6, and #8 would be attacked by the EAR a few years later. About half of *this* burglar's home-intrusions occurred in this same small geographic area, which seemed to be "ground zero" for the East Area Rapist.

The timing is also interesting, with incidents occurring in 1972, stopping for several months, and then resuming for a short time in the spring months of 1973. It seems they stopped for good just about the time that the Visalia Ransacker crimes started up in May 1973.

A detailed suspect description is unavailable, but reports generally put him as a white male, in his twenties, 5'6" to 6', with a slender to average build.

When all was said and done, over thirty incidents had been tied through M.O. to this offender. None of the crimes in this series can be prosecuted anymore, so police have implored the public to bring forth more information or a confession. So far, nothing additional has materialized. Whether this offender went on to become the Visalia Ransacker / East Area Rapist or not is unknown.

The East Sacramento Flasher

At the same time that the 1972-1973 Cat Burglar incidents were occurring, the Rancho Cordova and Carmichael areas were being preyed upon by a man who committed several flashings/indecent exposures.

The M.O. of the flasher varied, but it usually involved him standing near a door or a window, waiting for a period of time, and then when he felt that it would have the most shock value, he'd knock on the window or do something to get the resident's attention and flash them. He would sometimes speak to the victims, and would sometimes linger near their property and commit "lewd acts" for a period of time.

There's nothing tying him directly to the Visalia Ransacker or East Area Rapist series, but he very well might be related to the 1972-1973 Cat Burglar incidents. Many of these flashing incidents occurred on or near the same street and on the exact same day as Cat Burglar offenses.

The subject was described as a white male, early twenties, 5'8" to 6', 160-170 lbs, with a thin to medium build. His hair was described as light brown, reddish brown, or dark brown. He was usually described as wearing only a t-shirt – he had no pants or underwear on his person or nearby. He didn't appear to be armed.

This criminal has never been identified. Like the 1972-1973 Cat Burglar series, none of the crimes can be prosecuted anymore, so police have brought this information to the public in hopes that someone can help answer these lingering questions.

The ties to East Sacramento are interesting and the timeline matches up fairly well, but whether this offender went on to become the Visalia Ransacker / East Area Rapist or not is unknown.

Cordova Meadows Burglar

The "Cordova Meadows Burglar," a criminal with a different M.O. than both the Flasher and the 1972-1973 Cat Burglar, began operating in East Sacramento in 1973. There were *some* overlaps and similarities between these serial offenders, but investigators and researchers have yet to determine if this series was related to any of the other ones that we've discussed in this chapter.

This particular burglar didn't seem to care whether a resident was home or *not* for his intrusions, though most of his crimes were committed in empty houses. He also didn't care whether it was day or night, and he was quite a bit messier at crime scenes than the 1972-1973 Cat Burglar seemed to be. Calendar-wise and geography-wise, these incidents overlapped a bit with the Cat Burglar, though a large number of them occurred in the first couple of months of 1973 while the Cat Burglar was on some kind of break. The Cordova Meadows Burglar scenes could be differentiated from other serial crime sprees by the time of day, the more extensive ransacking that would occur at the scenes, the leaving of burnt matches behind, and the fact that he would move women's undergarments about the house.

He also stole different items than the Cat Burglar. The Sacramento Sheriff's department lists the following items as having been stolen by the Cordova Meadows Burglar: "coins, piggy banks, jewelry, binoculars, hunting knives (some in scabbards), photographic cameras and movie cameras, two-dollar bills (numerous,) Blue Chip stamps, handguns, food, alcohol, and prescription medication." They also added that "larger items, most electronics, and other items of value were noted to be disregarded by the suspect." He sometimes stole photos of the women who lived at the house as well, and he frequently stole weapons.

Most interesting of all – the Cordova Meadows Burglar would sometimes steal single earrings from a pair.

This obviously sounds a *lot* more like the Visalia Ransacker than anything we've discussed up to this point. If this *was* an early version of the VR, and many folks think that it was, then a tragic detail needs to be brought up: after the Cordova Meadows Burglar entered a home, he would sometimes murder the family dog.

This burglar was rarely seen by anyone, but on one occasion, a witness did see a man possibly related to the burglary. She could describe him only as a white male in his late twenties with long brown hair. His vehicle seemed to be a green Opel Kadett.

At another sighting, a woman described him as a white male, over sixteen years old, between 5'8" and 5'10", and between 160 and 170 lbs. He had brown hair and was wearing a brown jacket, blue jeans, and black tennis shoes. It should be noted that this was similar to how the Ransacker was often described.

In one of the more dramatic burglaries, the homeowners interrupted the thief. One of them chased after him and got a good look at the subject. The police recently re-interviewed the witness, and he gave the following description of the burglar: he was a white male, 18-22 years old, between 5'8" and 5'10", and 180 lbs. His build was "slightly pear-shaped," with wide hips. He had brown hair "touching his ears." He wore a white t-shirt, jeans, and boots that left a waffle-print impression.

This description is interesting because it includes several elements of the most common Visalia Ransacker *and* East Area Rapist descriptions.

Those who feel that the Cat Burglar and the Cordova Meadows Burglar are the same point out that the M.O. may have only seemed to switch back and forth between an offender who rummaged extensively and one who did not because of the nature of each of the crimes he was committing. If he entered an occupied home at night, he probably kept the rummaging and noise to a minimum to avoid encountering the homeowners. If no one was home, he was free to ransack as he pleased.

The Flasher series might not seem to correlate with anything that the Visalia Ransacker / Golden State Killer was known to have done, but there's an interesting parallel in at least one of the events – in one of the flashing incidents, the Flasher knocked on a door. When the resident opened it, the offender was, of course, without pants or underwear. He asked the woman if she had a match – an odd thing to ask considering that the Cordova Meadows Burglar, who was operating at roughly the same time, left matches behind on occasion.

There was an interesting connection to the East Area Rapist crime series at one of the burglaries committed by the Cordova Meadows Burglar. One of these crimes, occurring March 7th, 1973, was at the home of a teenage girl who actually became an East Area Rapist victim three and a half years later. And when the East Area Rapist attacked her, he stole a single earring from a pair – the only time he was known to do that in the East Area Rapist crime series. It's an astounding parallel that, along with the overwhelming M.O. similarities, seems to possibly link the Cordova Meadows Burglar to the VR/EAR series.

Another parallel was that one of the victims of this burglar, a seventeen-year-old girl, received strange communications (hang-up phone calls, a letter, a threatening phone call) during this burglary series. This girl lived next-door to the home where the VR/EAR killed Brian and Katie Maggiore a few years later.

But again, the cases we've discussed in this chapter may not be related to each other and they may not be related to the Visalia Ransacker / Golden State Killer series at all. But several M.O. factors, along with the incidents happening in key areas and timeframes, seems to indicate that there *may* be something important to discover here.

One more point that might help tie all of these together – the burglaries and the rape that occurred in mid October 1975 in the East Sacramento area had several hallmarks of the 1972-1973 Cat Burglar series, the Cordova Meadows Burglar, the Visalia Ransacker, *and* the East Area Rapist series. Bedrooms were ransacked, food was eaten, burnt matches were left, an offender entered a home and stole a purse (which he left nearby) while a family was sleeping, coins were taken from a piggybank, a birthstone ring and a high school class ring were stolen, and a home-invasion rape occurred that had all the hallmarks of the East Area Rapist series of attacks. Those incidents, detailed earlier in the book, seem to tie many of these possibilities together and top them with a nice bow. Out of everything we've discussed in over a thousand published pages on this criminal, the answer to several mysteries in this gigantic, sweeping crime series might be found in that one week of October 1975.

The Sarda Way Assault

One more Sacramento-area incident should be discussed – an attempted home-invasion rape that occurred on Sarda Way in Rancho Cordova on September 14th, 1973.

At 11:00 AM, a woman in her late twenties spotted a man in her backyard. She thought he was a utility worker, but something about the sighting was unnerving enough for her to retrieve her handgun.

A few minutes later, she heard a knock at her front door. She wasn't expecting anyone, so she didn't answer it. A few minutes after the knocking stopped, she heard a noise coming from the master bedroom. Checking on the noise, she saw the man from her backyard attempting to enter her home through the window. Once he realized he'd been spotted, he ran away, leaving behind the screen that he'd removed from the window.

The woman called her husband to tell him what had happened, and as she did, the man entered her garage (the main overhead door was already open). He then forced his way through the door between the garage and the kitchen – pushing it so hard that the nails holding the chain lock were pulled out of the doorframe.

Pointing her gun straight at him, the woman told the intruder that if he approached her, she would shoot him. The intruder backed off and walked away.

The woman called the police. When she hung up the phone, the man came back through the same door, rushed her, and attacked. She fought to retain possession of the handgun but the man took control of her arms and pointed the gun straight at her. Just as it was about to go off, she pushed with all of her might and forced the aim of the gun upward. The gun went off, and the bullet missed her. The intruder then made his escape as the woman passed out onto the floor.

The police arrived a few minutes after she woke up. Apparently the man had fled without harming her further.

The assailant was described as about twenty-seven years old, 5'8", and 140 pounds with a thin build. He had a "big, thin nose," sunken cheeks, pockmarks and a scar or mole near his mouth, and "narrow deep-set eyes with bags." He seemed "sick" or "tired-looking."

He had medium brown hair that was neck or shoulder length and "neatly combed," and he was dressed "neatly" in a brown jacket, a beige shirt, trousers, and white shoes. He wore ladies white dress gloves and had a blue scarf in the right pocket of his jacket.

The intruder's tenacity, description, geography, and even facial composite resembled other East Area Rapist descriptions quite a bit, but this assailant didn't resemble physically Visalia Ransacker descriptions. It should be noted, however, that in the EAR/VR case the physical descriptions do vary quite a bit in incidents that we *know* are related through other types of evidence. In light of the Visalia Ransacker case being connected to the East Area Rapist case, this assault was worth mentioning.

The Jennifer Armour Murder

On the night of November 15th, 1974, a fifteen-year-old Visalia-area girl named Jennifer Lynn Armour disappeared while on her way to a local football game. She was last seen at about 8:30 PM while on her way to meet friends.

Her nude body was found over a week later in the Friant-Kern Canal near Woodlake – an area located northeast of Visalia and a fair distance away from where she'd disappeared. Her bra was wrapped around one of her wrists, and her clothing was found on the bank nearby.

Investigators were able to determine that the girl had died by drowning, but at first they couldn't agree on whether it had been accidental or whether there was foul play involved. They ended up determining that Armour had been killed, and the Fresno Bee (along with the Fresno Guarantee Savings and Loan Association) set aside $2,500 for information leading to the arrest and conviction of her killer. The money was never claimed. The case got very little press, and unfortunately, it was never solved.

A year later (on December 27th, 1975), the partially-clad body of fourteen-year-old Donna Richmond was found in an orange grove near the Friant-Kern Canal, roughly two miles from her Exeter home and in the same broad, general area as Armour's body. Richmond, who'd last been seen on the afternoon of December 26th riding her bicycle home from her boyfriend's house, had been stabbed to death.

Her father, Tulare County Assessor Donald Richmond, was notified within hours that an arrest had been made in his daughter's case. Oscar Clifton, a man living in Farmersville (an area between Visalia and Exeter), was booked and arraigned for the crime. Clifton subsequently stood trial for the murder and was found guilty in August 1976.

It wasn't the first time that Clifton had been in a courtroom – he'd been convicted of an attempted rape in the mid 1960s. In that case, it was alleged that he'd rushed an eighteen-year-old woman while she was sunbathing in the afternoon. A car pulling off the road interrupted the attack – the driver let the woman into his vehicle and rescued her.

Oscar Clifton appealed that conviction in 1967 and again in 1969, but the appeals were unsuccessful. He also appealed his conviction in the Richmond case several times, but that conviction too was upheld. He died in prison in 2013.

In November 2017, Tulare County Sheriff's cold case detectives released a statement announcing that there were looking at Clifton in the Armour murder, and that they would like anyone who knew him in the 1970s to come forward with information that might have bearing on the case. No further information was provided.

Despite the conviction of Clifton in the Richmond case and his apparent status as a person of interest in the Armour case, many researchers feel that the Armour case should be looked at again through the lens of possible Visalia Ransacker / Golden State Killer involvement. With the VR series now an official part of Golden State Killer canon and a better picture of the offender's crimes and murders coming into focus, more attention is being given to the areas where the VR/GSK committed his crimes. Due to similar geographic ties and similar victimology between known VR targets and the Armour case, an exploration of it and even another look at potential ties to the Richmond case is in order.

In the 1990s, some evidence was catalogued from hair found in the Richmond case. DNA testing at the time failed to come up with anything because the samples were too degraded, but if the samples are still in evidence, it's possible that modern technology can generate a profile.

When it comes to all of the known and all of the possible victims of the Visalia Ransacker / East Area Rapist / Golden State Killer, court proceedings due to take place in the immediate future will soon tell us if justice is being served. It's our hope that the focus brought to this offender will help bring a resolution to the crimes discussed in this book, and that these efforts will help bring a new understanding to how these types of serial offenders operate. With the wheels of justice still turning, the hope is that someday our awareness will reach a point where we as a society can prevent these types of tragedies from ever occurring.

A Final Note

The information contained in this book has been culled and collated from police reports, documentation, news articles, interviews with investigators (former and present), experts, court transcripts, archived correspondence, and research materials like phone directories, maps, and property records.

Writing a book like this was a team-effort. A special debt of gratitude goes to the community surrounding this case – particularly the dozens of people that we've come to know as friends. Many researchers and investigators have been more than generous in sharing information, materials, and expertise with us. This book is the sum total of their generosity.

We've done everything in our power to ensure that this information is accurate, which can be quite a challenge in a case that's over forty years old. No personally identifying information about victims or witnesses is contained in this book that hasn't already been revealed in other places or hasn't been signed off on by the people involved. Keeping up a privacy standard was a primary goal in compiling this book. The victims are, first and foremost, the reason why so many people have worked so hard on this case.

If you'd like to keep up with the latest information in this case or view more materials, you can find more at the following venues:

Twitter: https://twitter.com/coldcasewriter
Trial Website: http://www.goldenstatekillertrial.com
VR Website: http://www.visaliaransacker.com
GSK Website: http://www.goldenstatekiller.com
Discussion: http://www.reddit.com/r/VisaliaRansacker

If for any reason you feel that you have a tip that has relevance to this case, we urge you to contact the FBI:

Phone: 1-800-CALL-FBI (1-800-225-5324)
Web: https://tips.fbi.gov/

Mail:
FBI Sacramento Field Office
2001 Freedom Way
Roseville, CA 95678

For questions or comments related to this book, you can reach us at:

E-mail: coldcase.earons@gmail.com

Acknowledgments

This small page near the end of the book doesn't even begin to do justice to the impact and contributions made by so many incredible, selfless, and supportive people. We can't thank you enough for your tireless and unwavering dedication to this case and for your support of our efforts to help bring some clarity and organization to it.

Special thanks goes to Bill Harticon, Brad, Paul Holes, Erika Hutchcraft, Jeff, Ken ("Drifter"), Loria, Marjorie, Mike Morford, Andrew Nelms, Larry Pool, Donnie Priest, Renee, Richard Shelby, Mason Tierney, Tim, Melissa Trussell, John Vaughan, and "Zforce."

You've all contributed so much, both directly and indirectly, to every word written in this book. The contributions you've made (and continue to make), the dedication you show, and in many cases the friendships we've forged have been the foundation of this book and of this case. You've changed the way that many of us approach a cold case in the twenty-first century, and you've truly made a difference. Thank you for everything.

–Kat Winters and Keith Komos

Supplemental Material

LIST OF VISALIA RANSACKER INCIDENTS

"*" indicates that there isn't enough evidence to be sure of the Ransacker's involvement in this incident.

VR#	Date	Street
1*	May 1973	S Demaree St
2*	June 1973	S Demaree St
3*	September 3rd, 1973	W Kaweah Ave
4*	September 10th, 1973	W Kaweah Ave
5*	September 1973	W Feemster Ave
6*	September 1973	W Feemster Ave
7*	January 1974	W Feemster Ave
8*	January 1974	W Feemster Ave
9*	March 19th, 1974	W Walnut Ave
10	April 6th or 7th, 1974	S Linda Visa St
11	April 6th or 7th, 1974	S Whitney St
12	April 1974	S Whitney St
13	April 1974	S Whitney St
14	May 4th, 1974	S Dollner St
15	May 5th, 1974	W Feemster Ave
16	May 10th or 11th, 1974	W Tulare Ave
17	May 11th, 1974	S Whitney St
18	May 17th, 1974	S Emerald Ct
19	May 17th, 1974	W Dartmouth Ave
20	May 18th, 1974	W Feemster Ave
21	May 18th, 1974	W Cambridge Ave
22	May 21st, 1974	W Howard Ave
23	May 25th or 26th, 1974	W Sue Ave
24	May 24th-27th, 1974	S Redwood St
25	May 25th or 26th, 1974	W Cambridge Ave
26	May 26th, 1974	S Sowell St
27	May 26th, 1974	W Howard Ave
28	May 24th-27th, 1974	W Cambridge Ave
29	June 22nd or 23rd, 1974	S Conyer St

30	September 14th, 1974	W Princeton Ave
31	October 4th, 1974	S Grant St
32*	October 16th, 1974	S Verde Vista St
33	October 19th, 1974	W Cambridge Ct
34	October 19th, 1974	S Oak Park St
35	October 19th, 1974	W Cambridge Ave
36	October 23rd, 1974	S Giddings St
37	October 23rd, 1974	S Oak Park St
38	November 1st, 1974	W Vassar Ave
39	November 1st, 1974	W Vassar Ave
40	November 1st, 1974	W Cambridge Ave
41	November 1st, 1974	S Giddings St
42	Oct 30th-Nov 2nd, 1974	W Paradise Ave
43	November 2nd, 1974	S Mountain St
44	November 2nd, 1974	W Laurel Ave
45	November 2nd, 1974	W Campus Ave
46	November 2nd, 1974	S Whitney St
47	November 29th, 1974	W Princeton Ave
48	November 29th or 30th, 1974	W Tulare Ave
49	November 29th or 30th, 1974	W Meadow Ave
50	November 30th, 1974	W Meadow Ave
51	Nov 30th or Dec 1st, 1974	S Encina St
52	Nov 30th or Dec 1st, 1974	W Paradise Ave
53	Nov 27th to Dec 1st, 1974	W Paradise Ave
54	Nov 30th or Dec 1st, 1974	W Paradise Ave
55	Nov 30th or Dec 1st, 1974	W Cambridge Ave
56	Nov 29th to Dec 1st, 1974	S Sowell St
57	Nov 29th to Dec 1st, 1974	S Sowell St
58	Nov 30th or Dec 1st, 1974	W Kaweah Ave
59	Nov 30th or Dec 1st, 1974	W Kaweah Ave
60*	December 14th, 1974	W Vassar Ave
61	December 14th, 1974	S University St
62	December 14th, 1974	W Cambridge Ave
63	December 13th to 15th, 1974	W Cambridge Ave

64	December 16th, 1974	W Seeger Ave
65	December 21st, 1974	W College Ave
66	December 21st, 1974	W Meadow Ave
67	December 20th to 27th, 1974	S Divisadero St
68	December 21st, 1974	S Fairway St
69	December 21st, 1974	W Iris Ct
70	December 21st to 29th, 1974	W Fairview Ave
71	December 22nd, 1974	S Terri St
72	December 22nd, 1974	W Laurel Ave
73*	December 22nd, 1974	W Beverly Dr
74*	December 22nd, 1974	S Oak Park St
75*	December 22nd, 1974	S Oak Park St
76	January 25th, 1975	S Verde Vista St
77	January 24th to 27th, 1975	W Pecan Ave
78	February 2nd, 1975	S Whitney St
79	February 2nd, 1975	W Whitney Dr
80	February 2nd, 1975	W Gist Ave
81	February 5th, 1975	S Whitney St
82	February 16th, 1975	S Sowell Ave
83	February 16th, 1975	W Meadow Ave
84	February 16th, 1975	W Kaweah Ave
85	March 1st, 1975	W Howard Ave
86*	April 1975	S Redwood St
87	May 24th, 1975	S Mountain St
88	May 24th, 1975	S Mountain St
89	May 24th, 1975	S Redwood St
90	May 24th, 1975	W Kaweah Ave
91	May 31st, 1975	S Sowell St
92	June 1st, 1975	W Harvard Ave
93*	June 1975	S Verde Vista St
94*	July 24th, 1975	W Kaweah Ave
95	July 25th, 1975	W Fairview Ct
96	July 25th, 1975	W Campus Ave
97*	July 25th, 1975	S Whitney St

98	August 1st, 1975	W Campus Ave
99	August 23rd, 1975	W Howard Ave
100	August 23rd, 1975	W Howard Ave
101	August 23rd, 1975	W Feemster Ave
102	August 24th, 1975	W Princeton Ave
103	August 24th, 1975	W Cambridge Ave
104	August 29th, 1975	W Dartmouth Ave
105	August 30th, 1975	S Redwood St
106	August 31st, 1975	W Royal Oaks Dr
107*	September 1975	W Myrtle Ave
108*	September 6th, 1975	S Whitney St
109*	September 9th, 1975	S Whitney St
110*	September 9th, 1975	S Redwood St
111*	September 10th, 1975	S Cornell Ave
112*	September 10th, 1975	W Whitney Dr
113*	September 11th, 1975	W Campus Ave
114*	September 11th, 1975	S Locust St
115	September 11th, 1975	S Whitney St
116*	September 22nd, 1975	S Verde Vista St
117	September 22nd, 1975	W Royal Oaks Dr
118	October 3rd, 1975	S Redwood St
119*	October 4th, 1975	S Verde Vista St
120*	October 6th, 1975	S Verde Vista St
121*	October 20th, 1975	S Whitney St
122*	October 20th, 1975	S Emerald Ct
123*	October 21st, 1975	W Royal Oaks Dr
124	October 24th, 1975	W Campus Ave
125	October 24th, 1975	W Campus Ave
126	October 24th, 1975	S Redwood St
127	October 24th, 1975	S Redwood St
128	October 24th, 1975	S County Center Dr
129	October 24th, 1975	S County Center Dr
130	October 24th, 1975	S County Center Dr
131	October 29th or 30th, 1975	W Kaweah Ave

132	November 2nd, 1975	W Evergreen Ave
133	November 2nd, 1975	W Country Ave
134	November 2nd, 1975	W Country Ave
135	November 2nd, 1975	W Evergreen Ave
136	November 2nd, 1975	W Evergreen Ave
137	November 6th, 1975	W Seeger Ave
138	November 6th, 1975	W Tulare Ave
139	November 6th, 1975	S Oak Park St
140*	November 9th, 1975	W College Ct
141*	November 20th, 1975	S Wellsley Ct
142*	November 23rd, 1975	W Royal Oaks Dr
143	Nov 30th to Dec 3rd, 1975	W College Ave
144	December 1st, 1975	W Beverly Dr
145	December 1st, 1975	S Central St
146	December 1st, 1975	W Kaweah Ave
147	December 8th, 1975	W Sue Ave
148	December 10th, 1975	W Laurel Ave
149	December 10th, 1975	W Kaweah Ave
150*	January 18th, 1976	S Burke St
151*	October 24th, 1976	W Kaweah Ave

EAST AREA RAPIST / GOLDEN STATE KILLER
ATTACKS

Attack	Date	City	Street
NA	10/21/75	Rancho Cordova	Dawes St
1	06/18/76	Rancho Cordova	Paseo Dr
2	07/17/76	Carmichael	Marlborough Wy
3	08/29/76	Rancho Cordova	Malaga Wy
4	09/04/76	Carmichael	Crestview Dr
5	10/05/76	Citrus Heights	Woodpark Wy
6	10/09/76	Rancho Cordova	El Segundo Dr
7	10/18/76	Carmichael	Kipling Dr
8	10/18/76	Rancho Cordova	Los Palos Dr
9	11/10/76	Citrus Heights	Greenleaf Dr
10	12/18/76	Carmichael	Ladera Wy
11	01/18/77	Sacramento	Glenville Cir
12	01/24/77	Citrus Heights	Primrose Dr
13	02/07/77	Carmichael	Heathcliff Dr
NA	02/16/77	Sacramento	Ripon Ct
14	03/08/77	Sacramento	Thornwood Dr
15	03/18/77	Rancho Cordova	Benny Wy
16	04/02/77	Orangevale	Richdale Wy
17	04/15/77	Carmichael	Cherrelyn Wy
18	05/03/77	Sacramento	La Riviera Dr
19	05/05/77	Orangevale	Winterbrook Wy
20	05/14/77	Citrus Heights	Merlindale Dr
21	05/17/77	Carmichael	Sandbar Cir
22	05/28/77	South Sacramento	4th Parkway
23	09/06/77	Stockton	North Portage Cir
24	10/01/77	Rancho Cordova	Tuolumne Dr
25	10/21/77	Foothill Farms	Golden Run Ave
26	10/29/77	Sacramento	Woodson Ave
27	11/10/77	Sacramento	La Riviera Dr

28	12/02/77	Foothill Farms	Revelstok Dr
29	01/28/78	Sacramento	College View Wy
NA	02/02/78	Rancho Cordova	La Alegria Dr
30	03/18/78	Stockton	Meadow Ave
31	04/14/78	South Sacramento	Casilada Wy
32	06/05/78	Modesto	Fuschia Ln
33	06/07/78	Davis	Wake Forest Dr
34	06/23/78	Modesto	Grandprix Dr
35	06/24/78	Davis	Rivendell Ln
36	07/06/78	Davis	Amador Ave
37	10/07/78	Concord	Belann Ct
38	10/13/78	Concord	Ryan Rd
39	10/28/78	San Ramon	Montclair Pl
40	11/04/78	San Jose	Havenwood Dr
41	12/02/78	San Jose	Kesey Ln
42	12/09/78	Danville	Liberta Ct
NA	12/18/78	San Ramon	Thunderbird Pl
43	03/20/79	Rancho Cordova	Filmore Ln
44	04/05/79	Fremont	Honda Wy
45	06/02/79	Walnut Creek	El Divisadero Ave
46	06/11/79	Danville	Allegheny Dr
47	06/25/79	Walnut Creek	San Pedro Ct
48	07/05/79	Danville	Sycamore Hill Ct
GSK1	10/01/79	Goleta	Queen Ann Ln
GSK2	12/30/79	Goleta	Avenida Pequena
GSK3	03/13/80	Ventura	Highpoint Dr
GSK4	08/18/80	Dana Point	Cockleshell Dr
GSK5	02/05/81	Irvine	Columbus
GSK6	07/27/81	Goleta	Toltec Wy
GSK7	05/04/86	Irvine	Encina

LIST OF ITEMS STOLEN BY THE VISALIA RANSACKER

VR#	Date	Items Stolen
10	April 6th or 7th, 1974	Piggybank
11	April 6th or 7th, 1974	Piggybank
12	April 1974	Several items (no report)
13	April 1974	Several items (no report)
14	May 4th, 1974	Coin collection, cash
15	May 5th, 1974	Piggybank, money
16	May 10th or 11th, 1974	Coin bank, money, .380 Remington automatic pistol, ammunition
17	May 11th, 1974	Cash, wedding cards
18	May 17th, 1974	Coins, man's ring
19	May 17th, 1974	Coin bank, cash, possibly Blue Chip stamps
20	May 18th, 1974	Coins, cash, piggybanks, broken necklace, pantyhose, cologne
21	May 18th, 1974	Nothing
22	May 21st, 1974	Nothing
23	May 25th or 26th, 1974	Coin collection, regular coins
24	May 24th-27th, 1974	Coins from a piggybank, cash, single earrings from sets
25	May 25th or 26th, 1974	Coins from a piggybank
26	May 26th, 1974	Nothing
27	May 26th, 1974	Collectible coins, regular coins
28	May 24th-27th, 1974	Piggybank, cash, 8-track tapes

29	June 22nd or 23rd, 1974	Nothing
30	September 14th, 1974	One single earring
31	October 4th, 1974	Coins, a Ruger .22 revolver, three boxes of .22 ammunition, one and half boxes of 12-guage ammunition
33	October 19th, 1974	Nothing
34	October 19th, 1974	Coins
35	October 19th, 1974	Cash
36	October 23rd, 1974	.32 revolver, two low-end Kodak cameras
37	October 23rd, 1974	Piggybank, coins
38	November 1st, 1974	Coins from a piggybank, collectible coins
39	November 1st, 1974	Coins, cash, Blue Chip stamps
40	November 1st, 1974	Coins, cash
41	November 1st, 1974	Money from a piggybank, cash
42	Oct 30th-Nov 2nd, 1974	Coins from a piggybank, cash, a single earring, alarm key to victim's place of employment
43	November 2nd, 1974	Coins from a piggybank, Blue Chip stamps
44	November 2nd, 1974	Coins, single earring from a pair, four tubes of epoxy glue
45	November 2nd, 1974	Nothing
46	November 2nd, 1974	Coins, collector's coins, Blue Chip stamps, new men's t-shirts

47	November 29th, 1974	Piggybank, two boxes of .22 rifle shells
48	November 29th or 30th, 1974	Regular coins, collectible coins, costume jewelry, a bra, a ladies' wallet, a single earring, two photos of children
49	November 29th or 30th, 1974	Cash and coins from a strongbox
50	November 30th, 1974	Coins
51	Nov 30th or Dec 1st, 1974	Coins from a piggybank, collectible coins
52	Nov 30th or Dec 1st, 1974	Nothing
53	Nov 27th to Dec 1st, 1974	Coins
54	Nov 30th or Dec 1st, 1974	Coins two rings, one earring, a check payable to the victim
55	Nov 30th or Dec 1st, 1974	Coins from a piggybank
56	Nov 29th to Dec 1st, 1974	Money, a ring
57	Nov 29th to Dec 1st, 1974	Regular coins, collectible coins, possibly alcohol
58	Nov 30th or Dec 1st, 1974	20-gauge shotgun shells and .22 ammunition
59	Nov 30th or Dec 1st, 1974	Coins, small stereo
60	December 14th, 1974	Coins from a piggybank
61	December 14th, 1974	Cash, two rings
62	December 14th, 1974	Nothing
63	December 13th to 15th, 1974	Coins and cash
64	December 16th, 1974	Nothing
65	December 21st, 1974	Cash, a coin collection, a shaving kit

66	December 21st, 1974	Coins from a piggybank, coin collection, four single earrings, Blue Chip stamps, binoculars
67	December 20th to 27th, 1974	Collectible coins, two rings, two earrings, small transistor radio
68	December 21st, 1974	Ten-cent postage stamps, Blue Chip stamps
69	December 21st, 1974	Coins from a piggybank, cash, keys
70	December 21st to 29th, 1974	Piggybank, coins
71	December 22nd, 1974	Piggybank, coins
72	December 22nd, 1974	Coin collection, silver bracelet, two rings, two transistor radios, a pair of men's pajamas, new men's t-shirts, a suitcase
76	January 25th, 1975	Coin collection, Blue Chip stamps
77	January 24th to 27th, 1975	Cash and coins
78	February 2nd, 1975	Jewelry, a purse, a razor, twenty books of Blue Chip stamps, .22 ammunition
79	February 2nd, 1975	Nothing
80	February 2nd, 1975	Coins
82	February 16th, 1975	Coins, cash, single earring
83	February 16th, 1975	Coins and cash
84	February 16th, 1975	Coins and cash
85	March 1st, 1975	Coins, cash, rings, and a broken revolver
87	May 24th, 1975	.38 Taurus revolver

88	May 24th, 1975	Coins and cash
89	May 24th, 1975	Blue Chip stamps
90	May 24th, 1975	Cash and coins
91	May 31st, 1975	Coins from a piggybank and sixteen rings
95	July 25th, 1975	Coins cash, coin collection, ring, 20-gauge shotgun shells
96	July 25th, 1975	Coins, cash, stamps, and a credit card
98	August 1st, 1975	Coins from a piggybank, cash, Blue Chip stamps, two single earrings from a pair
99	August 23rd, 1975	Coins from piggybanks, cash, Blue Chip stamps, photo of daughter, engraved gold locket with a photo, a jar of cherries
100	August 23rd, 1975	Coins from a piggybank
101	August 23rd, 1975	Coins, cash, Blue Chip stamps, a ring
102	August 24th, 1975	Coins from a piggybank
103	August 24th, 1975	Coins from a piggybank
104	August 29th, 1975	Coins, cash, rings, nine single earrings
105	August 30th, 1975	Flashlight
106	August 31st, 1975	.38 Miroku revolver, coin collection, necklace, two boxes of 12-gauge ammo, three hundred rounds of .38 ammo
115	September 11th, 1975	Cash

117	September 22nd, 1975	Single earring, perfume, makeup, a bra, two photos of daughter
124	October 24th, 1975	Coins, cash, single cufflink, two single earrings, new men's sleeveless t-shirts, two nightgowns, a knife, old policeman's baton
126	October 24th, 1975	Hammer
128	October 24th, 1975	Coins, cash, three rings, three single earrings, a pin
131	October 29th or 30th, 1975	Empty brown leather suitcase, a dozen cans of vegetables and fruit
133	November 2nd, 1975	12-gauge shotgun shells, an empty purse, a man's wedding ring
134	November 2nd, 1975	Coins from a coin bank
137	November 6th, 1975	Cash
138	November 6th, 1975	Several cans of food, antique plates
139	November 6th, 1975	Food, canned goods, large suitcase
143	Nov 30th to Dec 3rd, 1975	Holiday postage stamps, a briefcase, binoculars, shaving kit
144	December 1st, 1975	Coins, cash
145	December 1st, 1975	Man's ring
147	December 8th, 1975	Jewelry
148	December 10th, 1975	Cash, rings, Blue Chip stamps

Praise for "Case Files of the East Area Rapist / Golden State Killer"

Despite the fact that some books have been written about this case already, that "Magnum Opus" has been missing, that one book you could place in the hand of anyone who says "never heard of this guy - can you recommend a comprehensive book?"

Now we have that book.

Kat Winters and Keith Komos have done true crime aficionados a huge favor by compiling the information pertaining to the EAR/ONS in a concentrated, readable form, making the story read like the real-life thriller (or horror story, rather) that it is.

A surprising aspect of the book is how much previously unknown information it entails. Before reading this book, I thought I knew everything there is to know about the case. You can imagine my surprise when page after page contained info I had never heard of before, such as sightings of the EAR/ONS before and after his attacks, statements from police detectives and surviving victims, etc.

Case Files of the East Area Rapist / Golden State Killer is the true crime literature event of the year, and I say that during a year when plenty of great books have been released in the genre. Whether you're a newcomer or a seasoned Internet sleuth on the terrifying EAR/ONS case, or just a fan of scary stories and unsolved mysteries, this book needs to be on your shelf.

- Books, Bullets, and Bad Omens

Kat Winters and Keith Komos, through exhaustive research of case files and interviews, have meticulously chronicled the brutal crimes committed by arguably the most elusive serial killer of the Twentieth Century - a psychopath and predator so steeped in criminal culture that some forty years later, his identity still remains a mystery. This remarkable work allows the reader to experience each crime scene down to the slightest of details. Most importantly, the information contained within this fact-filled book may very well be the impetus for a reader to provide the lead that uncovers this monster's identity and finally brings him to justice.

- David Paul, author of <u>Unearthing a Serial Killer</u>

A carefully researched account of a devastating series of unsolved rapes and murders over a ten year period in California in the 1970s and 80s. The author compiles information from a variety of historical resources and helps the reader analyze the patterns and nuance of the offender without pushing a specific agenda or conclusion. As someone who dislikes the "my dad did it" series of cold case books, it was refreshing to see this book isn't one of those. The author does the nearly impossible by taking thousands of data points and organizing them in a manner that is accessible to the reader whether they are new to the case or someone who has researched it for years. This book is the definitive resource for information on the EAR/ONS series of attacks.

- Amazon Review

Terrifying and fascinating examination of a brutal and twisted criminal. Well documented, and lots of credit for not being too sensationalistic about wild details.

- Amazon Review

Winters shows her passion for this case by maintaining a professional tone while presenting all of the verifiable facts of this case. While internet forums are rife with misinformation and misguided speculation that plagues those searching for this phantom rapist-turned-killer, Winters' book finally presents all of the available information for the case in a logical format for all to understand. I believe this book should be the foundation upon which non-LE sleuths conduct any and all research/investigations.

- Amazon Review

A simple retelling of the events would have been a good book, but Winters goes well beyond this. Like a skilled tour guide in a uniquely bizarre museum, she shows her guests characteristics of the crimes worthy of note, points out patterns where they appear, dispels common myths, but all without telling the guest how to interpret the facts themselves.

And that is important to more than just selling books. This is a guide through one of the most destructive criminal careers in American history, and these crimes remain unsolved. Winters does not demand you see these crimes or the criminal who committed them the same way she does. She gives you all the information at hand in hopes you will see it in a new way - perhaps in a way that brings us one step closer to this monster, his victims just a little closer to the justice they deserve.

Having explored some of the more well-known work out there on this subject, my recommendation for anyone just coming to this real-life mystery is to buy this book first. There are other good books on the subject, but this one is the best I've seen.

- Amazon Review

Proof

Made in the USA
Columbia, SC
25 June 2018